VĀDIRĀJA'S REFUTATION OF ŚAṄKARA'S NON-DUALISM :

Clearing The Way For Theism

A Translation of Vādirāja's NYĀYARATNĀVALĪ with a Commentary by the Translator

L. STAFFORD BETTY, Ph. D.

MOTILAL BANARSIDASS
Delhi :: Varanasi :: Patna

First Edition : Pune, 1978

ISBN: 978-81-2083-158-2

Also available at:

MOTILAL BANARSIDASS
41 U.A. Bungalow Road, Jawahar Nagar, Delhi 110 007
8 Mahalaxmi Chamber, Warden Road, Mumbai 400 026
120 Royapettah High Road, Mylapore, Chennai 600 004
Sanas Plaza, Subhash Nagar, Pune 411 002
16 St. Mark's Road, Bangalore 560 001
8 Camac Street, Calcutta 700 017
Ashok Rajpath, Patna 800 004
Chowk, Varanasi 221 0011

PRINTED IN INDIA
BY JAINENDRA PRAKASH JAIN AT SHRI JAINENDRA PRESS,
A-45 NARAINA, PHASE I, NEW DELHI 110 028
AND PUBLISHED BY NARENDRA PRAKASH JAIN FOR
MOTILAL BANARSIDASS PUBLISHERS PRIVATE LIMITED,
BUNGALOW ROAD, DELHI 110 007

TO

My parents, Mr. and Mrs. Samuel M. Betty;
My maternal grandparents, Mr. and Mrs. Louis Conover;
and my mentors at Fordham University,
Thomas Berry and Jose Pereira.

FOREWORD

I am happy to see that successive contributions made during the last four or five decades by Indian scholars writing in English to the Dvaita philosophy of Madhva have succeeded in rousing interest among scholars from England and America to take part in making his school of Vedānta much better known, studied and appreciated than it is now, in their countries also.

Western savants like Ninian Smart and the late Suzanne Siauve have already led the way in this direction. It is stimulating to learn that the American Institute of Indian Studies will shortly be taking up the publication of a volume on Dvaita philosophy in its project of the *Encyclopaedia of Indian Philosophies.* More students in foreign countries are now selecting topics of Dvaita philosophy for the Ph. D. degree.

It is gratifying to find Prof. Stafford Betty, of the California State College, making his debut at this propitious juncture with his English translation and Comments on the first section (*sara*) of Vādirāja Tīrtha's *Nyāyaratnāvalī.* His work is sure to be warmly received by students of Madhva philosophy and admirers of Vādirāja in this country and outside.

Vādirāja holds an accredited position next only to that of Vyāsarāja in Madhva's system. His *Nyāyaratnāvalī* is more or less a miniature edition of his own metrical *magnum opus* the *Yuktimallikā.* He is known for his scintillating exposition of the doctrines and arguments of Dvaita philosophy and its interpretation of the Śrutis with all the poetic graces of pun, alliteration and rhyme and for his fascinating critique of rival theories of the Advaita school with his inimitable sallies of wit, humor and irony which make their appeal irresistible.

A terse Sanskrit philosophical treatise and a polemical one at that is rather difficult to translate—the more so when it is couched in almost epigrammatic Anustubh verses. Prof. Betty has achieved remarkable success in this task. The text of 421 verses of the selected portion of the original is arranged under 18 topics and each section is suitably broken up into its distinctive units of verses or parts thereof, dealing with a complete idea. The comments show a clear grasp of the intricacies of the subject matter. The treatment of Vādirāja's critique of the Advaita epistemology, its doctrine of Pratikarmavyavasthā, Biṁbapratibimbabhāva and other topics is clear and impressive and supported by suitable references by way of further clarification to the writings of modern authorities on Indian philosophy and the Advaita and Dvaita schools. It may incidentally be pointed out that Vādirāja has merely followed Madhva's etymological explanation of the term 'brāhmaṇa' in Bṛhadāraṇyaka Up. (viii, 3,4) to connote the supreme Brahman "which is known thro' the Vedas" (*brahmaṇā vedena aṇyate iti Brāhmaṇaḥ*)—the transposition of the sandhi vowel from the second to the first syllable being taken to be suggestive of the supreme glory of Brahman, as explained by Jayatīrtha in his *Tattvaprakāśikā* on Madhva's *Sūtrabhāṣya* (i, 3.42). It is not, therefore, a liberty taken by Vādirāja on his own initiative as supposed on p. 97. fn. 2.

Prof. Betty's painstaking work is sure to be received with warm praise by all students of Dvaita philosophy as a valuable contribution to the expanding literature on the subject in English and to call for an early completion of the remaining parts of the work on the same lines. Students of Advaita also stand to gain a better insight into its concepts from Vādirāja's lucid exposition of the subject and its intricacies, as brought out by Prof. Betty.

Ruparel College,
Bombay-16.

B. N. K. Sharma
(U. G. C.) Professor of Sanskrit
and Ardhamagadhi (*Retired*)

CONTENTS

INTRODUCTION

Vādirāja is a Hindu theologian and writer for the Dualist system of Vedānta. He was active in the Kanara district of India throughout all of the sixteenth century (a "life of 120 years is traditionally ascribed to him.")[1] His major work *Yuktimallikā* is well known to Dasgupta, K. Narain, and B. N. K. Sharma — the three twentieth-century scholars who are perhaps most responsible for exposing the West to Vedāntic Dualism (Dvaita). Nevertheless none of Vādirāja's works has until now been translated into any Western language. Indeed only one work from among the hundreds of volumes written over the centuries in defence of the Dualistic system founded by Madhva (13th century) has ever been translated and published.[2-3]

It is obvious then why I felt it worthwhile to translate a Dualist polemical treatise like the present one: to bring to light a philosophical/theological tradition and methodology all but overlooked by Indologists.

But why a work of *Vādirāja's* among the many followers of Madhva? Sharma, who probably knows him best, calls him "the most facile writer in Dvaita literature. His fine poetic faculty and human touch, the quick flashes of his wit and humor, his apt analogies from life and literature, and his racy way of putting things have made him the most popular and enthusiastically applauded writer in Dvaita literature."[4] Sharma goes on to say that Jayatīrtha and Vyāsarāya (or Vyāsatīrtha), while admittedly the two greatest defenders and interpreters of Madhva, were nevertheless "too learned and stiff to be of use to general

1. B. N. K. Sharma, *A History of the Dvaita School of Vedānta and its Literature*, II, p. 192. I am indebted to Sharma for all the biographical data presented here.

2. This is Jayatīrtha's *Vādāvalī* (or *Vedāntavādāvalī*), translated by Nagaraja Rao (cf. Sharma, *ibid.*, I, p. 337). I have not been able to acquire the work (published once in 1937, again in 1943) through any distributor or library.

3. A number of works from the hand of Madhva himself have been translated.

4. Sharma, *op. cit.* II, p. 192.

readers."[1] Anyone who has tried to follow Dasgupta's exposition of Vyāsatīrtha will at once recognize the truth of this judgment.[2]

I was only too happy then to acquire, quite unexpectedly, a copy of the lone published edition of Vādirāja's *Nyāyaratnāvalī* ("The Jewel Necklace of Logical Arguments"),[3] so that the thought of this intriguing philosopher-poet, and of his school, could be uncovered.

The *Nyāyaratnāvalī*, though not so well known as Vādirāja's *Yuktimallikā*, is inferior only in size to the latter. It has 901 verses (each thirty-two syllables long) in the anuṣṭubh meter, and is divided into five "saras" (or sections), as against the 5,379 verses of *Yuktimallikā*. The poetry, polemical flavor, and to a certain extent the actual arguments are the same in both works. Writing of the *Nyāyaratnāvalī* in his *History*, Sharma says that in it Vādirāja "tries to flabbergast his opponents by a clever and judicious mixture of theology and metaphysics. His homely analogies and persuasive rhetoric make an instantaneous appeal to the reader...."[4] As for the style of the work, it is "as usual with him alliterative and epigrammatical."[5] Not only that, it is highly elliptical: the 421 verses translated here (the first sara) comprehend much more material than would be possible without so condensed a style; indeed the style is in places almost like that of a sūtra. The work would be only partly comprehensible without the commentary provided by the editor.[6]

I have alluded to the polemical style of the work. What then is the polemics aimed at ? It is aimed exclusively and relentlessly at the Non-dualist (Advaita) Vedānta system built around Śaṅkara's philosophy. Like most of the polemical treatises written at the time, this work bristles with artful indignation

1. *Ibid.*, p. 200.
2. See Surendranath Dasgupta, *A History of Indian Philosophy*, IV, Chapters 29 and 30.
3. Udipi: Prabhākara Press, 1935. The monks at Sode Mutt in Udipi were kind enough to send me a copy.
4. Sharma, *op. cit.*, II, pp. 209-10.
5. *Ibid.*, p. 209.
6. The commentator appears to be a certain Viśvendratīrtha, the head of the Sode monks at the time the work was published. I will refer to him only as "the commentator" in my own commentary. Needless to say, my debt to him is enormous.

(the hostile style may or may not coincide with Vādirāja's actual sentiment). In any case, the present work is meaningless without a good knowledge of the Non-dualist school being opposed; for Vādirāja is not so much constructing his own metaphysics and epistemology as destroying that of his opponents. His contentiousness is understandable given a knowledge of his times. Then as today Non-dualism was the reigning philosophy among intellectuals in India: Before Dualism could live in its own right, it had to subdue this imposing Goliath. As for the unfortunate name-calling that we will see, Dualists claim that Non-dualists started the practice; some Non-dualists would even appear to agree.[1]

This introduction is not the place to explain in any detail the points separating the two schools; I reserve this for the commentary following. But several general remaks at the outset might be helpful.

There are four doctrines which to my mind form the core of the system Vādirāja opposed. They are (1) the doctrine that Brahman is the *only* ultimately real Being, whose nature it is to be perfectly conscious of absolute bliss; (2) the doctrine of identity, that is, that this Brahman is ultimately one with everything; (3) the docrtine of world-illusion, that is, that objects of sense or ideas of the mind, including that of our own individuality, are ultimately illusory; and (4) the so-called vyāvahārika-doctrine, which says that most things that we meet with our senses or mind are conventionally real (real in a sense, not wholly unreal) and are therefore to be distinguished both from the one Ultimate Reality, Brahman, and from utter illusions like a mirage or the stuff of dreams.

The first two of these doctrines do not logically imply each other; though they undoubtedly burst simultancously out of the same experience, they form altogether different statements about reality. It is quite one thing to say that Brahman is alone real,

1. The modern Non-dualist Ananta Krishna Sastri, for example, points out that in the controversy between the Non-dualist Madhusūdana Sarasvatī and the Dualist Vyāsarāya, it was the former who indulged in the practice, not the latter. As Sastri says, something impelled Madhusūdana "to throw his sense of decorum to the four winds and direct bitter attacks at his opponents" ("Introduction" to *Śrīnyāyāmṛtādvaitasiddhi*, Part I, p. 87).

and then to say that there is a"layer"in everything that is absolutely identical with this Reality. On the other hand, the latter two doctrines are logically required by these two basal intuitions. For if Brahman is alone real, then what is *not* Brahman *cannot* be real. Now obviously the world that we all know — the world of particulars, where there is everywhere friction between different, often opposing entities — cannot be this Brahman; for Brahman is by definition pure Bliss-Consciousness. But, comes the reply, there is the world before us, quite obviously real. Here the fourth doctrine applies. It states that this world before us is *not* altogether *un*real; it is real in a sense. But it is to be distinguished from what is ultimately real, Brahman, at the same time that it is to be distinguished from what is purely illusory (like a mirage). The world, then, is a metaphysical no-man's land — neither quite real on the one hand nor altogether unreal on the other.

This last doctrine is in many respects the most crucial of Non-dualism. If it can stand up to criticism, then its proponents have successfully anchored their entire system. On the one hand they will have secured Brahman's non-duality by showing the world's unreality compared to Brahman; on the other they will have made the essential distinction between one kind of unreality — the world's — and that of a more flagrant sort — a mirage's — and thus will have acquitted themselves at the bar of common sense.

You may have noted with some confusion that, judging from what I say, Non-dualists assert both that Brahman and all things are essentially identical, yet that these same things, supposedly identical with Brahman, are illusory. So which is it ? Is the world illusory or is it, since one with Brahman, real ? The answer given is that the *ground* of all things is real, is one with Brahman, but that things *as they appear*, that is, as entities different from, often clashing with, each other, are unreal. Thus the *secret essence* of all things is but one Reality, Brahman, while the *appearance* of all things is ultimately unreal. For this reason Non-dualists denounce *differences* wherever they appear. Where difference is perceived, one is dealing with mere appearance. It is only when one has intuited the Reality below the divided and divisive appearances of things that one has met with the Real.

Against these intuitions and arguments the Dualists, Vādirāja among them, pit themselves. Unlike the Non-dualists, who think that they intuit during the purest bliss realized during meditation both the ultimate Reality of what they perceive therein and their essential identity with It, the Dualists, though their meditative bliss may soar equally high, never forget their essential contingency upon and hence difference from what It is they are united with. Or rather, though they may forget this during the actual experience, they reassert it as soon as they "come down". At any rate, they bring a radically different mind-set to what may be a similar if not identical raw experience.

Where Non-dualists see Brahman as the only real Being, Dualists see Him (as opposed to "It") as no more *real* than anything else. Dualists distinguish God and the world not on the basis of *reality*, but on the basis of dependency. Just as in Christianity God and the world are not related as real to unreal, but as non-contingent, or self-existent, to contingent, so it is here.[1] Thus for Dualists there are realities as ultimately real as God Himself. Brahman is *not* the lone Reality. Nor are these realities identical with Brahman. There isn't any secret essence in everything which is identical with Him. It is certainly true that He is the Ground of our being, but not in any material sense: He is our Support, our Inner Controller; He pervades us; but He is by no means *identical* with us. As for the vyāvahārika-doctrine which supposedly anchors Non-dualism, Dualists have nothing but scorn for it. A conventional reality midway between Brahman and ordinary illusions like a mirage is, they say, unsupported by experience; for experience tells us only of realities and unrealities, not of different grades within reality. Thus the world cannot be regarded as that queer *tertium quid* postulated by Non-dualists. It is either real, in which case there is a real second to Brahman, or it is unreal, in which case the common sense distinction made by everyone between a real oasis and a mirage is baseless, both alike being illusory. Either way then, the Non-dualists are refuted on this point, say the Dualists.

1. "Contingency," however, has a "Christian ring" to it. It suggests not only the world's dependency on God, but its creation *ex nihilo*. Since in Madhva's system prakṛti (the stuff of which the world is made) is eternal, creation *ex nihilo* does not apply. It is perhaps wise to speak, therefore, only of the world's "dependency" on God in this system.

What is at the *root* of this divergence between these rival schools, both alike basing their doctrines on one and the same Scripture, namely the principal Upaniṣads ? Is the difference between a Śaṅkara and a Madhva ultimately based on a difference in the religious experience itself ? Did Śaṅkara have a monistic experience and Madhva a theistic ? Is the matter that simple ?

It does not appear so to me. In the first place, Śaṅkara was a Dualist at the same time he was a Monist. Zimmer correctly says, "His stanzas praising the Goddess (Śakti-Māyā-Devī) are among the most celebrated examples of Indian devotional verse ... he gives devout praise to the 'second' — Māyā, Mother of the world — and with all sincerity; expressing the mode of divine dualistic experience on the plane of bhakti...."[1] In addition, it is clear that a Non-dualist's meditation *starts out* dualistically: Brahman is initially meditated on as an object, even if a highly abstract object; it is only later that this experience of difference gives way to that of "non-dual absorption, absolutely devoid of any consciousness of a distinction between the perceiver and the thing perceived."[2] We must conclude, then, that Śaṅkara well understood the experience underpinning a philosophy of theism, in which a difference between the adoring and the Adored is perceived.

As for Madhva, there are indications that even while he remained a theist, he was not foreign to an experience like the absorption described above. His statement, "Release consists in shaking off all extraneous associations and regaining one's own selfhood,"[3] is more suggestive of a monistic than a dualistic experience. And the contemporary Dualist Sharma says that according to Madhva "release is the realization of the intrinsic bliss of selfhood by each one of us,"[4] while in another place he speaks of the "endless bliss of complete self-realization and God-realization"[5] as if the two were, in some way, synonymous. It

1. Heinrich Zimmer, *Philosophies of India*, edited by Joseph Campbell pp. 460-61.

2. *Ibid.*, p. 436.

3. Madhva, *Brahmasūtrabhāṣya* 1.1.17 (translated by B. N. K. Sharma, *Madhva's Teachings in His Own Words*, p. 144.)

4. Sharma, *Philosophy of Śrī Madhvācārya* p. 336.

5. *Ibid.*, p. 328.

is nowhere near as clear that Madhva had experienced something akin to Śaṅkara's non-dualism as it is that Śaṅkara experienced something akin, if not identical, to Madhva's dualistic theism. But the possibility is strong that each knew the other's experience even while denigrating it. In other words, it is entirely possible, if not probable, that the same relation between Śaṅkara and Madhva applies as that between, say, a Plotinus and a St. John of the Cross. Many students of mysticism (Stace for example) feel that Plotinus and St. John knew a like identity with what each conceived of as the Supreme. Yet, while Plotinus indulges himself in the mystical language of identity, St. John holds back. Stace believes that St. John and other great Catholic mystics "were submissive and managed to give an interpretation of 'union with God' which could be accommodated to strict orthodoxy [which was dualistic, of course]."[1] Stace's view is confirmed by Meister Eckhart's identity-talk when not under pressure combined with his more orthodox duality-talk when forced to defer to the Church.

The question then is, *if* Śaṅkara and Madhva, both highly realized mystics, had essentially the same religious experience — dualistic at times, non-dualistic during moments of mystical self-abnegation and self-transcendence — why does one emerge the enemy of the other ? Was Madhva deferring to the climate of bhakti — which characterized the Vaiṣṇava community he was a member of ? Was the dualism implicit in any relation between two beings — even two lovers in the most intimate embrace—too formidable an "obstacle" for him to rise above ? Was Śaṅkara (or Gauḍapāda, or whoever first enunciated an absolute Non-dualism), on the other hand, more free, for some reason, to be faithful to his experience, just as it was ? This is a possibility.

Or must we evoke a modernistic theory like Carl Jung's to explain the difference ? Following Jung's theory of psychological types,[2] we may ask whether Śaṅkara and Madhva were psychological opposites: Did Śaṅkara see the mystical oneness of his samādhi — the experience itself — as "more real" than the

1. Walter T. Stace, *The Teachings of the Mystics*, p. 128.

2. Cf. C. G. Jung, *Psychological Types*, from *The Collected Works of C. G. Jung*, VI. Chapter 10.

entities (Brahman and the soul) *grounding* the experience, while Madhva was irresistably drawn back to the *context grounding the experience* as the more primal datum?

Or finally, is their difference ultimately what it in fact seems to be — philosophical ? Do the Dualist and the Non-dualist each think the other a bad philosopher, the matter ending there ? Does the Non-dualist think the Dualist hopelessly incapable of philosophizing about the samādhi-experience *as it is* ? Is the Dualist too rigidly orthodox in his bhaktic religion to deal faithfully with the given ? In modern terms, is he unphenomenological ? Or, on the other hand, does the Dualist regard the Non-dualist as *mindlessly* phenomenological ? Has he forgotten that the very *condition* of his transcending individuality in the samādhi-experience is the very individuality he *seems* to transcend ? Was it not *he* who transcended, or forgot, or left behind, his individuality ? Was it not *he* as opposed to anyone else, who self-forgettingly experienced Brahman ? Wasn't that essential "he" still there even while it was lost sight of ? In other words, hasn't the Non-dualist confused the experiential domain (which may be non-dualistic) with the ontological domain (which is dualistic), and thereby landed himself in absurdity ?

I certainly do not know the answer. Any of these three possibilities seems plausible enough. In any case, I do not think that the last reason is the sole, or even the most telling, reason. And of course our problem is immensely simplified if we hold — I think simplistically — that Śaṅkara and Madhva had radically different religious experiences.

Whatever the case, the present work was meant by its author to be read by philosophers. I personally find that most of Vādirāja's arguments are potentially as disconcerting to the sophisticated Non-dualist philosopher of our own day as they probably were to Vādirāja's original auditors. The *Nyāyaratnāvalī*, in other words, is far from a period piece. Anyone interested in putting Non-dualism to the twin philosophical tests of internal consistency and reality-consistency could hardly do better than acquaint himself with Vādirāja's merciless dialectic.[1] His

1. My article "A Death-Blow to Śaṅkara's Non-dualism? A Dualist Refutation," *ReligiousStudies*, 12 September, 1976), 281-290, is based on one of Vādirāja's arguments presented in this work (see pp. 163 ff.).

methodology is of the most modern and potentially devastating sort: it is what Western philosophers call the *reductio ad absurdum*, and what Indian philosophers picturesquely describe as "slaying one's enemy with his own sword." Vādirāja asks only that his rival auditors take seriously the *necessary implications* of their own philosophy. Whether the present reader comes to feel that Vādirāja misrepresents Advaita Vedānta, and thus in effect vanquishes only a "straw man," or in fact succeeds in drawing out the real implications of the system, in the process destroying utterly its intelligibility and possible truth, one thing must be granted, I think, by all: Advaita has met a most formidable opponent.

A final point. The title suggests that this work is but a preamble to theism: it "clears the way." And that is in fact the case. Vādirāja is but clearing away the ungoverned jungle of Non-dualism. It remains for another work to erect the temple on the site of the clearing. Vādirāja frequently refers to his theistic beliefs in passing, but only as an architect might who can see the finished temple shining resplendently in his imagination but who has not yet drawn up the plans for its construction.

NOTES ON THE TRANSLATION

I have as much written this translation for the linguist as for the student of philosophy or theology. In most cases the unembellished, compact style of Vādirāja's Sanskrit is retained if the reader leaves out the parenthetical elements. I have usually succeeded in translating the verses so that they make as much syntactical sense without the embellishment as with it.

Throughout I have fought two opposite temptations: that of giving a mechanical, cramped translation which is more faithful to Sanskrit syntax than to English, and that of translating with abandon. It is difficult for me to say whether I am more likely to have sinned in the first or in the second way.

Another rule I have tried to follow is "clarity first." I have been unafraid to repeat myself in the commentary. I have tried to take nothing for granted; if Vādirāja makes an old point in a new context, I am apt to explain again how he arrived at the original point. I have also tried to remain always conscious of the broadest context of the arugments as they unfold. In other words, I am writing as if I assumed the reader were here making his first acquaintance with the Dualist system.

In this work Vādirāja is addressing his adversary in the second person. He is not actually debating with him but *reminiscing* an earlier debate. Thus he frequently speaks in the past (aorist, imperfect, or perfect) tense. He also alludes constantly to points made in the debate by his Non-dualist foe: the commentary is indispensable, needless to say, to follow much of what is going on here.

A word more about the format. According to Nyāya theorists, there are two modes of argumentation, irenic and polemic. The latter, here adopted by Vādirāja, is itself of two sorts — one which seeks to defeat an opponent by destructive criticism only, the other in addition to such criticism carefully presenting and defending an alternative. The present work is largely, but not exclusively, destructive of the opposition.

The polemics, as I indicated earlier, is occasionally insulting. Sometimes Vādirāja will mock his opponent with mordant irony which cuts to the quick; sometimes he will call him outright "stupid" (ajña). I have thought it fitting to preserve this contentious tone in my commentary as well as translation. In other words, I have appeared to take sides.

A look at the table of contents will reveal that the translation is divided neatly into sections. This is not Vādirāja's scheme, but my own. Vādirāja has provided us with only 421 consecutive verses.

Each of these verses is divided into two sixteen-syllable parts. I have labeled the first part "a", the second part "b".

I have adopted certain conventions throughout the translation and commentary, usually to avoid confusion, occasionally to prevent incessant repetition:

The word "identity" is usually a tag to designate the doctrine of the Non-dualist. An "identity-text" is one of his pet-texts, such as "One only, without a second," which he uses to advance his position. "Difference" on the other hand is usually a tag for the Dualist's doctrine; a "difference-text" is one which supports the doctrine of God's real difference from all His (real) creatures.

Dualists have many names for God: "Brahman," which has connotations of impersonality, is so distinctive (and so well known) that when it appears I leave it untranslated. "Viṣṇu", "Hari", "Nārāyaṇa", etc., are personal names of God, and as such are used indiscriminately by Vādirāja; I will almost always translate such names as "Viṣṇu" to avoid confusion. There are also certain words, especially "Īśvara", which are usually translated as "the Lord", and I will follow the custom. Finally there is the word "Kṛṣṇa", the name for the most widely revered manifestation, or avatāra, of Viṣṇu on earth; I will leave this word untranslated. What is most important to remember is that for a Dualist like Vādirāja, all these words signify the one same Being, God, the Supreme Being. There is, for example, no difference at all, as there is for a Non-dualist, between Brahman (Ultimate Reality) and Īśvara (the Lord).

Where a pronoun takes the place of "Brahman" either in the text or in the commentary, I have translated it as "He" if in a Dualist context, and as "It" if in a Non-dualist. This is the established custom.

I have deferred also to the custom of capitalizing synonyms for the Non-dualist Brahman. Thus "Consciousness", or "Pure

Consciousness", is usually used to translate "cit" or "cinmātra"; on the other hand, "consciousness" is used when it is clear that Brahman as limited by its soul-adjunct is exclusively being alluded to.

I have translated "śabda" as "Revelation", "śruti" as "Scripture", and "smṛti" usually as "the Purāṇa(s)" (since they are usually what is meant).

Finally, I should prepare the reader for a disappointment. Most of Vādirāja's brilliant word-play is lost in the translation. This poem is vaguely reminiscent of Alexander Pope's *Essay on Man*; several times it displays the verbal pyrotechnics of Byron's *Don Juan*. Yet almost all of this is missing in the translation — inevitably, I am afraid. For our best efforts will usually be spent trying to make clear a philosophical terminology usually quite alien to the English language. We can "acquit ourselves" of the task of translation, but we are a long way from "mastering" such a task. Indeed, we may ask ourselves if we will ever see the day that we can render "antaḥkaraṇavṛtti" into English poetry; and no wonder, for no one has ever rendered it well into English prose.

I. INVOCATION

1. To you, Man-Lion, who bear Lakṣmī on your breast, who chastised the demon (Hiraṇyakaśipu) with your fierce claws, who are committed to the defense of your doctrined — hail!

COMMENT: Vādirāja begins by invoking praise to Viṣṇu, or Hari, the supreme God of the Mādhva, or Dualist, school of Vedānta.

The "Man-Lion" refers to Viṣṇu's fourth of ten incarnations (see verse 6 below). Viṣṇu had to assume this form in order to destroy a demon named Hiraṇyakaśipu who was ravaging the world. Since by a dispensation from the god Brahmā the demon could not be killed by god or man or animal, the supreme God Viṣṇu, feeling Himself obliged to honor Brahmā's unlucky promise, solved the problem of the fiend's destruction by incarnating as *half*-man and *half*-beast. He then tore Hiraṇyakaśipu to pieces and ended his reign of terror.

Lakṣmī (śrī) is the goddess of fortune and, more importantly, the consort of Viṣṇu. Among beings she is second only to Viṣṇu, according to Dualist Vedāntins. The image invoked here is that of an adoring wife snuggled against her lord's breast and of the lord's gracious and tender acceptance of her devotion. Lakṣmī is frequently demythologized by philosophers and depicted as the *power* of God, or Viṣṇu.

Vādirāja's commentator mentions that the "position" protected by the Man-Lion is the true doctrine preached by the Dualists.

2. May the milk-ocean-resembling Madhva, whose heart of hearts is an abode everlastingly prepared for the triple-gloried (Viṣṇu), provide me with the light of true understanding!

COMMENT: In all of his works Vādirāja professes a towering gratitude to his school's founder, Madhva, one of the most important and original philosophers of India. Here Madhva is pictured as harboring within his heart the glorious presence of God; God in turn is called "triple-gloried" because He is the master of heaven (Vaikuṇṭha, His own abode), hell, and earth.

The word "milk-ocean" alludes to the great event during

Viṣṇu's second incarnation (see verse 6 below). After being conquered by demons, the gods, or Viṣṇu's regents, implored their Master to restore their strength lest they perish. They were instructed to churn the ocean (made of milk) until the "nectar of immortality" appeared. They did so, with Mount Mandara as the churning-staff and Viṣṇu Himself incarnated as a turtle supporting the staff on His back. When the nectar appeared, the gods drank it and, with strength renewed, "struck down their foes, who fell headlong through space to lowest depths of hell !"[1]

Madhva is compared to the "milk-ocean" for two reasons. First, as we just saw, his heart is the abode of Viṣṇu just as the milk-ocean was of the turtle. Second, his gift to men, his words of truth, bring eternal beatitude just as the nectar of immortality brought victory to the gods.

1. John Dowson, *A Classical Dictionary of Hindu Mythology and Religion, Geography, History, and Literature*, p. 14.

II. VIṢṆU'S SUPREMACY

3-5. In words like "this Lord of all," "this controller of all," "the ruler of all," and others, Viṣṇu's majesty is proclaimed.[1] Scriptural texts speak of "this eternal majesty of Brahman (brāhmaṇa)";[2] some have praised, "His majesty is true."[3] Another has sung, "Knowledge, power, activity are innate (to Him)."[4] Thus (His) eternally true majesty (consists in) knowledge, power, and activity through all eternity.

COMMENT : Most apparently these three verses (like the several which follow) are simple paeans. But they are also ballast for the arguments that follow. Vādirāja wants to show, first, that God's majesty is supreme, and therefore that there can be no identification with Him (as Non-dualists claim); second, that his majesty is not an illusion, not something which will someday disappear (say, at liberation),but that it is eternal; and third, that God has attributes — knowledge, power, and activity, as the Upaniṣad says — and is not, as Non-dualists hold, indifferentiated "Pure Consciousness."

Vādirāja, incidentally, interprets the word *brāhmaṇa* above idiosyncratically, not as indicating "one who is devoted to Brahman," as most modern scholars would judge, but rather as Brahman Himself.

He now gives examples of Viṣṇu's supremacy :

6. The Blessed One, the Lord over you, has been established as the rescuer of the Vedas, the supporter of Mount Mandara, the bearer of the earth, the slayer of the malignant demon.

COMMENT : The rescuing of the Vedas, etc., refer to the heroic actions of each of Viṣṇu's first four incarnations; each of these is mentioned in Epic or even in Vedic literature, but it is in the Purāṇas — particularly the *Bhāgavata Purāṇa* which is esteemed by Dualists almost as highly as the Upaniṣads — that the legends are fully developed.

1. All three quotations from *Bṛhadāraṇyaka Upaniṣad* 4.2.22.
2. *Bṛhadāraṇyaka Upaniṣad* 8.3.4.
3. *Ṛgveda* 8.3.4.
4. *Śvetāśvatara Upaniṣad* 6.8.

According to the *Bhāgavata Purāṇa,* Viṣṇu incarnated as (1) a fish during the great flood which submerged all the worlds; he recovered the Vedas from the demon Hayagrīva ("Horse-necked") and later slew him. As (2) a turtle he used, as we have seen, his hard back as the pivot of Mount Mandara, which in turn was used as a churning pole for distilling amṛta, the "nectar of immortality." As (3) a boar he lifted the earth to safety with his snout after it had been dragged to the sea-bottom by the fiend Hiraṇyākṣa ("Golden-eyed"). And as (4) the Man-Lion, as we saw above (in verse 1), he slew Hiraṇyakaśipu.

These heroic and splendidly imaginative deeds all show the supremacy of Viṣṇu, Vādirāja holds. Note how he reminds his Non-dualist opponent of Viṣṇu's superiority — in the second person. This reminder is appropriate because the Non-dualist's claim of identity with Brahman precludes Viṣṇu's superiority. (We will see more of this below.)

7-9. It has been established by the discriminating that the gods Brahmā, Śiva, and the others — who from moment to moment entreat this Lord above for (permission to carry out) their respective occupations — are unlike (Him) in power and knowledge and are obedient to Him. Human deeds modeled after the might of Viṣṇu are described in Scripture in this way : "Viṣṇu, you are beyond measure! They do not come close to (your) greatness !"[1] There is not, there has not been, there will not be the equal of Viṣṇu !

COMMENT : He is showing that gods and men are vastly inferior to Viṣṇu. This inferiority extends to Brahmā and Śiva, the chief of Viṣṇu's vassals, for they too are completely dependent on Him for deliverance from the powers of evil, specifically those conquered by Viṣṇu in his various avatāras. All creation, therefore, looks up to Him.

10. And furthermore, these sacred Epics and Purāṇas (smṛti) at all times (kālatraye) forbid equality with Kṛṣṇa. Then with whom would there be an identity, pray consider ?

COMMENT : He says that just as Scripture (mostly meaning the Upaniṣads) speaks of Viṣṇu's supremacy over and hence difference from all creatures, so the Epics and Purāṇas — later,

1. *Ṛgveda* 7.99.1.

not strictly canonical, yet highly regarded works dealing with the heroic exploits of God's avatāras, especially Kṛṣṇa — speak of *Kṛṣṇa's* supremacy. Indeed they speak so resoundingly of it that a mere question, a simple reminder to the Non-dualist, serves here as a refutation : how, Vādirāja asks, could all be identical, as Non-dualists claim, in the face of so much evidence showing our inferiority to, and thence difference from, Kṛṣṇa our deliverer ?

11-12. Scripture compelled (us to believe that) majesty is the Lord's entire nature, while Scripture (śruti) and the Epics and Purāṇas (smṛti) compelled (us to accept) its absence in any other. And it cannot be said, not in a hundred eons, that what is by nature only low and what is by nature eternally most high are identical.

COMMENT : He here sums up the significance of verses 3-12 with a single syllogism : God is most high; man is not most high; therefore God is not man. Thus there is a reality *second* to God, and Non-dualism is therefore untenable.

III. REFUTATION OF THE NON-DUALIST INTERPRETATION OF SCRIPTURE

With the introductory material now behind him, Vādirāja begins the refutation in earnest. His first concern is to expose the Non-dualists' erroneous interpretation of certain key texts in Scripture.

13-14. When it is said that every declaration of a difference (between Brahman and any other thing) is untrue and unrevelatory, (we admit that), *if* difference is invalidated by the non-secondness-text, it *is* to be maintained that the invalidated difference would somehow be unreal; and in that case a statement attesting difference *would* be untrue and unrevelatory.

COMMENT : Vādirāja is concerned over the charge made by Non-dualists that statements speaking of or assuming such a difference are, as Vādirāja puts it, "untrue and unrevelatory." Non-dualists "propose that all those texts and contexts which proclaim the reality of the Universe and the difference between Jīva [the soul] and Brahman are to be viewed as 'modes of restatement' (anuvādaka) or empirical facts which are to be refuted by those denying reality to the world of differences."[1]

One of the latter is what Vādirāja has in mind when he refers to "the non-secondness text." This is the celebrated text "one only, without a second."[2] If this statement, he says, does in fact assert non-duality, then any assertion of duality, since it contradicts infallible Scripture, is wrong; and difference, so palpable and so apparently obvious, must somehow be unreal. This, of course, is the very conclusion drawn by Non-dualists.

15a. But this (invalidated difference) cannot be concluded from an investigation of the purport of Revelation (śabda).

COMMENT : Vādirāja believes that the force of all the Scriptures taken as a whole points overwhelmingly in the direction of difference and dualism, and that the Non-dualists misinterpret

1. B.N.K. Sharma, *Śrī Madhva's Teachings in His Own Words* p. 58.
2. "ekamevādvitīyam." *Chāndogya Upaniṣad* 6.2.1, 2.

statements like "one only, without a second." He now tells why he believes difference is defensible and valid by analyzing a second text :

15b. The words "not this, not this"[1] indicate that (God's) Self (ātman) is neither the human soul (jīva) nor matter (jaḍa).

COMMENT : He is referring to the following quotation : "For the desire for sons is the desire for wealth and the desire for wealth is the desire for worlds; both these are, indeed, desires only. This Self [ātman] is (that which has been described as) not this, not this."[2] Vādirāja wastes no time in enlisting the quotation — which Non-dualists believe shows the unreality of everything not Brahman — to his cause. The first "this," he says, refers to "sons," or souls; the second refers to "worlds," or matter. Thus the statement clearly indicates the difference of God from all His creation, spiritual as well as material substances, and hence the validity of difference.

He now gives his opponents a grammar lesson on the text :

16-17. By putting a word with a nominative ending in conjunction with (the word signifying) Brahman, the (former) word, in the same case (as the latter), is by all means to be differentiated (from it) because of the meaning of "not". Just as by the statement, "A pot is not a piece of cloth," all understand that the pot is by nature the negation of the piece of cloth, so would the idea be in this case too.

COMMENT : He is referring specifically to the words "both" and "Self" in the statement,"...both [ete] these are, indeed, desires only. This Self [ātma] is...not this, not this." He points out that since "both" and "Self" are in the same case (nominative) and are linked negatively, we have a clear case of mutual exclusion. So how can the Non-dualists deny difference ?

18. Now in the statement, "There is not a world *in* the Self," the word ("world") *would* indicate something totally non-existent; but the word in the statement, "The Self is *not* the world," is a word indicating something different (from the Self) — no doubt about it.

1. "neti neti."
2. *Bṛhadāraṇyaka Upaniṣad* 4.4.22, as translated by S. Radhakrishnan, *The Principal Upaniṣads* p. 279.

COMMENT : Here he is contrasting the statement of difference analyzed in the previous two verses to a bona fide statement of non-duality. If the adversary can point to a text which says there is no soul, world, or whatever *in* Brahman, then Non-duality would be established, and the whole world would have to be regarded as illusory, as ultimately unreal, and hence as not a second to Brahman. But as matters stand, there is no such text. We have instead a statement indicating the *difference* between Brahman and creation.

He now describes more precisely the error of his opponent with regard to the text ("not this, not this") :

19. And according to you the meaning fulfilling the statement is to be arrived at by (treating the statement as if it were an) ellipsis. This is certainly not so with me; for the appropriate correlative (negated) in this (quotation) is arrived at, (in my interpretation,) by means of the double (negative — "not this, not this").

COMMENT : Unlike Dualists, he says here, who have carefully and impartially examined the text to determine what the "not this, not this" locution is referring to, and have accordingly determined that souls and matter are the correlatives (or recipients) of this double negation, Non-dualists mutilate the text's most obvious signification by saying that it declares the utter unreality of souls and the world rather than their difference from Brahman. He now gives a grammatical analysis of the Non-dualists' mistake through an example :

20-21a. Take the case of a word with a locative case-ending, as in the negation, "There is no cow *on* the earth," : the "earth" in the statement would be the *location* of the negated object (cow). (But) those who can discriminate the meaning of Revelation say that the (grammatical) character of "earth" does *not* apply to Brahman (in the scriptural text we are considering).

COMMENT : Here he says that the Non-dualists in effect interpret Brahman ("ātmā") as if it were in the locative case instead of the nominative — as if the relation between Brahman and the matter/souls different from Him was of the same order as that between the earth and cows in the statement, "There is no cow *on* the earth." But, he continues, there simply isn't any basis for such an interpretation. Therefore the obvious meaning — mutual exclusivity—is the true meaning of the text, and the doctrine of non-difference dependent on a locative interpretation of the word indicating Brahman is indefensible.

21b-22. Furthermore, the meanings of different words would certainly differ accordingly; for that reason your "non-secondness' text (in Scripture) would forbid a *second* (but) would not strike down the *difference* — conspicuous (precisely) *because* of the non-secondness — in Brahman.

COMMENT : Again he has in mind the first text, "In the beginning, my dear, this was Being, one only without a second."[1] Non-dualists hold that this text proves Brahman's non-duality, that nothing really exists except Brahman, that all earthly phenomena are merely apparent and are ultimately illusory. Vādirāja replies that, since we must take words at their face value whenever possible, and since "non-secondness" does not have the same meaning as "non-difference," then we had better not confuse the two. For non-secondness, he maintains, means only what it says: that there is no second, or *equal,* to Brahman; not that there is nothing different from Brahman. He then says that the non-secondness text, far from being a non-difference-text, is a difference-text; for in stressing Brahman's primacy with respect to all other things, his difference from them is obviously recommended as well.

23. Thus my speech declaring Brahman's difference as constituting the truth about Brahman was not untrue and unrevelatory. On the contrary, it was true and revelatory.

COMMENT : He feels he has successfully defended the doctrine of difference against the opponent's charge (see verses 13-14) that Dualists disregard the intent of Scripture and as a result miss the truth.

He now advances another argument based on linguistic analysis of the *Chāndogya* text :

24. By saying "One who *has* no second" when the negative meaning is united to Brahman, a genitively defined relation

1. *Chāndogya Upaniṣad* 6.2.1, 2, as translated by S. Radhakrishnan, *ibid.*, pp. 447-449.

(between Brahman and the second) emerges — but not non-difference.

COMMENT : He argues that the word *advitīyam* (*a*="not," dvitīyam="second") is an adjective genitively (possessively) related to the noun *ekam* ("One," Brahman), and not a noun in apposition with Brahman. (In grammatical terminology, it is a bahuvrīhi, not a tatpuruṣa.) The statement is saying that Brahman *has* no second, not that He is by nature non-seconded. Now if Brahman *has* no second, there must be an *existent* second for Him not to have; whereas if He is non-seconded, the "non-secondness" could refer, not to a different entity but to Brahman alone; and therefore Non-dualism is defensible only on this latter interpretation — which Vādirāja here rejects.

Vādirāja is not committed in this verse to proving the dualistic intent of the passage; he wants merely to show that a case can be made for it, that there is no basis for the unquestioned assumption that the text is an "identity-text."

He now delivers a wicked thrust at the opponent :

25-26a. From what you say, the (thesis of) Non-dualism itself would have to be a second; I believe that from the outset the text (as you interpret it) would annul even this second because there is no basis for abandoning (in this one instance) what (you claim) has been realized (i.e., non-duality).

COMMENT : This redoubtable argument catches the Non-dualist in a palpable self-contradiction: If Brahman is alone ultimately real, as Non-dualists maintain on the basis of the text we have been examining, then this very text is unreal, for obviously *it* is not identical to Brahman ! And if the text is invalid because ultimately unreal, then how can Non-dualists base their belief upon it ? Vādirāja concludes :

26b-27a. This interpretation of yours showing the invalidation of duality in the investigation of Revelation's purport was itself untrue and unrevelatory !

COMMENT : He now brings a new text to bear on the non-secondness text :

27b-30a. Just as in the statement "The lotus is blue" a lotus inseparable from the blue is signified, but the non-difference

> proper to a (literal) non-difference is not there by meant — rather there is (meant only) the quality of being the ground of what is "non-different" — so it is with respect to the text "Brahman is ..everything" : one should understand that Brahman is inseparable from all, not (that He is) one in essence (with all). Thus only in this (former) sense is there an identity; only a second taught with respect to being an aspect of Brahman (brahma-dharmatayā) was denied; the "non-second" text prohibits *this* (kind of secondness).

COMMENT : Here Vādirāja refers to a third scriptural passage, "This Brahman is truly everything."[1] He says that just as the blue of the lotus is never regarded as identical with the flower, so Brahman must never be regarded as identical with souls and matter. Rather, like the flower which is inseparable from the attribute "blue," Brahman must be regarded as inseparable from us. We are pervaded by Brahman, He is our inner controller, He sustains us at all times by His presence. Vādirāja is saying in so many words that to deny secondness to the soul is to deny its *independence* of Brahman; such a denial is of course laudatory by Vādirāja's standards.

It is interesting that he does admit an identity of a kind. All things, he says, are aspects, or properties, or qualities of Brahman. He means exactly what Madhva meant when he wrote centuries earlier that souls are the *body* of Brahman. Sounding ever so much like Rāmānuja (though in fact differing from him), Madhva writes :

> The Jīva [soul] is the body of Viṣṇu and therefore it is called Śārīra or body. But Viṣṇu has a body of his own, how is it then that the Jīva is said to be the body of Viṣṇu ? It is called His body because it is under His control (just as the human organism is under the control of the Jīva; so the Jīva organism is under the control of the Lord)."[2]

So both Madhva and Vādirāja allow that a case for the soul's non-secondness *can* be made, indeed *must* be made; but this is

1. *Chāndogya Upaniṣad* 3.14.1.
2. Madhva, trans. Sriśa Candra Vasu, *The Upaniṣads with the Commentary of Madhvācārya*, Part I (Īśa, Kena, Kaṭha, Praśna, Muṇḍaka and Māṇḍūkya); The Sacred Books of the Hinuds, Vol. I p. 80 (*Kaṭha* 6.17).

not to imply that there is an *essential* identity : As Sharma writes, "the intrinsic natures of the two are such that no merger is possible."[1]

30b-32. And thus every statement made by *you* was untrue and unrevelatory. And therefore (the charge of) "error-speaking" is applicable only to you, sir ! And thus, because of the certainty of the truth of difference, statements affirming difference, worthy of praise from the wise, doubtlessly won out at the Council of Truth. Thus only Truth-speakers (Dualists) were knowers of the truth.

COMMENT : This triumphant conclusion is pertinent to all material from verse 13 to here.

Dualists of Madhva's persuasion refer to themselves as *tattvavādins*, meaning both "speakers of truth" and "Realists" simultaneously. On the other hand, Dualists call a Non-dualist a *mithyāvādin* — which means both "speaker of error" and "Illusionist" simultaneously.

Dualists consider themselves Realists; they believe that the world, with all of its distinctions, is real— that is, it is not the stuff of dreams, or a projection of consciousness, or a phantasm. Non-dualists, on the other hand, call the world an illusion, or a creation of the power of Illusion, or māyā (hence *māyāvādin*, which means the same as *mithyāvādin*, is another name for the Non-dualist). Thus each term — *tattvavādin*, and *mithyāvādin* or *māyāvādin*—is at once a tag of identification ("Realist," "Illusionist") and an estimate ("speaker of truth," "speaker of error").

1. B.N.K. Sharma, *Philosophy of Sri Madhvācārya* p. 228.

IV. REFUTATION OF THE NON-DUALIST "VYĀVAHĀRIKA-DOCTRINE"

In order to make their monism plausible, Non-dualists muster all their efforts to explain away the seeming difference of the world from Brahman. They feel that if they can show it to be illusory, then the unique reality of Brahman is protected. Otherwise the world must be acknowledged as a second to Brahman, and Non-dualism fails. But it is not enough simply to "write off" the world as an illusion, they quickly perceived, for the world — or at least most phenomena observed in the world — is immediately distinguishable from an obvious illusion like a mirage or an absurdity like a rabbit's horn. Thus in evolving a doctrine which would show the world to be an illusion, Non-dualists had to be careful not to overlook the distinction between the world's illusion and these more obvious types of illusion. They therefore, like the Mādhyamika Buddhists before them, devised a system which postulated *three* levels of truth : (1) absolutely true (pāramārthika); (2) conventionally true (vyāvahārika); and (3) delusively true (prātibhāsika). This second, or vyāvahārika, level of truth, Non-dualists state further, typifies every aspect of the world's appearance and of human thought and activity in the world throughout eternity. We are freed of this "world-illusion" only upon liberation; or rather, it is the transcendence of such illusion that constitutes liberation.

Vādirāja now shows the consequences of such a theory :

33-36a. An error which characterizes what has been heard continually — day in and day out, in creation after creation through beginningless time — from the mouths of learned teachers, and (characterizes) reflection (on their words) as well, would never cease until liberation, and even clings to a Yogi-Prince in all matters (treated by him) because it is applicable to the omniscient. Indeed (your) "conventional" appraisals (vyāvahārikamānāni) would yield just such an error. And in that case the Vedas and other canonical works — (only) perpetrating the irreversible Great Illusion the whole world over — would be guilty of a monstrous fraudulence.

COMMENT : Vādirāja refuses to hold the conventional standpoint in esteem. He can find no consolation whatever in the thought that the world is only conventionally real, and that worldly distinctions — as between God and man, one man and another man, one object and another object — are only conventionally true. For the words of Scripture are a part of this world, their truth dependent at the very least on the distinctions they signify. If therefore the world is unreal and common distinctions signified by language untrue, what happens to Scripture ? And what are we to make of the supposedly omniscient teachers, like Yājñavalkya, whose words are preserved in Scripture ? They would be "omniscient" only with respect to illusory knowledge. They would ultimately be talking gibberish. Scripture would in that case be nothing but a compendium of lies, a hoax writ large.[1]

36b-38a. A purely delusive appraisal (prātibhāsikamāna), however, causes error a little at a time, here or there, once in a while, and only when there is a defect — not otherwise. Thus this (truth) hurts only fools, not yogis. Hence a "great fraudulence" of unending duration is *not* applicable to it.

COMMENT : Non-dualists assume that the conventionally true (vyāvahārika) is of greater value than the delusively true (prātibhāsika): for instance, the knowledge of silver is useful in the everyday-world, but when silvery shell is mistakenly identified with silver, such knowledge is not useful.

Vādirāja, like other Dualists, disagrees. Seldom is any great mischief done by a common error — and in most cases only fools suffer from their misjudgments. Moreover, ordinary illusions are the result of a defect (doṣa) — as when a person thinks the moon is small because of the "defect" of standing so far away from it; but defects can be removed or allowed for (as when the same man calculates the actual size of the moon) — thus they are short-lived. In any case, Scripture could be granted immunity

1. It is interesting that Non-dualists actually admit that Scripture is only conventionally true — even their precious identity-texts; but they claim that such texts, even though Vyāvahārika, can nevertheless *induce* in the hearer the requisite knowledge for liberation: "The roaring of the lion cognized in a dream is no doubt illusory; but, nevertheless, it enables the dreamer to wake up from his dream" (T.M.P. Mahadevan, *The Philosophy of Advaita* p. 62).

from such error. But if *all* knowledge not Brahman-knowledge is ultimately untrue, then not even the great yogis and saints, and therefore their utterances recorded in Scripture, are immune. Thus all they have said would be held in contempt. Certainly then the vyāvahārika is far more insidious than the prātibhāsika; yet Non-dualists have failed to see this.

38b-40. Moreover, if the Scripture — in case after case using words indicative of mutually distinct entities, and explaining all the sacrifices according to precepts — belong to a permanent illusion in the manner described above because of their merely conventional truth, (a spectacle of) unending depravity emerges, not (a world in which there is) the superiority of basic elements (guṇa). Therefore this (vyāvahārika-doctrine of yours) is absurd.

COMMENT : Congruent with the Non-dualists' theory of three levels of *truth* is that of three levels of *reality* — a point obvious to anyone who reflects a moment. The reason Scripture (or any statement) is ultimately false is that it reflects a state of things which is false. Now it is found that Scripture in fact reflects, and is indeed dependent on, *difference;* it uses different words to denote different things; its precepts everywhere presuppose knowledge of the peculiar characteristics of things before there can be any understanding. Moreover, it itself is obviously different from Brahman. Thus to say that Scripture is vyāvahārika is to say that the world is too. And that is exactly what Non-dualists do in fact maintain.

But it is absurd for Non-dualists to hold that the world is universally illusory, Vādirāja says. First of all, no man in his right mind would say that the Scriptures themselves (see verses 33-36a) were fraudulent. Second, it is absurd for Non-dualists to write off the world as depraved, as a gross fiction whose basic constituents (or guṇas) perpetrate the world-illusion; for they honor at least one of these guṇas — sattva — as the very dispeller of the ignorance which separates them from liberation.[1]

A further difficulty with the vyāvahārika-doctrine occurs :

1. Cf. K. Narain, *A Critique of Mādhva Refutation of the Śaṁkara School of Vedānta* pp. 97-98.

41-42. Certainly a circumstance which ensures the success of everyday life is what all describe as "true" if this circumstance alone applies, very well and good. But (in a situation) where all objects are equal with respect to annullability — precisely because of the remoteness of the annulment — there would be nothing whatever distinctive about this (circumstance described as "true"); on the contrary, there would be the objection spoken (above : that *all* circumstances are part of the universal illusion).

COMMENT : He says that what the world takes to be "true" is what works, or rather, what conduces to the good of people; for example, an action which resulted in good karma and a more auspicious birth in a future life would be "true," which an action with an opposite effect would be "false." Dualists concur in this taken-for-granted wholly unexceptionable assessment. But what about Non-dualists? It is illogical, says Vādirāja, for them to agree with the rest of the world. For their vyāvahārika-doctrine makes even "true" actions no more than part of the universal world-illusion. So on what basis would a Non-dualist discriminate between "true" and "false ?"

As the contemporary Dualist philosopher B.N.K. Sharma says, "there would be no distinction between truth and falsity in experience. There would be nothing to distinguish illusions from valid experiences. All experience would be suspect..."[1]

Vādirāja is referring to the Non-dualist version of liberation in verse 42. Liberation, at which time *all* objects and meanings irrespective of their conventional validity or invalidity are annulled from consciousness, is the beginning, according to Non-dualism, of the only ultimately valid, real, true experience : undifferentiated Brahman-Consciousness (see verses 314b-315). This Consciousness and the concomitant annulment of the world is said to be remote because liberation is regarded as many life-times away for most men. In any case, it certainly doesn't figure here and now in our attempts to distinguish truth from error at the everyday level.

Vādirāja now gives an example to show the defectiveness of the Non-dualist's vyāvahārika-doctrine :

1. Sharma, *Philosophy of Śrī Madhvācārya*, p. 138.

43-44. When an illusion (of silver in silvery shell) arises, a person desiring silver goes at that very moment to the place (of, the supposed silver) in order to inspect it and becomes aware, at that time, of the (error's) removal. But should the illusion again arise, a person *not* desiring the silver, having disregarded it and gone to his home, never experiences the removal (of the error). Tell me, what is the difference in the two cases ?

COMMENT : He asks how, if all alike is ultimately false — as the vyāvahārika-doctrine implies — there is any basis for distinguishing the experience of the first man from that of the second in the example above. Everyone but a Non-dualist would say that the first man *discovered* the error and removed it, whereas the second did not. Moreover, the first man discovered his error by closely inspecting the shell at the moment he saw it; the removal of the error did not occur at some far-off place in the distant future (as the Non-dualist's annulment of the world-illusion does).

The Non-dualist of course perceives the distinction between the experience of the two men. But he says that the corrected knowledge of the first man is conventionally true (vyāvahārika), while the uncorrected knowledge of the second man is delusively true, or in other words conventionally false (prātibhāsika). Vādirāja is in effect saying that the vyāvahārika should be regarded by Non-dualists as no better than the prātibhāsika; for next to ultimate truth (pāramārthika) they are equally illusory. And for Vādirāja, as for all Dualists, it is only the *ultimate truth* which is of value.

For him, then, there is only "true" and "false." The perception of the shell is true, that of the silver false. That is all there is to it.

He concludes :

45-46. One who is afflicted with a mania producing (conviction in) an inextinguishable "Great Illusion," who moreover declares, while posturing as one grounded on the Scriptures, a (belief in the world's) depravity *based on* the depraved condition of the all-assisting Scriptures, kills his own mother ! I believe that he gets amusement by bringing harm to everyone.

COMMENT : He says that a Non-dualist is like a man who kills his own mother : while he claims an enormous debt to the Scriptures, as a man to his mother, he at the same time nullifies their worth by saying they are vyāvahārika—a classic instance of "biting the hand that feeds you." He also says that the Non-dualist is sadistically crazed. He is like one who gets pleasure from showing all that they are but phantoms acting out their parts on an unreal stage. He undermines their confidence that what they do here has any real significance. In short, he is the enemy of the people.

For these reasons, and for all the others listed earlier (starting from verse 33), the vyāvahārika-doctrine is fallacious, and the doctrine of difference carries the argument.

V. PROOF OF GOD'S DIFFERENCE FROM SOULS FROM AN ANALYSIS OF THE EPIC AND PURĀṆIC TRADITION

Having shown the consequences of the vyāvahārika-doctrin and thereby the absurdity of it, Vādirāja in the present section makes good use of some of the holy writings that he has saved from the noose of Non-dualism to advance the opposite doctrine of Dualism.

47-48a. Moreover, Kṛṣṇa is well known as "superior in intelligence to Brahmā, Śiva (Rudra), and the rest." And since Brahmā and the rest are for that very reason proven to be inferior in intelligence, then the intelligence of souls and the Supreme (Lord) was, to say the least, different !

COMMENT : Kṛṣṇa, perhaps the most celebrated incarnation of Viṣṇu, has almost as many epithets as Viṣṇu (the "thousand-named") Himself. "Superior in intelligence," etc., is one of them, according to the commentator. This name, Vādirāja says, proves Kṛṣṇa's (and Viṣṇu's) supremacy over Brahmā and Śiva, and hence His difference from them. And if these high gods are inferior to Him, then it is obvious that it is wrong to identify Viṣṇu's intelligence with any soul's, from Brahmā on down.

48b-49a. A lowness and a highness conditioning a (solitary) Pure Consciousness would cease only at the cessation of consciousness altogether, never otherwise. Therefore the difference between a soul and the Lord is eternal.

COMMENT : Non-dualists say that all differences between intelligences are merely apparent, are nothing more than transitory "adjuncts" conditioning the One Brahman, which they frequently label "Pure Consciousness" (see ahead to verse 69 for a fuller explanation). Thus there is no *ultimately real* difference between Viṣṇu, which is just an adjunct, and a soul, which in its merely apparent individuality is just another adjunct. For these adjuncts will fall away in time (at liberation). Vādirāja says, to the contrary, that consciousness considered as a whole must be considered as eternally bifurcated into the consciousness of the Lord and the consciousnesses of His creatures. This division is ultimately real; it is not a transitory, merely apparent result of the adjunct-conditioning of a so-called "Pure Consciousness." The disappearance of this division, or difference, could mean only that all consciousness whatever had disappeared; for consciousness exists in no form but *as* "divided."

It should not be thought that Dualists have a doctrine speaking of "consciousness as a whole." In fact they do not. This phrase is appropriate only in the present context and is to be interpreted metaphorically.

49b-50a. And Viṣṇu's universal supremacy, supported by the intrinsic natures of (the different) consciousnesses, is both inviolable and eternal. How was this not so, may it be asked ?

COMMENT : Each consciousness, he says, is *intrinsically* (svabhāva) what it appears to be. Thus God really *is* the Supreme Being, and souls really *are* contingent and limited, and their resulting difference is therefore inviolable and eternal.

He now dramatically brings out this difference by showing, not merely His difference from men, but from mighty gods :

50b-51. That one of great might, Rāma, whose arrow (slaying Rāvaṇa) brought a reverent salute from Brahmā, Śiva, and the others (assembled), conquered His foe with (but) a weapon of straw ! And we, His devoted followers, will conquer with but a straw in our meeting with the adversary!

COMMENT : This passage probably refers specifically to the defeat of the arch-fiend Rāvaṇa by Viṣṇu's avatāra Rāma, as recounted in the *Rāmāyaṇa*.[1] There it describes how Rāma slays Rāvaṇa with a "huge and dreadful shaft given by Brahmā

1. Book VI, Section 110. It is entirely possible that I have not located the right reference. The commentator says the passage refers to the episode in the *Rāmāyaṇa* dealing with the defeat of the "kākāsura," which literally means "crow-demon." I have not been able to find any mention of the "crow-demon" in various recensions available to me; nor does the word turn up in any dictionary I have consulted. Thus I have taken the word to refer metaphorically, especially since "kāka" often means "contemptuous," to Rāvaṇa. In any case, Vādirāja's intent is clear.

and highly useful in battle."[1] The sequel to the slaying tells how Brahmā, Śiva, and all the other gods and celestials saluted Rāma with hands folded in the traditional Hindu manner and sung His praises by recounting His exploits and reciting some of Viṣṇu's many names.[2] Thereafter Brahmā reveals who Rāma is, namely an incarnation of Viṣṇu. Brahmā says during the speech, which is replete with splendid honorifics, "I am thy heart, the worshipful Saraswatī (Goddess of Learning) is thy tongue and all other celestials, O lord, created by Brahmā are thy down." In a more philosophical vein Brahmā adds, "none hath got independent existence but thee."[3] Vādirāja believes of course that the *Rāmāyaṇa* proves Viṣṇu's supremacy, and hence His difference from all else.

He then announces with a pun *tṛna* ("straw") — which means "arrow" with reference to Rāma and "a minimum of effort" with reference to the Dualist philosophers rebutting their adversaries, the Non-dualists — that anyone denying the plain sense of this revered writing will certainly be defeated in any debate.

52. What god excells this God — who by only a touch of his hand (on the bow-string) makes (all) beings from Brahmā on down bow to a straw ?

COMMENT : The "straw," or arrow, is of course a symbol of Viṣṇu's, or Rāma's, incomparable might.

53. And therefore who would not substantiate at the assembly (both) Rāma's eternal difference from souls and sovereignty over the gods ?

COMMENT : After stating here the overall conclusion to be drawn from the pertinent passages in the *Rāmāyaṇa* — namely Viṣṇu's supremacy and difference — he taunts his adversary with these words :

54. Look at the efficacy of (reciting) Viṣṇu's name ! It is indeed an indicator of His essential character. If you disregard it, then your Śiva would become furious !

1. M.N. Dutt, *The Rāmāyaṇa* Vol. 3, p. 1512.
2. Book VI, Section 119.
3. Dutt, *The Rāmāyaṇa*, Vol. 3, p. 151 2.

COMMENT : Śiva, let us recall, was one of those who did obeisance to Viṣṇu after Rāvaṇa was slain and the threat to their existences thereby overcome: all the gods and celestials together praised Viṣṇu by reciting His names in one mighty chorus, Śiva among them. Śiva by so praising was admitting, says our author, his dependency upon Viṣṇu; he was at that time like every other soul appreciatively reciting the holy names in order to express his homage to the Supreme, the dispenser of all favors.

One of the names of Viṣṇu (not found in the *Rāmāyaṇa* incidentally) is "superior in intelligence to Brahmā, Śiva, and the rest," as we learned in verse 47. The commentator says that Vādirāja has this name in mind here. Because some Non-dualists, Śaṅkara among them, who preach *Śiva's* supremacy at the vyāvahārika level and the irrelevancy of the whole question of supremacy at the pāramārthika level, contradict the clear intent of this epithet, no matter what level they speak from, they act at variance with the example set by their very own deity who recited many of Viṣṇu's names in the *Rāmāyaṇa*. Thus Śiva, who himself acknowledged Viṣṇu's supremacy, is said to "become furious" at his own devotees for not doing so.

Vādirāja now turns from this episode in the *Rāmāyaṇa*, which emphasizes Viṣṇu's difference from all the gods and celestials, to a passage in the *Bhāgavata Purāṇa*, which emphasizes His difference from men.

55-61a. *The Bhāgavata Purāṇa* clearly states : "Once upon a time a powerful king of Benares (Kāśī) named Pauṇḍraka, flattered by fools shouting, 'You are Vāsudeva, the Blessed One descended (to earth), the Lord of the world,' thought himself the Imperishable (in the form of an avatār). The stupid man dispatched a messenger saying, 'I am Vāsudeva,' to Kṛṣṇa.... Hearing then the boast of the dim-witted Pauṇḍraka, (Kṛṣṇa's) court-members, Ugrasena and the others, laughed loudly."[1] Now since the sentiment "I am He" is so often reviled, what sensible man would ever foster it ? The Illusionists' sentiment, "I am the Imperishable, I am the Infinite, I am Govinda the Eternal," (recited) during

1. Book 10, Chapter 66.

their continuing spiritual exercises, and Pauṇḍraka's sentiment, "I alone am the Imperishable," "I am Vāsudeva" — tell me, what is the difference between them ? This sentiment, that is to say (this) illusion, is undoubtedly voiced by *imbeciles*.

COMMENT : The story of Pauṇḍraka, who thought that he, and not Kṛṣṇa, was the avatār of God for his age, is recounted to illustrate the error of the Non-dualists, who similarly identify the soul with Brahman. How are they different, he asks, from Pauṇḍraka, who identifies himself with the Lord ? And since Pauṇḍraka is clearly censured, why do the Non-dualists persist in their error ? In doing so they show themselves to be fools.

61b-62a. Moreover, the overreacher, namely the demon-descended (Pauṇḍraka), would ride on the roads masquerading as the Four-armed (Viṣṇu) and mounted on a chariot bearing (on its standard) the golden Garuḍa (of Viṣṇu).

COMMENT : Garuḍa is a mythical golden bird, Viṣṇu's mount. King Pauṇḍraka, riding in his chariot with an artificial Garuḍa painted on its standard, imagines himself to be riding the fabulous mount of Viṣṇu Himself.

"Four-armed" is one of Viṣṇu's thousand names. Viṣṇu is depicted in religious art as having four arms and hands, each holding a distinctive badge of his character and might.

62b-65a. He (Pauṇḍraka) is indeed a mindless cretin, and his speech, namely his empty boast, was hooted by the court (of Kṛṣṇa): so Śuka (the narrator of the story) says in censure time and again. (Now) if this (sentiment, "I am Vāsudeva,") is true, then why did Śuka, the prince of yogis, make repeated censure (of Pauṇḍraka) at the Great Council of the Yogis? Why did the Blessed Lord Kṛṣṇa, incensed by the messenger's report, cut off the head of this "sage" (Pauṇḍraka) even though a house-guest of this "god of wisdom ?"

COMMENT : The *Purāṇa* tells how Kṛṣṇa traveled to Pauṇḍraka's kingdom and, after first destroying two armies with his discus, severed the head of the ridiculous Pauṇḍraka. The gravity of Pauṇḍraka's crime is accentuated by the mention of Kṛṣṇa's status as a guest; normally a host and his guest are bound by a strict code of hospitality: obviously Kṛṣṇa must have had a very good reason for behaving so inhospitably.

Śuka is the narrator of the *Bhāgavata Purāṇa.* Within the work, a framework narrative, Śuka is presented by the author, said to be Vyāsa himself, as narrating its content to his father King Parīkṣit; there is an audience of many yogis, all of whom recognize Śuka as supremely wise.

After asking rhetorically what it was that made Śuka censure and Kṛṣṇa slay Pauṇḍraka, Vādirāja concludes :

> **65b-66.** Make no mistake about it : a way of thinking which is repugnant to Śuka, to Vyāsa (sūtrakāra), to the king (Parīkṣit), to (Kṛṣṇa's) court, *and* to Kṛṣṇa is a *false* way of thinking ! That knowledge which knows "I am a slave" (relative to the supreme God) — only that — is true knowledge !

COMMENT : The whole point of the last twelve verses, let us recall, is that Non-dualists, by holding that the Supreme Brahman and souls are one, are like Pauṇḍraka, who similarly identified himself with the Supreme Being. And since Pauṇḍraka was ridiculed and slain for his grotesque error, then Non-dualists too deserve to be ridiculed and slain (in argument) for their monstrous presumption.

VI. REFUTATION OF NON-DUALIST EPISTEMOLOGY

Vādirāja now undertakes the rebuttal of his opponent's epistemology :

67-68. The procedure (we will use here) strikes at the heart of the Illusionists' retaliatory formula. This (procedure of ours) invalidates the vyāvahārika-position (of the Illusionists) and establishes the ultimate reality of the world-appearance by (using) the very method (which they use on others). Who could fail to admire this procedure (of ours), which in the end disposes only of this (method of the Illusionists) ?

COMMENT : Vādirāja here promises to show how Non-dualist theories are self-defeating. He will show how Non-dualist doctrine establishes, not Non-dualism, but, of all things, the rival doctrine of Dualism itself. "One skilled in swordsmanship will slay his enemy with his enemy's sword" so writes the commentator of Vādirāja's argumentation.

69. Now he (the Non-dualist) said, "That which constitutes the illusion of some thing or another is nothing but the Substrate of that thing's illusory appearance." The congregation (here assembled) needs to look into this.

COMMENT : Vādirāja is assuming a thorough knowledge of the Non-dualist's epistemological position on the part of the reader. This information must be supplied before we can go any further.

We must always bear in mind that the Non-dualist is ever trying to establish Brahman's unique reality. He must do two things therefore: he must show, first, that what is real is absolutely identical with Brahman, for if this were not so the reality would be second to Brahman; and he must, second, show everything else to be an illusion. Here Vādirāja will investigate the Non-dualist's attempt to do the *latter*. More specifically, he will analyze his attempt to explain how phenomena can arise to consciousness and at the same time be illusory.

The theory goes like this : The appearance of a certain object, though ultimately illusory *as such*, as are all objects, is actually the Brahman-Consciousness (or "Pure Consciousness") itself; this Consciousness — the only ultimate reality, let us recall — is the *Substrate*, or Ground, or Basis of the object. The various objects that we see are "superimposed" on the Brahman-Consciousness; each object is said to arise by virtue of a "limiting adjunct" (upādhi), so called because it "limits" the Brahman-Consciousness in such a way as to make it appear as the object seen — the pot, the shell, or whatever. Pure Consciousness is regarded by Non-dualists as shining through, as making apparent the object contacted; in that sense it is the Substrate of the object.

Prior to this "shining through," the object, indeed Pure Consciousness itself, is obscured by Ignorance, or Nescience (*avidyā*). Before this Ignorance can be removed ("destroyed"), a vṛtti, or "modification" of the viewer's mind (antaḥkaraṇa), destroys the Ignorance enshrouding the object once the senses make contact with it. Non-dualists often say that the mind is modified in such a way as to take the actual shape of the object, just as air would fill a balloon. It is only after this mental modification, or vṛtti, has destroyed the obscuring ignorance, therefore, that an object can be seen; moreover, the vṛtti has such power only because the Brahman-Consciousness suffuses or pervades, or, as is often said, "is mirrored in" the vṛtti, thus lighting the object up as it were. Note how in this scheme it is not the senses that see an object, for a vṛtti is needed to make the object apparent; note further that is not even the vṛtti which sees the object, for a vṛtti is nothing more than the key which unlocks the door behind which is the floodlight of Consciousness, the one and only Reality.

One further question needs to be asked here. Who or what precisely *does* the seeing? The Non-dualist's answer is that the soul, or jīva, does. The soul, or "individual consciousness," sees the object by its identification with the Substrate-Consciousness, which, as we just saw, suffuses the vṛtti taking the shape of the object.

To sum up: All is Ignorance (māyā) until the senses make contact with an object — at which time a vṛtti (mental modification), which is suffused by Brahman-Consciousness identical with the seeing individual consciousness, destroys the Ignorance and the object is seen. On the other side, the object itself is really no more than Brahman-Consciousness, but limited at the phenomenal level by an adjunct which makes it, when seen, appear as an object. The only ultimately real entity in all this process is the Brahman-Consciousness. Vṛtti, mind, soul in its aspect of individuality, object in its aspect of separation from other things — all this is ultimately unreal, vyāvahārika.

It will be necessary frequently to develop particulars of this Non-dualist epistemology as we proceed,[1] but for now we are prepared to follow at least in a general way Vādirāja's long rebuttal, which, as he has promised, will proceed by the method of *reductio ad absurdum.*

His first argument :

70-71a. Now if, in the case of shell (mistaken for) silver, only the Substrate-Consciousness is involved in the illusion[2] through a perception of Consciousness particularized (exclusively) by shell (and not silver), how is the twofold condition of this (Substrate-Consciousness) explained ? And how is (such) a curtailment of It based on the scriptural passage speaking of "Him shining ?"

COMMENT : He asks how, if Brahman is the sole Substrate of the world-illusion, a single object can be seen in two ways. Why isn't shell always seen as shell if it is seen at all ? Why occasionally as silver ? Why doesn't everything shine forth in the same way — as appearing to be what in fact it is — if the self-luminous Brahman is the Substrate of all objects ? The prātibhāsika-illusion of silver is therefore unaccountable.

Moreover, the Non-dualists' prized proof-text indicating Brahman's mode of existence as Substrate of the world offers no help in the matter of the silver-illusion. This text, which Śaṅkara subjects to minute analysis in his *Commentary to the Brahma Sūtras,* reads : "The sun does not shine there, nor the moon and the stars, nor these lightnings, much less this fire. After him when he shines everything shines; by the light of him all this

1. The reader desiring a fuller understanding of the arguments to follow should consult Surendranath Dasgupta, *A History of Indian Philosophy*, Vol. I pp. 470-474; and Vol. IV (1949), pp. 230-246.

2. This "illusion" refers to the vyāvahārika-illusion of the shell, not the prātibhāsika-illusion of the silver.

is lighted."[1] Where is there any indication here of a principle within Brahman the Substrate which might explain the silver-illusion once the shell is made to shine forth? Where is there any indication of a curtailment of It?

71b-72a. Moreover, the "veiling" of the Substrate by Ignorance is certainly not the (cause of the shell's) vitiation; nor does the arising of an illusory object (like a shell) because of the power of "projection" constitute the vitiation (of the shell into silver).

COMMENT: Non-dualists maintain that Ignorance has two powers: the power to veil and the power to project. When it conceals an object from consciousness altogether, thus occluding the Substrate-Consciousness, it is exercising its first power; when it projects an object — say, a pot or a shell — onto consciousness, it is exercising its second. Vādirāja points out here that neither of these powers explains the appearance of the shell *as silver.* For if Ignorance is exercising its power to veil, nothing at all will be seen; while if it is projecting the illusory objects of the world-appearance (e. g., pot, shell), as Non-dualists claim it does, we are again left with only the shell, and the silver's appearance is inexplicable.

72b-74a. If you maintain that all (knowledge) whatever comes about only in the manner (prescribed, i.e., as grounded on the Substrate-Consciousness), by what means will you trace the various illusions (pot, shell) *to souls?* For it is impossible that such (a soul) could realize an identity with those parts conditioned by limiting adjuncts, since that part conditioned by (an object like) a pot and that having the vṛtti are, according to you, different.

COMMENT: Vādirāja now leaves aside the question of how to account for prātibhāsika-illusions. Here he addresses the question of how to account for pragmatically valid "illusions," vyāvahārika-reality. Just as he used the stock example of shell-silver above to exemplify prātibhāsika-illusions, he will here, and elsewhere, employ the stock example of the "pot" to represent vyāvahārika-reality.

1. *Kaṭha Upaniṣad* 2.2.15, *Muṇḍaka Upaniṣad*, 2.2.10, *Śvetāśvatara Upaniṣad* 6.14; quoted by Śaṅkara, *The Vedānta Sūtras of Bādarāyaṇa with the Commentary of Śaṅkara*, Part I, trans. George Thibaut p. 192.

Let us recall that Vādirāja's intent since verse 69 has been to show that the Non-dualists' theory that Brahman is the Substrate-Consciousness of the whole illusory world is baseless. In the present argument he begins by alluding to two different aspects of Non-dualist doctrine: first, that a "part" of Brahman-Consciousness limited by an adjunct, let us say a pot-adjunct, is the Substrate of the pot; and second, that this pot is manifested to the individual by a mental modification (vṛtti) of the individual consciousness. He then asks how the impression of such a pot can be transferred to the individual's consciousness; for Non-dualists everywhere treat the pot-adjunct as *different* from the adjunct known as the "individual consciousness" with its succession of vṛttis. There is nothing pot-like about the second adjunct; it can no more be identified with a pot than the pot can be identified with a piece of cloth. So even if the pot *were* identical somehow with the Substrate-Consciousness, and could therefore be manifest to this Consciousness, it nevertheless remains entirely inexplicable how the pot could be manifested to the individual consciousness.

74b-75a. Moreover, if this (individual consciousness) realizes the illusion (of the pot) through a vṛtti, then this (vṛtti) may as well by itself constitute the illusion (of the pot). What is gained by this unheard-of mechanism of illusion ?

COMMENT : This argument, which shows another reason for the untenability of Brahman's being regarded as the Substrate, is found (as many of the arguments of this section) in Vyāsatīrtha, one of the most brilliant Dualist philosophers, and is summarized by Dasgupta : "... if the consciousness reflected in the *antaḥ-karaṇa-vṛtti* be supposed to remove the veil of the object, *it may as well be held to manifest it*, and it is, therefore, unnecessary to suppose that the ground-consciousness or Substrate-Consciousness illumines the object"[1] (English italics mine). In other words, the generation of the pot's appearance by the vṛtti-reflected individual consciousness makes the assumption of a Substrate-Consciousness unnecessary, for since the former is acknowledged by Non-dualists to remove the veil of Ignorance covering the object perceived, it may as well be acknowledged

1. Dasgupta, *Indian Philosophy*, IV p. 235.

to *illumine* the object as well. Why adduce two consciousnesses when one will suffice ? So the thesis that Brahman is the Substrate of the world-appearance is superfluous.

But, the alternative is little better than the original hypothesis, Vādirāja challenges. For who has ever seen or heard of a "vṛtti" which takes the shape of the object cognized by consciousness ? And certainly no such bizarre mechanism is ever mentioned in Scripture!

Having disposed of one of his adversary's lines of argumentation, he now returns to consider the prize proof-text used by Non-dualists to show that Brahman is the Substrate of the world:

75b. The Scriptural passage, "After him when he shines (everything) shines," may as well praise the sun!

COMMENT : This text (first encountered in verse 71a) appears in three of the principal Upaniṣads and, in a slightly different form, in the *Bhagavadgītā* (15.12). So important is this passage to Śaṅkara that his interpretation of *Brahmasūtra* 1.3.22 is based on it. In his *Commentary* he writes :

> . . . the manifestation of this entire world consisting of names and forms, acts, agents and fruits (of action) has for its cause the existence of the light of Brahman; . . . whatever is perceived is perceived by the light of Brahman only, so that sun, moon, etc. can be said to shine in it; while Brahman as self-luminous is not perceived by means of any other light.[1]

It is clear that Śaṅkara believes that objects are seen by virtue of their identification with the Brahman-Consciousness, which serves as the objects' Substrate. Like the sun and moon mentioned in Scripture, they are visible ("shine") only by virtue of this identification.

Vādirāja will of course have none of this. He thinks that Non-dualists misinterpret the text. His commentator points out that the word *anu*, which here means *after*, indicates that the sun and the moon are not on the same footing as Brahman; thus they cannot be identified with Him. For He is the Source of their light, and they are but borrowers (they shine "after him"). In the same way an object seen with the aid of a vṛtti cannot be said to be one with the so-called Substrate-Consciousness.

1. Śaṅkara, *Commentary*, I, p. 194.

Now the meaning of 75b emerges. Non-dualists, Vādirāja is saying, give no higher status to Brahman than to the sun. For after all, according to them the two are really one. Thus the text, as they interpret it, "may as well praise the sun." But of course the text forbids such an interpretation; far from adhering to Scripture, therefore, Non-dualists contradict it.

Vādirāja now shows how they not only contradict Scripture, but defy sound reasoning as well:

> **76.** And your position is again discountenanced because of the contact of the eye with the object : the percept of an existent pot presupposes the reality of the pot.

COMMENT : Having just shown that Non-dualists negate Scripture by making Brahman identical to objects grounded on It, he now appeals to reason to show that it is illogical for Non-dualists to speak of these same objects as "illusions." Non-dualists explain that an object like a pot is manifested only after the senses make contact with the object. But that is to say that the pot exists *prior* to the vṛtti triggering the pot's appearance, indeed that there would never have been a vṛtti at all without the pot's prior reality. How then can the pot be spoken of as an illusion ?

The present argument and the preceding one are complementary. In the first case Non-dualism gives the pot *too much* reality by identifying it with Brahman, while in this case it gives the pot *too little* reality by considering it an illusion.

> **77.** If, after violating the Scriptural passage (of verse 75) and the argument (of the last verse), (you try to recoup by saying that) the illusion in the case (of shell-silver) consists of the *witnessing-self*, (we reply that) it should be just the same in the case of the pot; for nothing needs to be accounted for twice.

COMMENT : The Non-dualists' next move is to explain prātibhāsika illusions as composed, not of the Substrate-Consciousness, but solely of the consciousness of the witnessing person (sakṣi). Such a ploy, he imagines them to feel, would explain the difference between vyāvahārika and prātibhāsika existence and thus save them the drubbing administered earlier (verses 70-72a). In other words, under this scheme the vyāvahārika would be explained as grounded on Brahman and the prātibhāsika on the soul's consciousness exclusively.

Vādirāja's response is that if shell-silver can be so explained, the pot can be explained in the same way. To provide the pot with an additional grounding on a "Substrate-Consciousness" is to ground it on *two* consciousnesses. But obviously it takes only one consciousness to perceive an object like a pot, which is certainly no more difficult to see than shell-silver. So again the Substrate-theory is superfluous.

78. And this (last theory) is illogical on another score : the *internal* witnessing-self — which, according to you, would belong to objects witnessed, like the pot above because (this would follow from your theory) of the (pot's) superimposition on the one witnessing — is in something situated *externally*.

COMMENT : He says that even if Non-dualists heeded the warning given in the verse before — that the Substrate-theory was superfluous — matters would hardly be helped. For even if it were granted that the soul's consciousness was the ground of the object seen, via a supposed superimposition of the object upon this consciousness, we would be left with but a new kind of absurdity. For the witnessing-self is *inside* the person's body, while the object seen is *outside*. So how could the two be in any sense identical ? Therefore to say that the object is grounded on the inner consciousness is a palpable absurdity — as absurd as saying that out is in and in is out!

This verse complements the previous one. In the first case the absurdity consisted of having one too many consciousnesses to ground the pot's appearance. In this case the absurdity consists in the one consciousness' having to be in two places at the same time.

79. And if, abandoning (your) acknowledged view in the case of silver-illusion and the like, you say that (only) the general (vyāvahārika) illusion is the Substrate-Consciousness, this will not do either :

COMMENT : The same distinction is made by the Non-dualist here as in verse 77 — the distinction between prātibhāsika-illusion and vyāvahārika-illusion. Vādirāja's response here.

will be different, however. He will allow the Non-dualist his Substrate for the moment, but only at the price of reminding him of still another embarrassing inconsistency :

> **80-81a**. In your doctrine the veiling Ignorance of the Substrate-(Consciousness) is the material cause of things superimposed (on the Substrate). Because of the cause's destruction when this (Ignorance) is destroyed, the thing (whose material cause the Ignorance is) would of necessity be destroyed too. Thus the idea, "There is *no* pot," should arise!

COMMENT : We have not seen this Non-dualist view before. Dasgupta explains it :

> But how did the world-appearance manifest itself ? Śaṅkara does not seem to go deeply into this question and simply passes it over in asserting that this world-appearance is all due to ignorance (*avidyā*);....But Padmapāda [one of Śaṅkara's more illustrious commentators]... says... that there is a force of power or potency (*śakti*) of nescience [or Ignorance] which constitutes materiality (*jaḍātmikā avidyāśaktiḥ*), and that it is this potency which transforms itself into the stuff (*upādāna*) of the world-appearance.[1]

It is this view — that ignorance is the stuff, or material cause, of worldly phenomena — that Vādirāja intends to expose and destroy here.

His argument is simple. If ignorance really were the material cause, or stuff, of the universe, then when ignorance is destroyed by the vṛtti, so would be the object constituted of the stuff! Therefore the destruction of ignorance should be accompanied, not by a knowledge of the object, let us say a pot, but by a void: one could say only, "There is *no* pot."

The contradiction pointed out here by Vādirāja is so egregious that one might suspect a misunderstanding on his part. This is not so. Non-dualists do speak of the Brahman-Consciousness as illuminating an object only after the Ignorance veiling it has been destroyed. And they do indeed, on the other hand, speak of Ignorance as the material cause (upādāna) of objects! The only way out for Non-dualists is for them to make a

1. Dasgupta, *Indian Philosophy*, II, pp. 8-9.

distinction between the two kinds of Ignorance. Some do make such a distinction; Bhāratītīrtha, for example, distinguishes Ignorance which is an adjunct of the soul and Ignorance which is an adjunct of the Lord — in other words, a kind of prātibhāsika ignorance (removed when an object shines forth) and a kind of vyāvahārika Ignorance (removable only at liberation). Bhāratītīrtha later says, however, that the very distinction itself is vyāvahārika.[1]

81b. She who is the wife of the illusion "There is a pot" was a widow twice over.

COMMENT : This locution, awkward in English, is hilariously effective in Sanskrit : bhramastrī ("wife of the illusion") is a pun on Brahmastrī ("a Brahman's wife").

The meaning is that the appearance of an ordinary object like a pot remains inexplicable despite two attempts by Non-dualists to account for it. For it was shown that the pot could be constituted neither of the witnessing-self in association with vṛtti nor of the Substrate-Consciousness. The pot's appearance, therefore, is inexplicable twice over; it has died two deaths, widowing Lady Illusion twice.

82. Even if it is true that you wish to preserve the doctrine of the elders, still there would be the matter of its (proper) teaching. Survey (your) skill today.

COMMENT : There is no argument here at all. He is saying merely that it is not enough for one to claim that he is preserving the doctrine of his elders, specifically Śaṅkara.[2] Such appeal to authority is worth little by itself; for it is necessary that Śaṅkara's doctrine first be understood and then rationally elaborated. Well, let us see, he says, how much sense the modern-day (sixteenth-century) Non-dualist can make :

83. Since Ignorance, by nature veiling the (Substrate-) Consciousness, would vanish, then undoubtedly the Substrate-Consciousness of the pot *is* the pot-superimposition!

1. Cf. Mahadevan, *Philosophy of Advaita*, pp. 229-231.
2. It is worth remarking that Vādirāja seems to hold his contemporaries in greater contempt than Śaṅkara. Whether anything more than the usual reverence for antiquity is reflected here is difficult to say.

COMMENT : If the pot manages to appear even though Ignorance was destroyed, then the pot *is* the Substrate-Consciousness; one should not therefore speak of the pot as *superimposed* on Consciousness, but simply *as* Consciousness. For the pot-superimposition can be accounted for in one of only two ways : as consisting of Substrate-Consciousness or of Ignorance. But Ignorance is destroyed. The result is that Brahman is the world-illusion. A more absurd result could not be imagined even by Non-dualist standards.

84-86. In addition to the defect (of your theory) voiced above — namely that the destruction of the object would result should Ignorance be destroyed — another defect is voiced : The ability in your defect-ridden Ignorance to *engender* illusions (like shell-silver) follows logically, but the beatific attribute the nature of which is to *annul* (such) illusions does not. Furthermore, how could this malignant demoness "Ignorance," which is provided with only the two-fold power of veiling (Consciousness) and projecting (illusions), bestow the good quality "knowledge ?"

COMMENT : Two blatant contradictions are presented here. First, though the Non-dualist is entitled only to say of the pot, "It is not," because of the destruction of its material cause (see verses 80-81a), he nevertheless says, "It is." Secondly, even though he admits that Ignorance possesses a defect (doṣa) which gives rise to the world-illusion, he nevertheless holds that the validly known pot arises from the defective Ignorance; in other words, jñāna (knowledge) comes from ajñāna (Ignorance, more literally "non-knowledge").

The choice of the word "defect" (doṣa) to indicate the Non-dualist's two fallacious arguments, by which he deduces things from their exact opposites, is probably a conscious mockery of the two kinds of defect — that yielding the vyāvahārika world-illusion and that yielding a local prātibhāsika illusion — ascribed to Ignorance by Non-dualists (see verses 89-90).

A piśācī, or "malignant demoness," is described by Dowson as belonging to "the vilest and most malignant order of malevolent beings."[1] She apparently has delusive powers of her

1. *Dictionary*, p. 235.

own, which Vādirāja here compares to the veiling and projecting aspects of Ignorance.

87. (Your) vacillating opinion is therefore in the disastrous circumstance called "self-refuting". Your guru forgot the doctrine that Ignorance is the material cause (of the world-appearance).

COMMENT : The implication is that, had the Non-dualist remembered this doctrine, he at least wouldn't have made the world-appearance contingent on the *destruction* of Ignorance, thereby refuting himself. But since he has so forgotten, all that Vādirāja has to do is spell out for the opponent the implications of his own doctrine. Vādirāja is of course laughing all the while; he adds insult to injury by implying that his opponent can't do his own thinking and is dependent for all his knowledge on his teacher.

The following verse logically takes up from verse 86 :

88. Since the means of knowledge, the Substrate-Consciousness, is flawed, on account of its being veiled (by Ignorance), the comprehension of material things is sought for by means of the defect called Ignorance.

COMMENT : Vādirāja wants to show here more clearly just how bizarre and wrong-headed his opponents are. Their illusionism, he explains, eventually seduced them into postulating Ignorance as the material cause of material objects, since it just wouldn't do to have Brahman as the unconditioned Substrate of an illusion. So Brahman is regarded as flawed somehow — as incapable of manifesting Itself purely — while Ignorance is regarded as the cause of the flaw; in other words, as the veil which prevents the Substrate from shining out in its native light, and instead perverts this originally pure light into the ordinary objects of the world which present themselves to consciousness. So Non-dualism ends by playing out its part in the theater of the absurd: Ignorance, not consciousness, is the means of valid sense-knowledge!

89-90. "But there is no additional defect there," say your traditional oracles. (We answer that) since both the veiling of the Substrate and the condition of being the material cause of matter refer to the same identical thing (Ignorance), then undoubtedly the destruction of the object (of Ignorance) would ensue. Only because of the existence (in your system) of the additional defect is there mention (of the rebuttal supplied here).

COMMENT : "There is no additional defect there"—that is, there is no such defect when a pot is seen as a pot. The only defect in such a case is the *general* defect of the world-illusion; sometimes referred to as "the beginningless defect of avidyā."[1] But Non-dualists also speak of another sort of defect, that which results in illusory perceptions like shell-silver. Dasgupta makes the distinction clear : "The difference between vyāvahārika and prātibhāsika is that the doṣa [defect] of the vyāvahārika perception is neither discovered nor removed until salvation, whereas the doṣa of the prātibhāsika reality which occurs in many extraneous forms (such as defect of the senses, sleep, etc.) is perceived in the world of our ordinary experience, and thus the prātibhāsika experience lasts for a much shorter period than the vyāvahārika.'[2]

Now by their insistence that vyāvahārika knowledge is *not* in need of an additional defect to explain its arising, Non-dualists, says Vādirāja, seal their own doom. For if such knowledge does not consist of such a defect, then it must consist of Ignorance unqualified in any way; but Non-dualists make it emphatically clear that this Ignorance is *destroyed* when empirically valid knowledge (of the pot) arises. So how could the pot appear precisely when its material cause is destroyed ?

This argument is essentially a repetition of verses 80-81a, but with a different twist. Vādirāja suggests here that if the Non-dualists had grounded the pot's appearance on an "additional defect," then, because a distinction had been made between the "beginningless defect" that is Ignorance and the stuff of the pot, there would be no contradiction between Ignorance's dissolution and the pot's appearance; for the pot's material cause would no longer be Ignorance, but this "additional defect."

In reminding his enemies of such missed opportunities he is showing them that he can play their game even better than they

1. Dasgupta, *Indian Philosophy*, IV, p. 254.
2. *Ibid.* I, p. 487.

can. His concluding remark seems to be saying: "Actually the additional defect would have helped you little even if you had invoked it to ground the pot's appearance. The problems with it would have proved insuperable in their own right. But its invocation would have at least indicated you were aware of the difficulty I have exposed and would have done you some credit."

91-95. And your doctrine has it that this cessation of Ignorance is contingent on a union (of Consciousness) with a defectless object through the agency of a vṛtti shaped like the thing seen. Yet it is universally agreed, because we are ignorant of an object distinguished by a flaw, that sense-experience not corresponding to the object contacted — like silver — is completely illusory, while in other (valid) instances the cause (of sense-experience) is the conjunction of the senses with the (actual) object: a union (of seer and seen) is experienced only when there is an object (already there), nowhere else. Come now, consider: why isn't shell-silver in (actual) contact with the eye ? And therefore both you and I must grant that the (defect-free) pot, really existing *prior* to super-imposition, was *non-superimposed*, and, because of its non-superimposition, was indissoluble, hence like the Ātman (i.e., Brahman).

COMMENT : The first sentence restates a familiar aspect of Non-dualist epistemology (see verse 76 in particular). He then contrasts their false theory of perception to the "universally agreed" truth — the theory of realism. He says that when we have valid knowledge, say of a pot, we contact the *pre-existing real* pot with our senses, and our senses and the pot become "united," at which time we "see" the pot; on the other hand, when we see illusory silver instead of the actual shell that our senses are contacting, what we "see" is not the object but a "defect," perhaps the remembered phantasm of real silver we have seen before; when we later discover our error, we call the silver an illusion and contrast it to the real shell.

How do we know that the defect-free pot or shell is independently real, really "out there" so to speak ? How, specifically, could anyone know that the silver, once discovered for the illusion that it is, *was* an illusion, and know by the same token that the shell is now rightfully perceived as shell ? Doesn't that judgment presuppose something (the shell) really present independent of the viewer for something else (the illusory silver) to be contrasted to ? Vādirāja thinks it does. And Sharma says : "Illusions...serve as foils to valid experience and give it its significance and value....The occurrence of illusions, at times, only confirms the possibility of true experiences at other times."[1]

This realistic analysis of sense-objects is inconsistent with the Non-dualist theory of superimposition. That theory says that an object is an illusion superimposed on the only Reality — Brahman. But if the object is there *prior* to superimposition, at which time Consciousness illumines the object, it must be capable of existing *independently* of superimposition. Even the Non-dualist himself implies the prior reality of the pot, we are reminded, when he makes the vṛtti dependent on the shape of the pot, which must therefore exist prior to the vṛtti.

All these considerations require us, and indeed the Non-dualist, to regard objects like the pot and the shell as *real.* Therefore they will not be destroyed, along with the rest of the so-called world-illusion, at liberation (as Non-dualists teach), but only left behind. They are as *real* as our own souls, indeed as real (though contingently real) as Brahman.

Vādirāja now more clearly spells out the implications of the opposing doctrine, then states his conclusion:

> **96-99.** Come now, consider: what would then be the status of the vyāvahārika? Now in your doctrine you say that a prātibhāsika reality (like shell-silver) would be a reality which is made known (as having been prātibhāsika) through an annulled illusion (as when the silver-illusion is annulled); the vyāvahārika-state refers to a reality (like the pot) which is made known through an enduring illusion. But (I say that) that reality which exists prior to superimposition can be compared only with the reality of Brahman. How marvellous! Look: the very method which was adopted by you to refute the opposition proved the doctrine of the opposition! Hence there can be no doubt that *your* beliefs were the laughing stock of the council!

1. Sharma, *Philosophy of Śrī Madhvācārya*, pp. 131-132.

COMMENT: In these verses Vādirāja re-establishes the larger context of the argument, which began back at verse 67. What has the Non-dualist succeeded in doing ? he asks. Only in establishing the doctrine of Dualism ! For since vyāvahārika objects exist prior to superimposition, as we learned above, they must be real. And if they are real, they exist alongside of Brahman, and are seconds to Him. Thus the Non-dualists are refuted — and by their own doctrines, as Vādirāja promised in verses 67-68.

100-101a. Furthermore, the blessed Vyāsa (the omniscient compiler of the Scriptures) said, "There is indeed dread over a foe." Look ! Since (you are) a foe to all, your dread extends even to yourself ! How much more (urgently) would this fear have been noted by Vyāsa (had he thought ahead to the day Non-dualism would flourish)!

COMMENT: This ingenious insult complete with scriptural deposition rubs more salt into the wound. The adversary set out to harm the world by saying it was only provisionally real. But his methodology backfired, and not only did he arouse the ire of the whole world, but he also succeeded (with an assist from his opponents) in refuting himself. How singular then must be his dread. He cannot live in peace even with himself. Such exquisite dread not even the omniscient Vyāsa thought necessary to describe!

101b-103a. The pot-superimposition is not Consciousness, which depends on a prior object. Nor is the pot-superimposition the vṛtti, for it too depends on what is prior. Hence according to your (own) belief superimposition, etc., failed also on two counts. Therefore the vyāvahārika-thesis has been exiled to a foreign country.

COMMENT: The passage harks back to verses 80-81a. There we saw that the appearance of the "world-illusion" could not be accounted for as consisting of either the vṛtti (mental modification) or the Substrate-Consciousness. Here the thought is basically the same though the language is more technical. In place of the word "illusion" substitute "pot-superimposition," and the meaning is the same: neither vṛtti nor Substrate-Consciousness constitutes the pot, for the pot pre-exists both. Thus the pot, or the world-illusion, remains inexplicable on Non-dualist terms; and the theory that the world-illusion is merely provisional (vyāvahārikata) must be considered invalid because based on this now exploded theory of superimposition.

103b-104. If the pot's manifestation should reside in the "pot-Substrate-Consciousness," then how is there the activity (of seeing) in the consciousness of the soul situated in the heart ? If by identity (of Substrate-Consciousness and individual consciousness), the activity should always be experienced by all souls.

COMMENT: In other words, even if it is granted that the appearance of the pot is accounted for by its Substrate, the Brahman-Consciousness (which manifests it), there is no accounting for the appearance of the superimposed pot to the individual consciousness. For the pot is outside the body, while the individual consciousness is "situated in the heart." If the Non-dualist then replies that the two consciousnesses are identical, in which case what was superimposed on (and manifested in) the Substrate-Consciousness would also be superimposed on (and manifested in) the individual consciousness, then *every* individual experience or perception should be experienced by *every* individual consciousness simultaneously since, as the Non-dualists would have to admit, *all* individual consciousnesses are one with the manifesting Substrate-Consciousness. Thus the Non-dualist epistemology completely fails to explain one of the most common of experiences: the mutual exclusivity of sense-impressions, the fact that only I see the paper in front of me, while my wife in the next room does not.

In the next passage Vādirāja straightforwardly presents the Non-dualist's answer to the charge:

105-107a. Now (you say that) when the inner mental organ with the eye's assistance comes forth, the modification by a vṛtti formed like the pot, etc., discriminates the object's shape like water (would if) situated in a field (under irrigation), and that as a consequence there would necessarily be a reflection of this (vṛtti) on the consciousness situated within the body; and this consciousness becomes the *knowledge* of this (object) by means of a perception of identity with the (Substrate-) Consciousness of the pot.[1]

COMMENT: With this explanation the Non-dualist thinks he has shown why the perception of the pot is not known by all individual consciousnesses even though all are one with the Brahman-Consciousness underlying the pot. Simply put, only that consciousness associated with a vṛtti of the pot will perceive the pot.

Vādirāja's sketch of Non-dualist epistemology gives us a chance to look more penetratingly at three of its leading concepts. I will rely in part on T.M.P. Mahadevan's masterly grasp of post-Śaṅkarian Non-dualist philosophy in outlining them.

(1) "The jīva-intelligence ..obscured by nescience [or ignorance]...does not by itself illumine objects like a pot. It is only through association with the internal organ [antaḥ-karaṇa] that the self apprehends objects."[2] But how does the "internal organ" apprehend objects ? we may ask. "....a transformation [vṛtti] of the internal organ is needed in order that the association of the self with the object may be effected."[3] But how does this vṛtti work ? It "goes through the senses to the object and pervades it. Thence arises the cognition of the object."[4]

In other words, the vṛtti takes the shape of the object perceived, just as "water situated in a field" — as Vādirāja says — takes the shape of the low-lying furrows it fills. But why is knowledge of the pot called a *reflection* ? In Non-dualist epistemology the consciousness perceiving the pot is spoken of as "reflected" in the vṛtti which it pervades: thus the consciousness 'mirrors" the object, thereby bringing about perception.

(2) The consciousness which perceives the pot, says Vādirāja, is "inside the body." Mahadevan explains that "the subject-intelligence which is within and the object-defined-intelligence which is without" are contrasted as such by Non-dualists; it is

1. For an illuminating "demythologization" of this Non-dualist view, see N.K. Devaraja, *An Introduction to Śaṅkara's Theory of Knowledge*, pp. 100-101.

2. Mahadevan, *Philosophy of Advaita*, p. 17.

3. *Ibid.*, p. 16.

4. *Ibid.*, p. 14.

this relation of inner to outer which makes them speak of the vṛtti's going "out to the object through the channel of the sense."[1]

(3) "In the perception of an external object, there has to be brought about the non-difference of the subject-intelligence [seeing the pot]... and the object-defined-intelligence [the Substrate-Consciousness of the pot]...."[2]

Vādirāja will attack, and has already attacked, his opponents' doctrines on each of these three fronts. He begins by (once again) pointing out the weakness of the vṛtti-theory.

107b-108a. If (the explanation of perception which you have given is) true, how does the knowledge belonging to this (individual consciousness) arise in cases of inference and the like ? For this (outward-moving) activity (of the vṛtti) does not apply in this case as in the other.

COMMENT: Vādirāja immediately finds an exception to the vṛtti-theory outlined in the previous passage. Take the case of inferential knowledge: where is there any object pervaded by the vṛtti ? Where is the field for the water to settle in ? In cases like this there is no object at all, but only a concept in the mind.

108a-109. Moreover, if one should acquire knowledge in such a case by a "mediate vṛtti" as you believe, then the *actual perception* may as well arise by the vṛtti, the only thing necessary in this case as well. Give up this useless insistence on handcuffing (perception to consciousness).

COMMENT: In order to account for inferential knowledge, Non-dualists hurry to distinguish between an ordinary vṛtti which relates to an actual object (aparokṣa-vṛtti) and one which doesn't (parokṣa-vṛtti). The latter, called a "mediate vṛtti" by Dasgupta because the knowledge it facilitates lacks the *immediacy* of direct perception, is not supposed to pervade anything at all like its sister vṛtti; nevertheless it is necessary for *non-perceptual* knowledge to arise.

Vādirāja responds to this new ploy in exactly the same way he did when the first vṛtti was encountered (see verses 74b-75a):

1. *Ibid.*, p. 34.
2. *Ibid.*

in short, if this vṛtti can "facilitate" perception, it may as well be held to "constitute" it; for if it can remove the Ignorance veiling the notion now understood, it may as well be held to illumine the notion. Thus the Substrate-Consciousness is superfluous.

As in verse 75a, where he quickly dispatched with the aparokṣa-vṛtti on the basis that such an explanation of perception was unscriptural and absurdly bizarre, he similarly brushes aside the parokṣa-vṛtti *mutatis mutandis*; only he calls it the "bonds of a rogue" ("handcuffs") in this case.

110-111. Just as the Scriptural passage, "After him when he shines everything shines," was hostile to you in the previous case, so it would be in this case too, and that (sun) should *acquire* its brightness; for the "shining," when accommodated (to the true meaning of the passage), shows that there are two different realities (spoken of). The undertaking of (still) another discussion having to do with this matter of the sun is getting fatiguing.

COMMENT: The "previous case" refers to the discussion of the aparokṣa-vṛtti in verse 75b. There Vādirāja said that the Substrate-theory, which has it that the vṛtti effects a oneness between the soul and the Brahman-Consciousness grounding the object, did not do justice to the text telling of Brahman's shining. For the text clearly differentiates Brahman the Source of the sun's light from the sun itself, which merely borrows the light. There is no oneness at all. And by analogy there is no oneness between Brahman and objects seen by souls. All alike "borrow" His light, to be sure, but none is self-effulgent, none is one with Him, as the Substrate-theory of the Non-dualists in effect says.

Now what was true with regard to objects, he says, is likewise true with regard to notions. Nothing is effected by the vṛtti in the first case, for there is no grounding of the objects on the Substrate in the first place. And the same is true *mutatis mutandis* in the present case.

In the last sentence Vādirāja needles his opponent. He implies that the Non-dualist, like a dunce, failed to learn his lesson the first time; and now he, the teacher, has had to cover the same ground again. He hopes he won't have to do it again!

112. Moreover, how did (the Substrate-) Consciousness' state of being reflected in a vṛtti lasting but an instant — (a state) which disappears the moment this (vṛtti) is destroyed — enter into the heart (or soul) again ?

COMMENT: He is saying this: How can a particular object, the appearance of which is made possible only when a vṛtti reflects that object onto consciousness, reappear (as objects commonly do) after the vṛtti facilitating its appearance is destroyed ? For there is no hope that the vṛtti will resurrect itself. And if you say that the object's appearance can be explained by a different vṛtti, then why does the object look the same ? Quite a coincidence, to say the least. How much more satisfactory, then, to explain the reappearance of an object in the way men commonly do: as the result of recontact with something existing in its own right and presisting in its existence.

113-114a. Moreover, how are the two (kinds of consciousness) identified when Ignorance is destroyed, since these two are conditioned by two (different) limiting adjuncts, namely the pot and the vṛtti ? And the adjuncts being different, there is necessarily a difference (between the two kinds of consciousness) even for you.

COMMENT: Non-dualists speak of the Substrate-Consciousness as "conditioned by a pot"; they make this Consciousness the permanent material cause of the pot. But they never say that the individual consciousness is conditioned by a pot; rather it, if anything, is conditioned by the pot-vṛtti, an entity which is confined to a definite point in space and time. How, asks Vādirāja, can two consciousnesses conditioned simultaneously by two different entities ultimately be one and the same Consciousness, as Non-dualists would have us believe ? No, the two are ultimately different, and the epistemological doctrine which makes perception contingent on an identity between the Substrate-Consciousness and the individual consciousness therefore fails.

You may recall that Vādirāja used this argument once before (verses 73b-74a).

114b-115a. And if the consciousness situated in the vṛtti should behold the pot by its own power, then the union of the two (pot and Substrate-Consciousness) through superimposition is redundant.

COMMENT: He has just shown that if Non-dualist doctrine is strictly adhered to, the Substrate-Consciousness and the consciousness reflected in the vṛtti could not be the same. But if they are not, he now says, then the vṛtti-consciousness must see the object by and of itself — i.e., independently of the misnamed "Substrate-Consciousness." Thus there is no reason to assume an identity of this Consciousness with objects like the pot through a so-called "superimposition." That doctrine becomes redundant, for the appearance of the pot has already been accounted for.

This argument repeats in slightly different language, and in slightly different contexts, the same ideas of verses 74b-75a and 108a-109.

115b-117a. And so what is the purpose of these rows of disconnected fragments ? Why couldn't the perception of such and such an object consist of the required vṛtti by itself ? Any relation whatever (between consciousness and object) could arise strictly on the strength of the resultant of these two (vṛtti and object). In what imaginable way is this rationale inconsistent with the perceived effect ?

COMMENT: The "rows" that he speaks of refer to three different consciousnesses, all of which supposedly are instrumental in perception. They are (1) the Substrate-Consciousness, (2) the consciousness reflected in the vṛtti, and (3) the consciousness "peculiar to the mind (antaḥkaraṇa)," as Vādirāja's commentator puts it. Vādirāja depicts each of these as parallel to the other two. In this way he gets across the idea of redundance, of superfluity, of a sprawling lack of economy in their doctrine — which is especially surprising (and reprehensible) because a posture of "non-dualism" would naturally suggest simplicity. The "disconnected fragments," the commentator goes on to explain, refer to the constituency of *each* of these parallel consciousnesses — all of which are Brahman, let us not forget. Each Brahman-Consciousness is composed of *parts* — pots, cloth, shell, you name it. Brahman is like an infinitely long string of beads, each bead corresponding to a perception. The word *abaddha*, here translated "disconnected," also carries the connotation "absurd."

Vādirāja is confident that his opponent will have to reject any explanation of perception which results in such a caricature of Brahman. He himself suggests the direction in which the opponent must go to be rid of this absurd and embarrassing consequence. "Trust that the vṛtti can account for perception by itself and that the Substrate-Consciousness and all the other battered paraphernalia in your arsenal are superfluous, are irrelevant to the problem of perception": this is Vādirājas' thought here.

But the vṛtti, this last refuge of respectability is booby-trapped.

117b-119a. How could a consciousness hidden within a body by nature non-transparent be reflected, when near a pot, in a vṛtti undergoing transformation outside (the body)? Since a face reflected in a mirror hidden by the hand has never been seen by anyone, then what is hidden by the body shouldn't be either.[1]

COMMENT: The vṛtti-theory doesn't hold up. For the consciousness of a man is supposed to perceive an object through its "mirroring" in the vṛtti, which in turn takes the shape of the object. But how, he asks, can consciousness which is inside a thick-skinned body be reflected (or mirrored) in something outside the body? And how, therefore, could it see the object supposedly pervaded by the vṛtti? To say that it could, would be like saying a man's face could be reflected in a mirror covered by his hand: everybody knows that the only thing visible is the hand. So how does the pot appear to consciousness, which is similarly reflected?

This argument elaborates the earlier one of verse 78.

119b-120. Otherwise (i.e., if a man's consciousness could be so reflected), a consciousness (having an experience) situated strictly within the body, framed inside the body (as in the case of a feeling of joy), yet producing its results in a perceptual vṛtti (i.e., as if it were perceiving

1. The commentator gives a passive meaning to *īkṣate*, and I follow him. The word *kasyāpi* seems to demand the passive; so does the sense of the sentence.

an exterior object), would know an (external) object visible to it exactly as this (interior feeling of joy). What is there to fear in an unconfined interior ?

COMMENT: Vādirāja has just argued that it is inconceivable that, even if there were such a thing as a vṛtti, a man's consciousness could ever be reflected in it. Here he presents the complementary argument. If that is the way consciousness behaves, then it would follow that a feeling (such as joy) perceived as interior should be experienced exactly as an external object. But everybody knows, to the contrary, that such a feeling is not.

The true view assumed all along by Vādirāja is that consciousness always stays "inside," and that the reason a pot is perceived as external is not because consciousness is being reflected in a *vṛtti* outside one's body, but because the object — as opposed to a feeling of joy — is *really present* outside one's body. This view of course postulates a *real difference* between consciousness and object — a difference which Non-dualists cannot recognize.

121. Also, since a face's reflection in a mirror would be different (from the face), that is all the more reason that reflection (in a vṛtti) would entail two consciousnesses.

COMMENT: The analogy from reflection is a bad one in the first place, he says. For it is common knowledge that a face is *different* from its reflection. For example, when a face smiles, matter is moved; there is no similar movement in the mirror *reflecting* the now-smiling face, however. How then can the Non-dualist use this analogy to explain the *identity* of the soul's consciousness and the consciousness "reflected" in a vṛtti ? Rather the analogy points to two ultimately *different* consciousnesses, and hence to the inexplicability of all perceptual phenomena engaged by an individual's consciousness.

122. Moreover, the Substrate-Consciousness would see this pot after having "superimposed" on the pot a sharing of its nature with it. If not, your guru would get angry.

COMMENT: In the "Introduction" to his *Commentary on the Brahma-Sūtras*, Śaṅkara says that the "real" and the "Unreal" have "superimposed upon each the characteristic nature and the attributes of the other."[1] Vādirāja lets his opponent know

1. Śaṅkara, *Commentary*, I, p. 4.

that he expects him to adhere closely to this orthodox Non-dualist teaching — or "your guru would get angry."

Vādirāja will now, as usual, make excellent use of this doctrine to reduce his adversary's position to absurdity:

> **123-124a.** In that case the thought "I am the pot" would be like (the thought) "I am fair-skinned," and the soul abiding within the body should observe, "I am the pot". Why (then) does that (soul) act (as if it were thinking), "I *perceive* the pot ?"

COMMENT: Non-dualists, he says, hold that the body, mind, etc., is superimposed on the Substrate-Consciousness just as objects like pots are. So why, he asks, should Consciousness say on one occasion "I am fair-skinned" of the *body* superimposed on it, but *not* say "I am the pot" of the *pot* superimposed on it ? After all, one superimposition is like another. So why in the second case does Consciousness say "I *perceive* the pot" rather than "I *am* the pot ?" And why, moreover, does it *act* not as if it were the pot, but as if it saw the pot ? This is just one more illogicality in the adversary's doctrine.

VII. FURTHER REFUTATIONS OF THE DOCTRINE THAT OBJECTS WE SEE ARE ILLUSIONS

Vādirāja now shows that the Non-dualist epistemology is inconsistent with the doctrine that the world we experience is an illusion.

124b-126a. (You say that) when Ignorance vanishes, every Substrate-consciousness without exception would be an illusion of some object or other; and when Ignorance acts as a veil, these (consciousnesses) are incapable of making the objects visible; and that has been the lot (of these consciousnesses) from all eternity. They (the Non-dualists) said, "Veiling, it abides": that was their belief.

COMMENT: In this passage he merely states his opponents' position.

This is the only place where he refers to the Substrate in the plural. Non-dualists would of course never do so, though they would be forced to admit it had its plural aspect conventionally speaking. In any case, what Vādirāja means by a particular Substrate-consciousness is the Substrate limited by a particular adjunct, such as that of a pot.

The rest of the portrayal is unexceptionable even by Non-dualists' standards.

He continues the sketch of his opponent's doctrine:

126b-128. Those (powers) which due to their natures are termed "Ignorance-projecting" and "Consciousness-veiling," have characterized the ongoing world, with its obstructed appearance, from the beginning; this illusory world-appearance was (explainable, you said, as) a transformation of (something whose) nature (is) distinguishable (from the Substrate-Consciousness underlying it). And this, (you continued,) the Substrate-Consciousness, because then veiled by Ignorance, (and therefore) comprehending material things in a flawed manner, could not manifest these (material) objects.

COMMENT: This is an accurate presentation of the vivarta-vāda ("illusion-doctrine") of Non-dualism. It states that "the world is an illusory appearance superimposed by *māyā* on Brahman."[1] The "something whose nature is distinguishable" from Brahman, mentioned in this passage, is just this māyā, or power of Illusion, and has always been presented as the very antithesis to Brahman, or Substrate-Consciousness, by Non-dualists. The exact relation between the two has never been settled, but it is generally agreed (1) that the stuff transformed into the actual objects of the world is this māyā (or Ignorance, which comes to the same thing), and (2) that "the effect has no reality apart from the underlying ground or substance [meaning the Substrate-Consciousness]."[1]

The Substrate-Consciousness, as we have seen, is unable to manifest objects without the aid of a vṛtti. Thus left to itself It comprehends material things "in a flawed manner."

Note in this sketch of Vādirāja's that the "illusory world-appearance" is said to exist, yet at the same time the Substrate-Consciousness is precluded from manifesting objects. It is this very conflict of ideas that he has in mind as he begins his rebuttal:

> **129-130a.** Since the author (you cited) says himself in his retaliatory formula that down to this present day the destruction of this (Ignorance) has been required for objects to be discriminated, then when Ignorance is acting as a veil, the Consciousness of such (an object) cannot constitute the illusion of it — (because Consciousness is not manifest).

COMMENT: He begins his rebuttal by asking the Non-dualist to face up to the consequences of his own doctrines. The Substrate-Consciousness and Ignorance, according to them, are mutually exclusive. If Ignorance is present, then the Substrate is obstructed; and if the Substrate shines through, then Ignorance is destroyed. But in that case, Vādirāja says, the world-illusion described (in verses 126b-127) as a product of the powers of Ignorance necessarily exists, prior to its manifestation, independently of the Substrate. Thus the Substrate is not the locus, or ground, of the illusion at all. It merely assists in creating the illusion.

The "author" mentioned in the verse could refer to any of a

1. Dasgupta, *Indian Philosophy*, II, p. 224.

great number of Non-dualist champions writing between the thirteenth and sixteenth centuries. Prakāśātman, Akhaṇḍānanda, and Vidyāraṇya were authors whose works were honored by Non-dualists philosophizing in the sixteenth century, when Vādirāja lived.

130b-132a. And thus (you say that) Ignorance veils the (Substrate-) Consciousness in its capacity as material cause (of the world-appearance). But you should therefore whole-heatedly affirm that *non*-illusoriness — of the whole universe, moreover — is proven just because that is so. Hence there is no illusion to creation. Think: how could it be otherwise on the very strength of your own rationale ?

COMMENT: Since Non-dualists say that Ignorance veils the Substrate-Consciousness, that is reason enough by itself to say that Ignorance, and the world constituted of it, is real. For it exists *prior* to the Substrate's comprehension of it and therefore independently of it. Thus it is altogeher wrong to speak of Ignorance, granted it exists, as an illusion. Hence the world constituted of Ignorance, its material cause, is real; it is a valid second to Brahman. Non-dualism is refuted.

He explains a further consequence :

132b-133a. The doctrine of superimposition has fled from the doctrine that Ignorance is the material cause; and when super-imposition was examined, (it was found that) the doctrine of material causality could not coexist with this.

COMMENT: These two classic Non-dualist doctrines are mutually contradictory, he says. He tells why:

133b. According to you, when a mental modification (vṛtti) *turns back* Ignorance, a superimposition on the (Substrate-) Consciousness will occur.

COMMENT: Recall that the Non-dualist holds that a vṛtti destroys the Ignorance veiling an object; in other words, only after Ignorance is destroyed by the vṛtti can there be a superimposition of the object on Consciousness, this superimposition resulting in the manifestation of the object to Consciousness. So for the object to be manifested Ignorance must be destroyed.

134. And what sensible, knowledgable man would predicate material causality of something (Ignorance) the effect of which is visible to everybody when it has ceased to exist ?

COMMENT: The meaning is this: If the Non-dualist is to cling to his doctrine that Ignorance is the material cause of the world, then he will have to admit that the material cause of manifested objects doesn't exist even while the objects obviously do. And that is strange logic.

135-136a. Therefore neither was the world illusory from being an effect of Ignorance, nor was it illusory from being a super-imposition. When one (of your theories) strives to associate itself (with the supposed world-illusion), the other shakes loose.

COMMENT: To sum up, the Non-dualist maintains two theories concerning the world-appearance: (1) superimposition and (2) the material causality of Ignorance. If ignorance must, according to the first, be *destroyed* in order for objects to appear, but must, according to the second, be *present* before the object can even exist, then the two theories are mutually destructive of each other. And since both are thereby invalidated, the theory of world-illusion is unsupportable; the world is real and thus a second to Brahman. Non-dualism fails.

136b. Moreover, the sunshine of knowledge would not scorch the top of a firmly rooted tree.

COMMENT: The "firmly rooted tree" is a metaphor here for any valid sense-knowledge. The "sunshine of knowledge" is a metaphor for any valid sense-perception. Vādirāja is thus saying that it is altogether wrong— opposed to Scripture and to immediate experience, says the commentator — to hold that valid sense-knowledge destroys the object sensed; which is exactly what Non-dualists are in effect holding by saying that Ignorance, the material cause of valid sense-objects, is destroyed when valid vṛtti-knowledge occurs.

This argument says poetically what verse 134 said in the abstract.

137. Unintelligibility is not only the ornament (or trade-mark) of your (category) Ignorance; it is also the ornament of your methodology, which contradicts an earlier (doctrine) with a later.

COMMENT: This verse is an ironic reference to a statement made by the Non-dualist Vimuktātman (writing in the thirteenth century): "Unintelligibility is the ornament of Ignorance, not an objection (to it)"[1] Vimuktātman meant that since the nature of the world itself, which is neither altogether real nor unreal, is unintelligible, then it is quite apt to describe its material cause, Ignorance, unintelligibly.[2] In this way Vimuktātman turned the tables on his opponents, who contended that the Ignorance-doctrine was objectionable *because* of the unintelligibility of the Non-dualist category Ignorance.

Vādirāja now turns the tables on the likes of Vimuktātman. Would the adversary also want to applaud the unintelligibility — or worse, the contradictoriness — of his own methodology ? He'd better; for he is guilty, as we have seen, of formulating two positions which logically exclude each other — namely, the doctrine that Ignorance is the material cause of the world and the doctrine that Ignorance must be destroyed before objects of this same world can appear.

138. Certainly an "effect of Ignorance" would be no more than *ignorant*. Where would *illusion* enter in ? Is the child of an untouchable *illusory* ?

COMMENT: This argument says that just as it is unreasonable to hold that knowledge destroys illusion, so it is to hold that Ignorance is illusion. For if one maintained the latter, he must as well maintain that the child of an untouchable (a member of the most abject class in India) is illusory just because he is descended from an ignorant mother. But that would be absurd. For it amounts to a confusion of what is worthless with what is illusory, or more generally, of evil with unreality.

139. Otherwise even your Brahman would be illusory because of Its association with Ignorance. If (you say that) Brahman is real because not superimposed, by the same token the world is real.

1. Suzanne Siauve, trans., *La Voie vers la Connaissance de Dieu* (*Brahma-Jijñāsā*) *Šelon l'Anuvyākhyāna de Madhva*, p. 72.

2. Cf. Dasgupta, *Indian Philosophy*, II, pp. 12-13.

COMMENT: In other words, if the untouchable's child in the example above *is* illusory, then Brahman should be too. For both alike are closely associated with Ignorance, and Ignorance, say Non-dualists, is synonymous with illusion.

Of course no charge could be more outrageous than to call Brahman, the One Reality, an illusion. The opponent is thus quick to reply that Brahman is not superimposed, as are illusions. Rather Brahman is that *upon which* the world-illusion is superimposed.

But if non-superimposition is a sufficient reason for the reality of a thing, then the world too must be real, Vādirāja rejoins. *Recall that in verses 130b-132a he showed how the world*-appearance had necessarily to exist independently of its superimposition on, and hence appearance to, the Substrate-Consciousness, and that therefore it had to be *different* from the superimposition. Hence, if Non-dualists say that Brahman is real precisely because non-superimposed, they must say the same of the world; for their doctrine implies necessarily the non-superimposition of the world.

140-141a. If (you say that) Ignorance is to be destroyed by knowledge, there would be only an opposition between them characterizable as destroying-versus-destroyed. How could there possibly be illusoriness ? Do you ascribe illusoriness to darkness because it can be destroyed by light ?

COMMENT : Non-dualists say that the world is illusory because it is the effect, or product, of an Ignorance which is illusory. How do they know that this Ignorance is illusory ? Because it is eradicated, or "destroyed," by knowledge, they say. But this reasoning is illogical, Vādirāja says. For things which are destroyed are not on that account said to have been illusory ! Is darkness illusory because light takes its place ? Thus there is every reason to suppose that the world, even if it *were* a product of Ignorance, is not illusory.

141b-142a. Since only a destruction of something *previously real* is experienced, as in the case of a pot or a piece of cloth, etc., then it is appropriate to think of what is destroyed as *real,* not as unreal.

COMMENT: Not only, he says, is it *un*reasonable to regard the world as illusory, supposing for a moment that it is a so-called product of Ignorance; it is *reasonable* to regard it as real. For in our experience we see *real* things destroyed, as when a pot is shattered or a piece of cloth burned. So what should dispose us to regard a pot as anything but real even if it is to be destroyed ? And since it is real, it is a real second to Brahman, and Non-dualism fails.

142b-143a. Whatever exists *without* being superimposed does not belong to this (illusion); unreality can't be ascribed (to such a thing) by a billion strategems. Otherwise Brahman's unreality would result.

COMMENT : We saw in verses 130b-132 (and again in 139) that Non-dualist doctrine necessarily implies the existence of the world prior to superimposition, and that therefore the world must be something other than a superimposition. Vādirāja says here that, since the Non-dualist is irrevocably committed to the doctrine that phenomena are illusory precisely because and inasmuch as they are superimpositions on Brahman, then there is no way that he can proclaim the non-superimposed world to be illusory; for Brahman, like the world, isn't superimposed either. So what could distinguish the two ? In other words, as the world goes, so goes Brahman. And this of course is exactly opposite to what Non-dualists want to say.

143b-145. In your creed, therefore, there is no end to the series of absurdities. Nevertheless, this rehearsal of absurdities in order to show their errors is to be stopped. I stop because (these errors are now) clear and out of a concern over the size of the work. Just as censure of that sentiment "I am He" was made in the *Bhāgavata Purāṇa,* so also (the truth of) difference will shut out fear of you with but a hiss !

COMMENT : A more literal translation of *abaddhamālā*, which I here translate as "series of absurdities," is "disconnected rows." This latter translation, which was employed in verse 115, has the merit of suggesting that the Non-dualist system is a mélange of mutually contradictory doctrines.

This passage is a general, wholesale denunciation of Non-dualism, particularly of the doctrine of world-illusion.

The "I am He" reference is to the Pauṇḍraka-episode recounted above, specifically to verse 57 where Pauṇḍraka's boast

"I am Vāsudeva" is greeted by the contemptuous laughter of Kṛṣṇa's court.

The buzzing sound *"huṁ"* (which is translated here as "a hiss") signifies strong disapproval, if not contempt. The "huṁkāra" may have been widespread at debates in Vādirāja's day and no doubt would have been used with great effect when one's opponent was found guilty of a *non sequitur*. Vādirāja here shows his contempt for the arguments of his opponent by condoning the practice.

VIII. DEMONSTRATION OF THE IMPOSSIBILITY OF VALID SENSE-KNOWLEDGE WITHOUT A SUBJECT-OBJECT-RELATION

The theory to be investigated and systematically discredited here is the Non-dualist thesis that, as Vidyāraṇya writes, "there is no conjunction of the jīva [knowing soul] with objects...,"[1] or as the contemporary Non-dualist expositor Mahadevan says, "The distinctions of cognizer, means of cognition, etc., are the creation of *avidyā*."[2]

Non-dualists are of course logically required to deny reality to objects because of their overarching doctrine of Brahman's oneness without a second. For that reason, as we know, the doctrine of illusory superimposition was invented to explain the appearance of the world. To this monism Vādirāja contrasts Madhva's realistic ontology. In the words of the latter's disciple Jayatīrtha, "There can be no knowledge in the absence of an object."[3]

It should be remembered that Non-dualists deny only *real* objectivity to worldly phenomena. They grant a provisional, or pragmatic (vyāvahārika), reality to the object-world.

> **146-147a**. Given that superimposition (as you say) is considered at variance with the seeing-seen-relation (which exists between subject and object), then according to the theory of superimposition (1) how is anything known in the absence of (such a) connection, and (2) (how is) the union intended characterized by "super imposing" and "superimposed ?"

COMMENT : Vādirāja has begun the section by asking two questions. The first he takes up now. (The second is answered starting with verse 168).

> **147b-148a**. In the first case, according to your way of thinking, what is known in the silver-illusion may as well be the rope-snake; and what is seen when the pot appears may as well be the cloth.

1. Mahadevan, *Philosophy of Advaita*, p. 14.
2. *Ibid.*, p. 13.
3. K. Narain, *An Outline of Mādhva Philosophy*, p. 22.

COMMENT : The meaning is that unless a particular perception, either valid (vyāvahārika) or illusory (prātibhāsika), is "tied down" to a real object, there would be no reason for seeing one object, or one illusion, rather than another.

The "rope-snake" is another classical illustration of prātibhāsika illusion — in this case of a snake when in fact a rope is present.

148b-149a. If, as you hold, knowledge of something is possible only because it is an effect of Ignorance, then what is (validly) known in the shell may as well be the shell-silver.

COMMENT : Non-dualists hold, as we have seen, that Ignorance is the material cause of objects like a pot or a piece of cloth, while the Substrate-Consciousness accounts for the manifestation of this or that particular object. Therefore the appearance of an object before consciousness is contingent on a particular product, or effect, of Ignorance, let us say "pot-ignorance." But in that case, argues Vādirāja, why shouldn't the appearance of shell-silver be as valid as the appearance of the real shell ? For the appearance of the silver instead of the shell is precisely due to, according to Non-dualism, the deluding powers of Ignorance attaching itself to the shell; but the shell is *itself*, is *already*, a product of Ignorance. Therefore a distinction between the shell and the silver-illusion would be groundless; and the Non-dualist theory of objectivity would suffer from over-inclusiveness (ativyāpti): illusions would have to be regarded as no less valid than the objects on which the illusions are based. Therefore this way of characterizing objectivity is fallacious.

149b-150a. Or explain this: how would what is known through Self-knowledge be Ignorance ? And how can Brahman be known in the Final Knowledge ?

COMMENT : The "Self" according to Non-dualism is "the silent witness, eternal and everlasting," which is manifest in the "state of superconsciousness," or samādhi; this Self is the "changeless Ātman,"[1] and "Self-knowledge" is the direct realization of it. The "Final Knowledge," according to Non-dualism, is the immediate and unqualified Brahman-knowledge which

1. Mahadevan. *Philosophy of Advaita*, p. 14.

commences at release; it is the pure Bliss-Consciousness which is the result of a realized identity with Brahman.

Vādirāja asks how such knowledge could be accounted for. For obviously it is not an effect of Ignorance since it is by definition the exact antithesis of Ignorance. So how can such knowledge arise to a consciousness said to perceive things only when these, constituted of Ignorance, are superimposed on the Substrate-Consciousness ? In this instance the Non-dualist theory of objectivity would suffer from underinclusiveness (avyāpti): a certain type of valid experience, indeed the only ultimately valid experience, would be completely unaccounted for. The Non-dualist theory is again proven fallacious.

> **150b-151a.** If something can be known precisely because it is an effect of Ignorance, then the *knowledge* (jñāna) of it would be an effect of the Non-Knowledge (i. e., Ignorance, ajñāna) of it.

COMMENT: The implausibility of the Ignorance-theory is immediately obvious from the language of the verse: a thing's principle resides in its exact opposite; the Non-dualist's theory is as blatantly wrong as the equation of A and non-A. To say the least, here we have another instance of over-inclusiveness. For knowledge is obviously over-extended when it is said to pertain even to material engendered by the principle directly opposed to it!

He now gives a practical example of what would happen if intelligence and non-intelligence, or Consciousness and Ignorance, were coalesced:

> **151b.** In a pot, a product of clay adhering to earth, there would be the capacity of being known *by* the earth!

COMMENT: Up till now Vādirāja has avoided labeling the Substrate-Consciousness as the world's material cause. He has carefully presented his opponents as upholders of the view that *Ignorance* is the material cause (upādāna) but here he assumes in his readers a more complete knowledge of his opponents' doctrine of material causality. He assumes that we are aware that Non-dualism resorts to two views, sometimes simultaneously, of material causality: first, that Ignorance is the upādāna of the world, and second, that Brahman Itself is the upādāna.

The force of Vādirāja's argument here consists in treating the material cause as one thing. According to Non-dualism Ignorance is not so much a power as "a substance or entity which has certain powers by which it transforms itself into cosmic appearances like the pot";[1] it is the "stuff that actually undergoes transformation,"[2] and it is "a positive power or stuff."[3] Thus in the example of our text it is the most basic "stuff" in the pot, and Vādirāja calls this "earth" (bhū). At the same time Brahman as Substrate is also spoken of as the material cause; and since Brahman is Consciousness, then the material cause is *Conscious*, and indeed conscious of the object superimposed on It. But that leaves the opponent in the ridiculous position of having to speak of the *earth* as conscious of the pot. Such is the implication of Non-dualism, says Vādirāja.[4]

152. If (the earth does) not (know, you say,) because it lacks the capacity to know, then the capacity (of the pot) to be known would occur (simply) by virtue of the nature of knowledge. What is gained by this ?

COMMENT: Vādirāja knows that the Non-dualist will not grant earth a knowledge of the pot in the example above. But then look at the alternative, he says. If the pot is *not* known by the earth, then how does the pot appear ? Knowledge by itself means nothing; there must first *be* the pot before there can be knowledge of the pot; for knowledge doesn't create the pot, but is created by the pot. So nothing is gained by denying the pot's capacity to be known by the earth of which the pot is made — as ludicrous as this is.

153. Moreover, Ignorance by its nature would at this time be only producing, and not removing, (the pot's) unintelligibility.

COMMENT: Ignorance, *he reminds his opponent*, has been said to be the principle, not of an object's apperance, but of its

1. Dasgupta, *Indian Philosophy*, II, p. 11.
2. *Ibid.*, p. 10.
3. *Ibid.*
4. The Non-dualist Appaya Dīkṣita makes a distinction between Brahman and Ignorance with respect to material causality: objects get their "being" from Brahman and their "materiality" from Ignornce (*ibid*). Others speak of the two as two strands of a single rope.

non-appearance; for Non-dualist doctrine holds that Ignorance must be destroyed before an object can be intelligible.

This is the same argument we have seen on several earlier occasions.

154. But the vṛtti, expelling the Ignorance, would through (its) power provide the pot, etc., with intelligibility (you say). Therefore, (we reply), *it* has the power to know.

COMMENT: This also is the same argument with which we are already familiar (see verses 74b-75a, 108a-109, 114b-115a).

155a. Do you call the Myrobalan tree (a mere) ten forearms high just because you have a mouth (to talk with) ?

COMMENT: He is referring to a popular saying, "Since you have a mouth, you must talk"; he means that his opponent is voicing one inanity after another — as people do who mindlessly wag their tongues just because they like to hear themselves talk.

The Myrobalan tree is a metaphor for the capacity to know, while its skimpy size signifies the much heralded, yet puny Substrate-Consciousness, which cannot destroy Ignorance and illumine objects by its own power. Since the vṛtti is the real knower, it is no more plausible, Vādirāja says, to call the Substrate-Consciousness the knower of the pot than it is to describe as a mere fifteen feet high the giant Myrobalan tree.

155b-156a. If (you insist that) a state of knowledge *is* present in a Consciousness unable to throw off Ignorance and incapable of making its own objects shine forth, why (we answer) isn't this (state) present in the *pot*, etc., (instead) ?

COMMENT: He says that before holding that a Consciousness so severely curtailed could know the pot, it would be wiser to hold that the pot could know itself!

156b-157. For if, upon the destruction of Ignorance, which is accomplished by something else (i.e., the vṛtti), this (Substrate-Consciousness) is still (regarded as the seat of) knowledge, (still it would have to be granted that) only that which destroyed the Ignorance (really) deserved to (be regarded as) capable of knowing. In that case the thing *known* would delineate itself!

COMMENT: Vādirāja insists that, since the vṛtti is the true knower, the Substrate-Consciousness is null and void. It is not the knower: It neither destroys Ignorance nor lights up the object. Yet the object *does* appear! Well, then, what can the Non-dualist say but that the object lights *itself* **up** ? But —

158a. How does a *pot*, expelling darkness as if it had the power of a lamp, get the lamp-like capacity ?

COMMENT: This is the final absurdity: pots with the power to illuminate themselves. Who has ever seen such a thing ? With this Vādirāja feels he has closed off the last escape hatch.

In fairness to Non-dualism it should be pointed out that the arguments of verses 154-158a are based on a questionable assumption: that the Substrate-Consciousness ceases to be the knower because it does not expel Ignorance, and that the vṛtti is the true knower because it does. The Non-dualist in fact conceives of the relation between Consciousness and the vṛtti as he would that between the eyes and their spectacles: It is true that imperfect eyes could not see a distant face without the help of spectacles, but on the other hand the spectacles could not see the face no matter what happened.

In the next three and a half verses Vādirāja pleads for sanity on two very basic points:

158b-159. Since your forefathers do say that knowledge destroys Ignorance, let it be stated that knowledge and the thing known exist by virtue of the nature of knowledge alone. But the assertion that the state of knowing and the state of being known exist by virtue of the power of *Ignorance* is absurdly illogical.

COMMENT: He suggests that it is essential that Non-dualists rid themselves of the absurd doctrine that knowledge is dependent on Ignorance as the material cause of valid sense-knowledge. He reminds them that earlier, more sensible Non-dualist thinkers were more apt to speak of the *destruction* of Ignorance by knowledge as the condition of valid sense-data. This last position is ultimately unintelligible as formulated by Non-dualists (see verse 152), but at least it isn't flagrantly absurd.

160-161. If you want to come up with something which will succeed in breaking down the undue extension (of perception to all things at once), let it be regarded as existing in the vṛtti required before Illusion (māyā) can be suppressed. Set your heart only on drinking the pure water obtained at home! For this desire to drink water from a mirage in the distance is baseless.

COMMENT: This argument, which reaches back to material first encountered in verses 103b-107a, correctly explains that Non-dualists invented their vṛtti to account for the fact that objects appear only one at a time — not, as might be expected otherwise, all at once. Vādirāja has all along been insisting, as we know, that the vṛtti, not the Substrate-Consciousness, should be regarded as the true knower. For it is the vṛtti which in the last analysis destroys the Ignorance which enshrouds any particular sense-object.

So to say that the Substrate knows such an object, he says, even though it does not expel the Ignorance, is like desiring to drink water from a mirage in the distance; of course no such water exists. On the other hand, he says, to make the vṛtti the knower is to set the heart on drinking pure water.

Why the praise of the vṛtti ? Is Vādirāja being ironic ? For the most part no, for vṛtti-knowledge, as we have seen, presupposes the prior existence of the object it illuminates; in other words, it can operate only against a background of real objects. Non-dualists would of course shudder to see themselves so misrepresented, but Vādirāja believes, as we saw, that their doctrine of Ignorance, and the method of its removal, presupposes this "misrepresentation."

Vādirāja of course rejects the vṛtti-doctrine of his opponents, but he likes what it implies and will use it to suit his purposes.

Now Vādirāja begins to explain what he considers true doctrine: the alternative to all of the absurdities aired unremittingly since verse 95. He will be most interested in showing what an illusion *really* is, and how to distinguish it from valid knowledge.

162. Let it be said that whatever generates a percept through its contact with the eye is the *thing known* by this (percept): wise men understand that what is first known is in all cases the *actual substance there* (viśeṣya).

COMMENT: Sensible men, Vādirāja says, recognize that there is an object really present when contacted by the senses — something which stands over against the perceiver and exists independently of the mind, something moreover which is contacted *prior* to the mind's classification of it as pot, cloth, shell, silver, rope, snake, or whatever.

163-164a. The sages of old say that the emergence of silver is produced in cases when a shell which is silvery is known, (and that this is) due to the similarity of silver to the substratum (shell) — (a similarity) called "an aptitude for being perceived in the form of silver."

COMMENT: Illusions come about, he says, when the actual substance present (the viśeṣya of the preceding verse) — in this case the shell — is mistaken for silver because of its similarity to silver. In other words, illusions occur when there is present a defect, such as "excessive remoteness, excessive nearness, excessive smallness, intervening obstruction, being mixed up with things similar to them, being manifested, and being similar to other things (sādṛśya)."[1]

So a thing can be correctly perceived as what it in fact is — and in this case there is no illusion — o what it is not — in which case we legitimately label, not the Viśeṣya, but the phantasm superposed *on* the Viśeṣya an illusion. In this way a distinction is made between reality and illusion without any of the embarrassing logical difficulties (of under-or ever-exclusiveness) that plagued the Non-dualist analysis (see verses 148b-150a).

The commentator explains that any theory of illusion which makes no provision for truly existing external realities as this one does, inevitably fails to distinguish reality from illusion, or to use Non-dualist terminology, vyāvahārika (pragmatically valid) from prātibhāsika (invalid) existence. For there would be no real entity to provide a standard by which any such distinction could be made.

164b-165a. And the innately real existent underlying this or that illusion therefore gives rise to such an (illusory) form because (its actual attributes are) suppressed; but

1. Dasgupta, *Indian Philosophy*, IV, p. 175.

the primary idea (of this existent) is not regarded as being characterized by this (illusory form).

COMMENT: He here makes the distinction — made in the immediately preceding commentary — between things as they are and things as they sometimes erroneously appear. He affirms his faith in our ability to know things as they are.

165b-167. As right knowledge manifesting some object or another would be due to the contact of the senses with that (previously existing but) up-till-now unknown object, so also would this illusion (of silver). Either an idea arising because of a desire, etc., is what is known in this (percept), or else what is distinguished by a relation with the intrinsically real will be produced. But in the absence of something to be seen the effect in that case would be nothing more than one of *unseeing* (i.e., nothing at all would be known)!

COMMENT: In other words, either shell mistaken as silver or shell recognized for what it is will be known by the viewer of the shell. In either case there is an object really there, an object existing prior to its subjectively false or objectively true perception. If there is no such object, as Non-dualists imply when they speak of all objects as illusions, then nothing whatever is seen, and the question of true or false perception is irrelevant.

This verse completes the first part of the inquiry introduced in verses 146-147a. Now the second part is taken up.

IX. FINAL CONSIDERATIONS SHOWING THE INEXPLICABILITY OF KNOWLEDGE THROUGH SUPERIMPOSITION

168-170a. (Now let's take up) the second (part of the inquiry). By the word "superimposition" illusory knowledge is expressly intended; (moreover) intelligent men are aware that what is known by this knowledge (supposedly) "superimposed"; and knowing and the state of being known have come into being (you say) in no other way but that. Now how would you, in this (second) part of the inquiry, answer this question: "How could knowing possibly characterize the one (i.e., the action of superimposing), and how could the state of being known possibly characterize the other (i.e., the state of being superimposed) ?"

COMMENT: In the first part of the inquiry (starting at verse 146), Vādirāja challenged his opponent to show how anything could be known in the absence of a real relation between seeing subject and seen object. Here he challenges him to show how the doctrine of superimposition can accommodate itself to such a relation.

170b-172a. The totality (of the process) of knowing and being known subsists strictly in vṛtti-knowledge (you in effect admit). (Now) if some relation (of knowing subject to known object) were (known to be) brought about in that way on the strength of a result (such as the appearance of a pot to consciousness), it seems to me that the bringing-about would strictly reside in the vṛtti which all acknowledge. Otherwise, how would your Brahman be knowable in the final vṛtti ?

COMMENT: Vādirāja's first rebuttal centers around the vṛtti (modification of the mind). Again he reminds his opponent that the vṛtti, since it alone can expel Ignorance, is the knower of the object uncovered, and that this knower is not any so-called "Substrate-Consciousness." But vṛtti-knowledge can take place only in a subject-object context, which is to say only if there is an object existing prior to the vṛtti. But if there is an object existing prior to the vṛtti-knowledge, what can it possibly mean to say that the knowledge of the object consists precisely in the *superimposing* of the object on the Substrate-Consciousness ? How could what was *already there* be superimposed, when the superimposition of it is the condition of its being there ?

If Non-dualists, he then says, were to disagree that the mind (antaḥkaraṇa) through the vṛtti is the knower, and assert in spite of all that consciousness is the sole illuminator and knower, they would find themselves in a very embarrassing position. For they hold that even the final knowledge of emancipation is effected through a vṛtti. The brilliant Non-dualist Madhusūdana, for example, states unambiguously that "the knowledge that contradicts the *ajñāna* constituting the world illusion must be of the nature of a vṛtti cognition."[1] Vādirāja's argument here is that if Non-dualists under the sting of criticism tried — as they certainly must try — to resist the vṛtti's power to know, then the emancipatory knowledge of identity with Brahman could not be effected. For the vṛtti alone is the true knower since it alone can destroy Ignorance. If it does not know Brahman, nothing does.

172b-173a. Men say, "My knowledge of the pot came through my eyes." The origin of the pot's perception doesn't lie in any "pot-Consciousness"!

COMMENT: Here he ridicules the notion that valid objects are manifested by the Substrate-Consciousness, on which they are superimposed. No one has ever become aware of such a Consciousness when an object was contacted, he says. Where is any evidence of the pot's superimposition on a "Substrate" ?

173b. Nor is an illusion voiding the manifesting Substrate ever seen.

COMMENT: Not only are pots not seen against a background of Consciousness; silver-illusion is never seen blanking out this Consciousness. What then should make us take seriously the bizarre epistemology, completely unattested by any valid means of knowledge, of Non-dualism ?

1. Dasgupta, *Indian Philosophy*, IV, p. 251.

174a. Tell how the world-illusion is the Brahman-Consciousness unknowable to Itself.

COMMENT: Non-dualism holds that Brahman is "self-luminous" (svaprakāśa). Citsukha defines self-luminosity as "the capability of. being called immediate in empirical usage, while remaining at the same time a non-object of knowledge. That is self-luminous, which, while not being an object of cognition, is fit to be called immediate."[1] Ānandabodha, another Non-dualist, says that the Ātman (Self), which he of course equates with Brahman, is "not an object of cognition,...cannot be manifested by cognition."[2] In other words, Brahman, though self-luminous, does not know itself as an object which is seen or in any other way objectified.

Vādirāja asks how, in that case, the world-illusion can be regarded as superimposed on this Brahman-Consciousness. For if Brahman cannot be objectified to Self, how can It be objectified to others (in the guise of the world illusion) ? The commentator sums it up this way: "A king who can't be seen even in his own quarters is not seen in the market place."

174b-175a. Thus effort to care for a baby that is seen becomes everybody. (But) who would extend himself for a baby in the womb of a round-bellied wife ?

COMMENT: The fetus described here is a metaphor for the world-illusion grounded on the unseeing (and unseen) Substrate-Consciousness. The reason that no one would extend himself on behalf of such an "illusion" is that it would be invisible. In other words, the Non-dualist hasn't succeeded in explaining the world-appearance with his Substrate-doctrine. For, first of all, the world is supposedly composed of Ignorance, which is said to veil this Substrate; and secondly, the "self-luminosity" doctrine precludes Brahman's objectivity, and by implication should preclude the appearance of anything "grounded" on it, as the world supposedly is.

The doctrine of realism, on the other hand, makes good sense. For it accounts for our experiences of and reactions to objects by the objects' real presence. They are as real as a newborn

1. Mahadevan, *Philosophy of Advaita*, p. 140.
2. *Ibid.*, p. 137.

baby, the center of everyone's attention. Even a theory which explained experience through vṛtti-knowledge exclusively would be infinitely preferable to the Substrate-theory. For at least in this case an object would precede the vṛtti — there would be an object really present for the vṛtti to pervade. But of course Non-dualists find this latter theory unacceptable, for they hold that the Substrate is the true knower, the vṛtti being merely its tool.

175b. And therefore there is no fear of the (would-be) thief of the jewel of difference.

COMMENT: This sentence concludes the long refutation of Non-dualist epistemology. Their theories of Substrate-Consciousness, superimposition, Ignorance, its destruction through a vṛtti, and the other concoctions have been shown to be either intrinsically absurd or mutually destructive of each other. Thus the reality of the world and its difference from Brahman are as firmly established as ever.

X. THE TRUTH OF VIṢṆU'S SUPREMACY AND THE FALSITY OF THE DOCTRINE DECLARING HIS SUPREMACY "MERELY CONVENTIONAL"

176-177. "The sages, O King, were celebrating the great Soma sacrifice on the bank of the river Sarasvatī (when) debate arose among them (on the question), 'Who is preeminent among the three great Lords (Brahmā, Viṣṇu, or Śiva) ?'... On (later) hearing (the report of the sage sent to find out), the seers, marvelling, with all further doubts dispelled, were convinced that Viṣṇu, from whom comes peace, from whom comes security, was the mightiest."

COMMENT: Verses 176-177 is a *verbatim* quotation from the *Bhāgavata Purāṇa.*[1] Vādirāja summarizes this particular episode beginning in verse 183 below, so I will not elaborate it here.

Our author is attempting to demonstrate from a later Scripture revered by both Non-dualists and Dualists the supremacy of Viṣṇu over all other beings, gods and souls alike. His thesis is that if Viṣṇu is superior to other beings, then He is certainly *different* from them — in which case his opponents' thesis of non-duality would become untenable. Recall that Vādirāja, and Madhva before him, is a devout theist; unlike Śaṅkara, who relegated devotion to the vyāvahārika level, Vādirāja, like Madhva, argues that nothing is so significant as or more ultimate than devotion to the One God, Viṣṇu.

178-180a. (In these words) the *Purāṇa* (smṛti) establishes the eternal difference (of them) from the entire multitude of souls. Moreover, equality and identity among these three gods has definitely not been established, for One among them is greatest. Because of the skill in discussion of those making the inquiry — namely, "Who might He be ?" — the doctrine of the proponents of oneness (of the three gods) and the proponents of equality perished through miscarriage.

1. Book 10, Chapter 89.

COMMENT: Non-dualists hold that all talk of these gods is vyāvahārika. Their distinctions are ultimately unreal. All there really is is Brahman, and these three gods are but vyāvahārika symbols of Brahman's power and efficacy. Insofar as these symbols bear any relation to reality, they do so only with reference to Brahman, Which is One.

Vādirāja argues that any such equality-or identity-talk is transparently inconsistent with the truth as determined by the sages. Any such doctrine "miscarries," for it was dead before it was born; speculating about such an identity or equality is like suckling a fetus born dead. (Note how the infant-symbolism is developed here. Five verses ago the baby was unborn but living. Here it is dead.)

180b-182. If there was still uncertainty over this, then these (sages) would begin to determine if it was so. (The result is that) this sacred precept concerning greatness, having spurned this (rival doctrine), demolishes the twofold doctrine (of oneness and equality) by siding against it. This inquiry demonstrates the eternal difference (from souls) of the three taken together, the supremacy of One (of them), and the fact that what is accepted true was believed by seers.

COMMENT: The story in the *Purāṇa* records that after debating among themselves, the sages still could not decide which god was greatest. So they invented a strategem whereby they could determine for good what the answer was. This is now described:

183-184. At the end of their examination they resolved to send Bhṛgu to behold with his own eyes the power (of each). Thinking that in a test of their capabilities the one whose power was greatest would alone emerge superior, he (insultingly) approached (each of) the three.

COMMENT: The sages decided that one of their number, Bhṛgu, should approach each god disrespectfully; the way that each comported himself, it was decided, would determine which was the greatest.

185-186a. The two gods, Brahmā and Śaṅkara (Śiva) by name, not knowing what was intended by him who approached in order to test their capability, (and thus) incensed, were graded low on account of their betrayal of the essential attribute of Brahman known as omniscience.

COMMENT: As recounted in the *Bhāgavata Purāṇa*, Bhṛgu failed to honor Brahmā (Bhṛgu's father, incidentally) with a deep bow and hymn; Brahmā was enraged but did manage to control himself.

Bhṛgu then insulted Śiva by accusing him of treachery and by refusing to embrace him. Śiva was so outdone that he came close to killing the sage, who was saved only by the entreaty of the god's consort.

Both these gods failed their tests not specifically because they became angry, but because they failed to divine what the sage's intention was, and thereby became angry. In other words, they failed the test of omniscience, an essential attribute of true divinity.

186b-188a. (But) Viṣṇu, always supremely omniscient, (apparently) not seeing (Bhṛgu's approach), tolerated the intolerable vexation of this hostile sage and bowed with His whole heart. He (Śuka the narrator) says, concluding, that these (sages), after deciding that this One elevated over all souls was therefore greater than Rudra (Śiva) and Brahmā as well, took refuge in Him alone.

COMMENT: The *Purāṇa* relates that Bhṛgu, upon reaching Viṣṇu's abode, walked in on the God as He was reclining on the lap of His consort, the goddess Lakṣmī. Bhṛgu, acting as if he were offended at the sight of so intimate a scene, kicked Viṣṇu in the chest to chastise Him. Viṣṇu bore the outrageous insult with perfect composure; He apologized for his conduct, warmly received the sage, offered him a seat, and asked his blessing.

Viṣṇu's comportment toward the sage won him the praise of all the sages, the *Purāṇa* continues; for He alone knew that He was being tested and that the sage didn't really mean the insult. He alone, therefore, passed the test of omniscience. Thus He is entitled to recognition as the Supreme God, superior to Brahmā and Śiva, as to all others.

188b-189. And therefore Maitreya's address forbids only a difference between the three marked by opposition. How could the sage have forgotten this settled truth (of Viṣṇu's supremacy) ?

COMMENT: He refers to the long address of Maitreya to Vidura in the *Bhāgavata Purāṇa* (Maitreya's address constitutes Chapters 3 and 4 of that work).

He refers specifically to certain problematic features of that address such as the following words reportedly spoken to Viṣṇu by Śiva (Rudra) : "Salutation unto thee who art the same with the Lord Rudra, who are the soul of the consciousness of ego, who are enveloped with three-fold energies, and who are Brahmā from whom divine speeches have emanated."[1] Vādirāja is aware of the "ring" of Non-dualism in this speech and others like it, and he wants to explain exactly in what sense an identity is indicated.

He says that an identity of natures could not be the import of these words. For sages do not forget, as do Non-dualists, the infallible instructions laid down by other inspired sages or by the Lord Himself. Thus Maitreya would have been aware of the unambiguous teaching of Viṣṇu's supremacy over all, as exemplified in Bhṛgu's test of the three gods.

So what can the identity indicated by the sage mean ? Vādirāja says that we are to understand that there is no opposition, or contrariety, between the three; the three share a common bliss and a common interest in the creation, maintenance, and destruction of the world. Moreover, the supreme Viṣṇu supports the other two and pervades their being. But this is the extent of the "identity," he says. The essences of each are different; and Viṣṇu is especially distinguishable from the other two by His supremacy.

190-192. But a "wise man" who would say with eloquent words postulating a merely provisional reality of the world (vyāvahārikatā) that this truth (of the Lord's supremacy) guaranteed by the seer is (ultimately) false is to be publicly questioned by discriminating judges in this way: "Why do you renounce this path of the seer ?" If you want to

1. J.M. Sanyal, trans., *The Srimad-Bhagabatam of Krishna-Dwaipayana Vyasa*, II, Book IV, p. 121.

appropriate what is opposed to it on the strength of identity-texts in Scripture (like "One only, without a second"), then all I can say is that not one of the great sages, the visionaries (written of) in the Scriptures, beginning with Vasiṣṭha were acquainted with this novel (interpretation of) Scripture.

COMMENT: Non-dualists, as we have seen, say that scriptural texts speaking of Viṣṇu's supremacy are vyāvahārika utterances: though they lead men to salvation, they are not ultimately true. Non-dualists base this interpretation of such texts on the so-called "identity-texts" of the Upaniṣads ("I am Brahman," etc.), which declare the ultimately real existence of Brahman alone. Vādirāja argues that no sage—and certainly not the Viṣṇu-worshipping Maitreya—who is told of in the Scriptures ever enunciates the "novel" vyāvahārika-doctrine. Thus there is no reason to suppose that when the Scriptures speak of the Lord's supremacy over all (and therefore difference from all), they are speaking anything but the plain and simple truth.

193a-b. And how is it that the author of the *Brahmasūtra*, Vedavyāsa, he who *abridged* this (supposed) narration (of identity in the Veda), does not *understand* the meaning of the Veda ?

COMMENT: Vedavyāsa is the mythical sage and author of the Veda (here meaning the Upaniṣads) and the *Brahmasūtra*, which is a summary of the teachings of the Upaniṣads. Vādirāja is asking how Śaṅkara in his famous *Commentary* on the *Sūtra* could have found therein the doctrine of non-dualism, together with the underpinning vyāvahārika-doctrine. For since this doctrine does not appear in the Veda (as established in the previous verse), how could it appear in an *abbreviated version* of the Veda ? Could Vedavyāsa, the very writer of the Veda, have misunderstood what he wrote ? He must have if Non-dualists have *legitimately* found their doctrine in the *Sūtra*. But that is a preposterous assumption.

193b-196. How is it that the Lord, the Vedas, Vedavyāsa, and these Vedic visionaries never taught the meaning which you have proclaimed ? Certainly these learned ones are not frauds. Since they wouldn't proclaim this "truth" of yours, the great sages simply weren't aware of this "truth." Or why didn't Śuka, when opposition to Kṛṣṇa's sovereignty arose,(have the priests) say in response (to their awakening) on that occasion, "*Prayer* to Him is the delusion of men" ?

COMMENT: Vādirāja first says that the sage-teachers and sage-authors would have been deceivers if they hadn't taught what they knew. And that possibility cannot be seriously entertained either by Dualists or Non-dualists. Thus the reason that there is no mention of the vyāvahārika-doctrine is simply that the sages knew of no such truth. Had they, he goes on to say, then Śuka, the narrator of the *Bhāgavata Purāṇa*, would have written Book 10, Chapter 23, in quite a different fashion.

There Śuka tells how a certain community of Brāhmaṇas in their spiritual pride failed to honor a request by Kṛṣṇa for rice. These men, when they realized their offense, quickly repented, whereupon they regained a true perspective and were able to speak of themselves as "powerless selves" and Kṛṣṇa (Viṣṇu) as "the Lord of all benedictions."[1] After this perspective had been regained, they reflected, "Verily, the illusion of the almighty Lord is capable of infatuating even the Yogins."[2] Vādirāja here asks why, if Non-dualism were true, the priests, once their vision had been restored, should react in so unexpected a way — in a way obviously extolling Kṛṣṇa's absolute supremacy over men, not His identity with them. Why hadn't the priests spoken of entreaty or prayer to Kṛṣṇa as being delusive, as would be fitting in a Non-dualist universe ? Why, in other words, did they awake as theists and not as monists ?

197. Moreover, because of the truth of the scriptural passage, "(This Supreme Being) is unattached,"[3] and because of the truth of the scriptural passage, "From whom words (return)"[4] the (doctrine of the) identity with the Pure Consciousness of Brahman is not attached to (or consonant with) Scripture.

1. Sanyal, *Srimad-Bhagabatam*, IV, p. 104.
2. *Ibid*, IV, p. 103.
3. *Bṛhadāraṇyaka Upaniṣad* 4.3.15, 16.
4. *Taittirīya Upaniṣad* 2.4.1.

COMMENT: These two texts speak of Brahman's inaccessibility and ineffability, and are both quoted (the first thrice) by Śaṅkara in his *Commentary on the Brahmasūtras.* Moreover, Śaṅkara makes it clear that he takes the *Bṛhadāraṇyaka* text quite literally: After quoting it he immediately says that any text speaking of some quality of the Self, or Brahman, "is (not for the purpose of teaching that the Self really possesses those qualities, but is) merely meant to glorify the Self."[1]

Vādirāja wants to know how anyone who accepts the literal truth of these texts can turn around and declare on the basis of Scripture the non-duality of such a Brahman. For isn't the truth of non-duality communicated in words which *do* attach themselves to Brahman and make this Brahman quite precisely accessible ?

198. Also, because you say that your thesis predicating the partlessness (of Brahman) is true, the identity-texts cannot stand. What (valid) meaning do you expect to arrive at by *contradicting* Scripture ?

COMMENT: Brahman's "partlessness" (akhaṇḍatva) is an important doctrine in Non-dualism. In his *Commentary* Śaṅkara refers to the text describing Brahman as "without parts, without actions, tranquil, without fault, without taint"[2] to support the doctrine.[3] In the course of his exposition Śaṅkara makes it quite clear that he regards a literal interpretation of the text as the pāramārthika, or ultimately true, truth. But that interpretation, says Vādirāja, creates a difficulty for the Non-dualist. For the identity-texts themselves are *at most* merely a *part* of the oneness of Brahman; they are obviously not completely identical with the bliss-core of Brahman's inner nature. But Brahman is partless; so the only way of somehow subsuming the identity-texts under the august Oneness of Brahman, and in that way accounting for their truth, is lost to the Non-dualist.

Vādirāja then asks in irony how his opponent hopes to establish the truth of his identity by contradicting Scripture instead of following it.

1. Śaṅkara, *Commentary*, II, p. 248.
2. *Śvetāśvatara Upaniṣad*, 6.19.
3. Cf. Śaṅkara, *Commentary*, I, p. 349.

199. This holy text (in the *Purāṇa*), supported by the scriptural texts signifying difference, having outlawed (your) identity as unscriptural, would bring about an understanding of the very beliefs of the great sages.

COMMENT: He concludes that the texts of the Upaniṣads and the *Bhāgavata* together speak of a real difference between Brahman and all other beings and invalidate the non-duality of his opponents.

200-203a. Moreover, if the (doctrine of the) annulment of the scriptural texts (indicating difference) were merely conventional (vyāvahārika), there would be no fear for the *Purāṇa*-texts (smṛti); and the scriptural texts would certainly speak the real truth in an ultimately real way (paramārthatās), for according to your (own) teaching the annulment would not be (ultimately) valid; (and) just as my duality, (which you regard as) merely conventional, is not menacing to you, so also there is no menace (in my estimation) to the *Purāṇa*-texts over a merely conventional annulment. If (on the other hand) this (annulment) were ultimately real, then it annuls even the identity-texts; then too, identity being non-existent, there would be no fear for the *Purāṇa*-texts.

COMMENT: Non-dualists hold that Brahman-Knowledge alone is ultimately real (pāramārthika); it is Knowledge which consists in a conceptionless Bliss-Consciousness such as none but the liberated experience; it is precisely this Consciousness which *is* Brahman, the "Knowledge of Brahman" and Brahman being identical. Furthermore, this Knowledge, according to Non-dualists, annuls conventional (vyāvahārika) knowledge, including all knowledge of difference. Now Vādirāja wants to know if this annulment is merely apparent (vyāvahārika) or real (pāramārthika). If only apparent, then the difference-texts in Scripture and the testimony of the *Bhāgavata* examined above is unchallenged, for a merely apparent annulment is no annulment at all. If, on the other hand, the annulment is real, then since the identity-texts themselves are part of the world, and since the opponent's knowledge of identity is conceptual (and therefore to be distinguished from the annulling Brahman-Knowledge), the identity-texts and the knowledge acquired from them are no more valid than any of the difference-texts. That being so, how can one go about preaching identity ? Certainly there is nothing to fear from a doctrine based on scriptural texts which have been annulled.[1]

203b-204a. If this Scriptural passage ("This Supreme Being is unattached") were an injunction against the attribute of attachment (of karma in Brahman), then according to you the passage would be an injunction against the attribute of (Brahman's) difference (from all things).

COMMENT: He says that Non-dualists are prone to see non-duality in texts which have nothing to do with non-duality. He says that, for example, the text cited above in verse 197, which really purports to say that Brahman is free of any karmic attachment, is misconstrued by Non-dualists to indicate Brahman's non-secondness (or "freedom from difference"). In other words, the Non-dualist thinks that the said "non-attachment" indicates an opposition between Brahman and the world so radical that nothing less than a relation of Reality vs. non-reality is called for; for only so radical an opposition could explain why there is no residual attachment whatever of the world to Brahman. The Dualist, on the other hand, believes that Brahman can be free of any such "attachment" but at the same time the world be real — in which case it is correct to talk about a real (not merely an apparent) difference between the two.

204b-205a. Furthermore, in the event of a complete standoff (vyāsaṅga) because of the mutual contradiction between those Upaniṣadic statements indicating identity and those indicating difference, why shouldn't these words (in the *Bhāgavata*) establish the true meaning ?

COMMENT: In other words, the excerpts cited from the later work (see verses 176-189) unambiguously establish, he says, the real difference of Viṣṇu-Kṛṣṇa from all other beings, including Brahmā and Śiva.[2] He feels that, if it were true that the identity-texts and difference-texts in the Upaniṣads succeed

1. Cf. Mahadevan, *Philosophy of Advaita,*.pp. 60-62.

2. Actually the *Bhāgavata Purāṇa* is neither systematically dualistic nor non-dualistic. As Dasgupta (*Indian Philosophy*, IV, p. 26) correctly says, it is "a collection of accretions from different hands at different times and not a systematic whole."

only in annulling each other, thus resulting in an inconclusive draw, then the testimony of the *Purāṇa* (which Dualists regard as authoritative) should be invoked as the tie-breaker. In that way the truth of difference could be satisfactorily established. (Dualists more typically argue that for every one identity-text in the Vedas and Upaniṣads there are many difference-texts.)

205b-206a. If the (doctrine of the) annulment (of difference) has force through an alliance (of the doctrine) with an ultimately real identity, why isn't it just as easily impotent through a connection with difference *not* (ultimately real) ?

COMMENT: The opponent says that the doctrine of the annulment of difference at the final liberation, although vyāvahārika like every other doctrine or conceptual mode of thought, can nevertheless be regarded as "having force" because allied with the pāramārthika identity. Vādirāja believes his opponent is overlooking a different kind of alliance — that of the annulment-doctrine with difference. The doctrine is itself a particular, distinct entity in the universe of differences. In other words, though the doctrine may be *associated* with the ultimately real identity because it furthers the realization of this identity, the doctrine itself is an *instance* of difference. In that case there is every reason to assume that the Non-dualist would disregard the annulment-doctrine. Or at least he would if he were logical.

206b-208a. If the principle in (determining) ascendancy is (as you say) the force in what is antagonistic (to difference), then (we say that) difference too would be a truth, (and) with a force still more forceful: the real truth would be the falseness of your identity, implicated (as it is) by the contradicting *Purāṇa* texts signifying difference.

COMMENT: Vādirāja simply wants his opponent to know he can play his game. If the opponent can arbitrarily say that identity ("what is antagonistic to difference") has force, and that difference is thereby invalidated, on the basis of some identity-texts, then he (Vādirāja) has every right to say — and moreover is less arbitrary in saying, since he has the *Purāṇa* on his side as well as the many difference-texts in Scripture — that difference has a greater force, and that identity is thereby invalidated.

208a-209a. The *Purāṇa*-text, united with and articulated according to the difference-texts in Scripture, confirmed by the practice of wise men known as interrogation, will invalidate the doctrine of a merely conventional truth and demonstrate the actual truth.

COMMENT: He says here that after all the arguments are in, the identity-theory cannot stand. The difference of the Lord from all else is valid, for none of the Non-dualist ruses has succeeded in establishing the "merely conventional" truth of the *Bhāgavata*-passages declaring the real difference of God from his real universe.

209b-210. If truth is (said to be) inappropriate to either (identity or difference exclusively on the basis of Upaniṣadic declarations), difference alone, I say, would be true. For there is the sacred text making the imprecation, "Truth is difference (truth is difference)"; (such) language pressing home the truth of *identity* is known by neither you nor me.

COMMENT: Like the preceding verses, this passage attempts to resolve the supposed ambiguity in the Upaniṣads in the favor of difference by looking outside them. Vādirāja says that the demonstrative, unmistakable language declaring the truth of difference in the above imprecation is unmatched by any similar declaration of the truth of identity. Thus difference should be given the nod on the basis of that alone. (The statement in question, though labeled *śruti* by Vādirāja, is in none of the principal Upaniṣads or the *Gītā*. It may be in one of the Brāhmaṇas).

211-212a. If a oneness consisting of Brahman who is Truth were, as you say, the truth (propounded in Scripture), then tell me — how is this truth (supposedly) based on the real meaning (consistent with) the meaning of the injunction, ("Brahman is the Truth, Knowledge, infinite") ? By what means would this (meaning of oneness) supersede the truth of the more immediate sense of difference (conveyed by the passage) ?

COMMENT: In this passage Vādirāja rebuts one of the "two principal Vedānta texts by which the Śaṅkarites seek to establish their theory of absolute monism...."[1] In this text, "Brahman is Truth, Knowledge, infinite,"[2] Non-dualists find that, as Śaṅkara puts it, "intelligence constitutes the essential nature of the highest Brahman,"[3] or in other words, that Brahman *is* intelligence (or "Pure Consciousness").

Dualists ask of their opponents at this point:

> Is Brahman, to whom all these qualities are attributed, a simple unity in Himself, or is He a complex of many qualities, truth, knowledge, infinite, etc., which have different connotations and are not synonymous ? Pure intelligence (*caitanya*) is one, but these epithets are many.[4]

Vādirāja and Madhva both say that the plurality of Brahman's attributes is inescapable if the primary sense of such texts is taken seriously. Brahman, therefore, is not even *in Himself* non-dual.

212b. And in the possessive compound ("having no second"), there would be a union with It (Brahman), not an identity with It.

COMMENT: The text referred to here describes Brahman as "one only, without a second."[5] In verse 24 Vādirāja argued that "without a second" ("advitīyam") should be treated as a possessive compound; here he assumes that it is. Non-secondness should thus be treated, he feels, as an attribute of Brahman, just as were Truth, Knowledge, and Infinity above. The meaning of the text is, as we learned in verse 24, that there is no one equal (or second) to Brahman, not that all is identical to Brahman.

Thus there is no cause for alarm in either of these two classic "identity-texts."

213-214a. Furthermore, the truth would reside in the non-annullable meaning of the Scriptures, not in that (which is) annulled. If even you admit that the meaning of the scriptural non-duality statements is invalidated because of the

1. Dasgupta, *Indian Philosophy*, IV, p. 125.
2. *Taittirīya Upaniṣad* 2.1.
3. Śaṅkara, *Commentary*, II, p. 34.
4. Dasgupta, *Indian Philosophy*, IV, p. 126.
5. *Chāndogya Upaniṣad* 6.2.1,2.

contradiction (of them) by sense-knowledge, etc., how now is there truth in them?

COMMENT: Non-dualists do not in fact admit that their non-duality texts are *invalidated* because of their incongruity with what the senses tell us; they do, however, admit the incongruity, and that admission is tantamount in Vādirāja's mind to an admission of invalidation. At the very least it casts great doubt about the sense-defying interpretation given by Non-dualists.

This argument is a take-off on Non-dualist argumentation. A Non-dualist will say that all difference is ultimately invalid because contradicted by the identity-texts. Vādirāja figures he has at least as much right to argue that identity is invalidated by sense-knowledge, particularly when the latter is buttressed by the scriptural duality-texts.

A word about sense-knowledge (pratyakṣa) in relation to Dualism would be helpful. Madhva and all of the latter philosophers of his school had the highest regard for sense knowledge, and indeed for inferential knowledge, both of which attest the reality of a world of souls and material objects second to Brahman. Their regard is signalized by this quotation from Madhva's *Viṣṇutattvanirṇaya*:

> ...difference between Jīva [individual soul] and Brahman is given by the independent authority of Pratyakṣa and inference. In that case, identity-texts would be unable to set aside this difference, which has been duly established by Pratyakṣa and inference. The Bheda-Śrutis [duality-texts] would then be adding to the weight of the earlier perception and inference about the reality of the difference between Jīva and Brahman.[1]

214b-215 When (a meticulous concern for) the primary sense (of language) is out of place, one employs a non-literal sense adopted to the different manner of speaking that kinsmen use (among themselves), and (thereby) happily relaxes with them. (In this the chances of) quarreling in the family would not be (so likely), nor, on the other hand, would all the world (outside the family) condemn (the practice).

1. Sharma, *Madhva's Teachings*, p. 58.

COMMENT: In verse 212a Vādirāja challenged Non-dualists for resorting to a secondary sense to explain away the duality-passages in Scripture. Here he defends, in conjunction with the testimony of our senses, his own reinterpretation of the non-duality texts in Scripture. He is saying in so many words that the "identity-texts" are troublesome only if read literally. But men, particularly intimates, do not always depend on the literal meaning of language when conversing. Any man well acquainted with another is able to supply the context for any statements the other makes; he knows if the other is speaking figuratively or literally, cautiously or casually. Had Vādirāja known Christianity, he might have argued that just as Christ's "family" of disciples did not regard their master's human nature voided by his words, "I and the Father are one," so the reader intimately acquainted with the Upaniṣads should not regard the world as voided by the statement, "One only, without a second."

It is interesting that Vādirāja not only explains why occasional non-literal language is used; he also defends its use. It is more appropriate among kinsmen, he says, than formal, cautious language; for the relaxation that this more casual approach to speaking affords keeps tempers down and spirits buoyant. So it is perfectly understandable, even commendable, that such "family-statements" as "I am Brahman" or "That art thou" appear in the Upaniṣads. And there is good reason not to interpret these identity-texts literally, particularly in light of our own sense-knowledge which makes it all but certain that such texts should not be taken literally.

216-217. Furthermore, how can this word "merely conventionally true" (vyāvahārika), spun out of your own head (svakapola), be applied to the utterly transcendent (apauruṣeya) words of Scripture and to the *Purāṇa* fashioned by the Supreme Spirit (mahāpuruṣa), merely out of bias for your own doctrine ? Analogously, who would put rhinestones on a priceless necklace of jewels ?

COMMENT: The only ultimately valid knowledge according to Non-dualism is *anubhava*, or direct experience of Brahman; sense-knowledge, including knowledge of the Scriptures, is according to them, as we are well aware by now, ultimately invalid (vyāvahārika). But how, Vādirāja asks, can Scripture be considered invalid ? As Dasgupta, explaining Madhva's view on the subject, says: "The Vedas are regarded as having by themselves independent force of knowledge. They are uncreated (*apauruṣeya*) and eternal (*nitya*). They are valid means of knowledge, and yet, since their validity is not derived from the speech of any person, they must be regarded as uncreated."[1] According to Dualists, the *Bhāgavata Purāṇa* is hardly less authoritative; although not "uncreated," it was created by God Himself. So how, Vādirāja asks, can Non-dualists dare to apply the concept "vyāvahārika," which is based on nothing but their own selfish needs, to these inspired words ? They may as well fashion a necklace of supposedly priceless jewels with cheap, pretentious rhinestones.

218. O ignorant man ! Though born into the family of sages (whose teachings are recounted in the Scriptures and Purāṇas), you vainly revile them, the very founders of the family; you are this noble clan's destroyer — of this there is no doubt.

COMMENT: All Vedāntins—Dualists and Non-dualists alike—are members of one family: all profess to base their belief on the Vedas, particularly the Upaniṣads, and most revere certain of the Purāṇas. Vādirāja is saying that the Non-dualist doctrine declaring these Scriptures to be non-ultimate is detrimental to the family. Not only does it split up the family, but by its very nature — as something which cuts of the hand that feeds it — it makes the Vedānta an object of ridicule.

219-221. "Thus the inspired sages on the Sarasvatī, worshipping the lotus-like feet of the (Supreme) Spirit in order to remove man's doubts, went to His protection." Think over this verse concerning the reward (of His worshippers). You may be sure that this worship of the Supreme Spirit, which destroys the doubts that men are prey to, *does* bring about the attainment of Him. What man of learning out of some perverse obstinacy would call this speech from the celebrated chapter (in the *Bhāgavata*) "only conventionally true" in the midst of an assembly of the wise ?

1. Dasgupta, *Indian Philosophy*, IV, pp. 202-203.

COMMENT: Verse 219 is the conclusion to the story telling how the sages ascertained Viṣṇu's supremacy.

This passage throws into relief the mischief that the vyāvahārika-doctrine can work. Since all of Scripture would be invalidated, the race of men would flounder: It would be unrealistic to expect a reward for a life of devotion; it would be absurd to look to the Lord in awe of his might or in expectation of his succor. For to do these things would be to act according to a "revelation," the content of which is ultimately unreal (vyāvahārika). But, on the other hand, if the identity-doctrine and its facilitating vyāvahārika-doctrine are repudiated, this bleak picture changes; for Scripture, true once again, is a valid guide to lead men through their lives into eternity. How, then, asks Vādirāja, can any wise, not to mention religious, man hold a doctrine so perfidious ?

222-224. Moreover, why don't you openly acknowledge that this nebulous term ("vyāvahārika") renders (Scripture) untrue and unrevelatory ? If the vyāvahārika-doctrine is considered in this way, (then), because (your own interpretation of) the identity-speeches is contradicted, the whole of Scripture — even that part which relates to ceremony and sacrifices (karmakāṇḍa) as well as that part which deals with Brahman (brahmakāṇḍa), (the first) revealing the observances both obligatory and optional, (the second) establishing the difference (of Brahman from his creatures and the world) and such like — (the whole of Scripture) brings happiness to good people (everywhere).

COMMENT: This passage shows the circular thinking of his adversaries: If, as Non-dualists say, all of Scripture, since distinguishable from the direct experience of Brahman-Consciousness, is vyāvahārika along with the rest of the world, then the identity-texts in Scripture would be vyāvahārika too. But the vyāvahārika-doctrine itself was born precisely because Non-dualists took these texts *as* true. In other words, this doctrine was invented specifically to accommodate, to make possible, a doctrine of identity which was consistent. That is why Vādirāja says in effect that, when the vyāvahārika-doctrine "renders Scripture untrue and unrevelatory," the doctrine paradoxically *certifies* this same Scripture and, because Scripture assumes the validity of difference in all its pronouncements, certifies the truth of difference as well. Thus Scripture is dependable, and good people everywhere are happy.

The same argument appeared in verse 202b-203a.

225-226. Why don't you ever come out and say within an assembly, "All these (words about the Lord and about religious duty) are *untrue* and *unrevelatory* !" If you are afraid to say that it is obvious that Scripture is unauthoritative, then the fault would be compounded because the censure of Scripture is veiled; in that way, you fool, there is the additional deception of good people.

COMMENT: Non-dualists teach that much of Scripture — particularly ritualistic and theistic statements — is merely a series of concessions made to the common man in his half-earnest search for salvation. This teaching, Vādirāja has made clear above, is a grave error. But what makes matters worse is that Non-dualists refuse to part with the Scriptures; they regard them (particularly the identity-texts) as man's means of release. Vādirāja believes that this stance is hypocritical; it would be better to openly declare the Scriptures' fraudulence once for all and then dispense with them, rather than to hamstring them with the disabling vyāvahārika-doctrine yet at the same time cling to them either for a false security or in order to stand tall in the deceived eyes of the world. For in that case the enemy would at least be recognized for what he was and his statements presumed suspect rather than trustingly adopted. (This passage repeats the theme of verses 45-46).

227-229. And when the same (vyāvahārika-doctrine), opposing both (identity-and-difference-) texts alike, sets aside (their) validity, then how can you abandon the many (difference-texts in favor of a few identity-texts) ? Your texts would deserve to be invalidated because not conforming to the rule (imposed by your own vyāvahārika-doctrine which nullified *all* texts). If not, why is a Buddhist, valuing the (few) scriptural statements favorable to him, ignoring all the rest of Scripture opposed to him — (why is he) not right while you, sir, are ? Hence this filthy demoness-of-a-sophistry (the vyāvahārika-doctrine) is not to be brought into an assembly of the wise.

COMMENT: He says that a Non-dualist Hindu who nullifies all of the Scripture with his vyāvahārika-doctrine, but then champions certain texts in this same nullified Scripture, is exactly like a Buddhist. For a Buddhist also rejects the Vedas (though for a different reason) while nonetheless believing certain doctrines (reincarnation, karma, etc.) originally taught in the Vedas. Is it logical, Vādirāja asks, to assume that the Non-dualist can pick-and-choose the few scraps of truth in Scripture with any greater accuracy than the Buddhist ? Of course not. So the Scripture-devouring vyāvahārika-doctrine must be dropped; the Non-dualist must reassert the full and ultimate truth of all of Scripture — or else be as arbitrary as a Buddhist in choosing what in Scripture he values.

230. Therefore, according to those seers who know all things, Viṣṇu, so vastly different from the (myriad) souls whose state has been determined to be low, was of a nature judged (by the seers as) supreme.

COMMENT: Vādirāja here rests his case. The vyāvahārika-doctrine having been rebutted, men can rely on the words of the Upaniṣads and, in particular, of the *Bhāgavata Purāṇa* to speak the unblemished, ultimate truth. Thus the *Bhāgavata*-passage declaring Viṣṇu's (Kṛṣṇa's) supremacy and man's inferiority relative to Him can be confidently regarded as true.

XI. A DILEMMA FOR NON-DUALISM: EITHER BRAHMAN ITSELF OR MERE MATTER SUFFERS KARMIC DEBTS*

231-232. If the Supreme Being and a soul are identical (as you claim), then the soul baking in hell (naraka)[1] for its sins will experience the harsh pain, and te Blessed One, dwelling eternally in the heart (here meaning the soul) in order to incite both the activity and the experience of this (soul), would (Himself) suffer by virtue of its suffering.

COMMENT: With these verses Vādirāja begins to explore another absurd consequence of Non-dualism. He acknowledges along with his adversary that certain souls suffer in hell, accordint to the law of karma,[2] for their sins. But if that is the case, he goes on to say, then Non-dualists are in for an embarrassment. For they take Yājñavalkya literally when he says, "On the heart, Your Majesty, all beings are supported. The heart, verily, Your Majesty, is the Supreme Brahman."[3] Thus they are compelled to draw the conclusion, Vādirāja claims, that Brahman itself must suffer the very pains of hell that the soul (or "heart"), with which it is identical, is suffering. And how can Brahman, which Non-dualists regard as unimpeded Bliss-Consciousness, do that ?

233. It is proper to hold that only the soul can sin but that matter cannot sin. Ask yourself whether expiation (for sins) is proper to a man or to a can.

COMMENT: Vādirāja is wary lest his Non-dualist opponent, in order to protect the Ātman from the imputation of sin and

*Part of this Ch. has already appeared in my article in *Religious studies* (Cambridge Uni.) Vol. 12, No. 3 (Sept. 1976), pp. 281-90.

1. Naraka, usually translated "hell", is one of the devices by which souls which have led wicked lives are justly punished. As in Christianity, it is popularly regarded as a fiery pit where the guilty souls are tormented. Unlike Christianity, Hindus (with the lone exception of the Dualists of Vādirāja's school) regard hell as temporary — really more of a purgatory than a hell.

2. The karma-doctrine states that a soul will in the end reap precisely what it sows in a perfectly just moral universe.

3. *Bṛhadāraṇyaka Upaniṣad* 4.1.7; Radhakrishnan, *The Principal Upaniṣads*, p. 252.

suffering due it, since either of these would hardly befit Brahman said to be identical with it, should maintain in the course of argumentation that it is not the soul (jīvātman) which sins (or commits any act, for that matter), but rather the antaḥkaraṇa, or inner mental organ. Vādirāja reminds his opponent that Non-dualism maintains that this organ is an extremely transparent *material* stuff; by itself, therefore, it is not conscious, it is not intelligent; as superimposed on the Pure Consciousness (Ātman-Brahman), it merely *conditions* this Consciousness; it may be considered as the lens focusing the light of Consciousness.[1]

It would be useless, therefore, for the Non-dualist to point to the antaḥkaraṇa as the seat of sin and suffering. Can matter experience the suffering of hell ? If so, then one may as well say that a can is capable of suffering as well as a man.[2]

234. Furthermore, the body's inner mental organ and the like (i.e., buddhi, ahaṁkāra) cannot be the seat of sin, as you would require, because in deep (dreamless) sleep, when everything (except the Consciousness of Bliss) is dissolved, the basis of sin would happen not to exist.

COMMENT: Non-dualists distinguish the blissful Ātman that is our "real Self" from the antaḥkaraṇa ("inner mental organ") manas ("mind"), buddhi ("intellect"), and ahaṁkāra ("ego"), all of which are matter and in themselves unconscious. They say that ordinary consciousness is a result of the reflection of Pure Consciousness on these material instruments of perception. Now Non-dualists regard the state of dreamless sleep as the one instance in the life of an ordinary man when Brahman-Consciousness shines through unhindered: "According to them, no one has the experience of 'I' in the deep-sleep-state."[3] In other words, all of the machinery of ordinary consciousness is dissolved.

1. Cf. Dasgupta, *Indian Philosophy*, II, pp. 76-77, for a detailed explanation of the relation of Consciousness to antaḥkaraṇa.

2. Actually Vādirāja asks the Non-dualist to consider whether a man or an *arrow*, not a can, is able to suffer. But since the verse in Sanskrit is especially effective because *narāṇām* (of men) and *śarāṇām* (of arrows) rhyme, I have rendered the rhyme rather than the literal meaning into English.

3. Narain, *Mādhva Refutation*, p. 71.

Vādirāja retorts that this teaching is inconsistent with the karma-doctrine as interpreted by Non-dualists, at least as long as they insist on regarding the antaḥkaraṇa as somehow the seat of sin. His argument is the same as Vyāsatīrtha's, reported by Narain:

> The denial of the ego in the deep-sleep-state entails the discontinuity of the "I" that enters this realm of oblivion with the result that it is difficult to be convinced that the same sleeper has awakened. In other words, the ego in the deep-sleep would make the recognition of personality impossible.... Because the individual before sleep was a different personality, all his actions must be supposed to have remained fruitless. Not only this, the enjoyments of the awakened individual would appear to be due to no *karma* at all.[1]

Simply stated, the existence of karma is inexplicable if the seat of sin is the egoistic mental organ; for this organ is said to dissolve during deep sleep, and the new one that would replace it upon awakening would be discontinuous with the first.

235. Moreover, since this (antaḥkaraṇa) is dissolved, the dissolution (in turn) of deep sleep (and subsequent return of ordinary consciousness) would be inexplicable; for, as the clear-sighted say, it is karma which is the cause of everything that happens.

COMMENT: He says that if the antaḥkaraṇa, the seat of sin and repository of karma, is dissolved, then the routine karmic effect of waking would in itself be inexplicable. There should be an endless sleep!

236-237a. Furthermore, you hold that Ignorance clings to the reflection (of Pure Consciousness, namely the soul); (in that case) certainly sin and the rebirths marked by duḥkha (suffering) which result from it would pervade the soul itself. Talk it over with children: "What is responsible for doing right and wrong ?" (They'll tell you!)

COMMENT: Vādirāja is here asking the Non-dualists merely to heed the consequences of their own teaching. If the soul is, as

1. Narain, *Mādhva Refutation*, p. 73. See Dasgupta, *Indian Philosophy*, IV, p. 236, for a shorter exposition of the same argument, and *ibid.*, p. 243, for a Non-dualist counter-argument.

they say, the locus of Ignorance (avidyā), then the soul itself must experience the effects of this Ignorance, which are sin and the round of rebirths resulting from sin. The mechanical, insentient antaḥkaraṇa (mental organ) may indeed be a necessary cause of sin and so forth, but certainly it does not *experience* the sin or its consequences; only the soul can do that. Even children, he concludes, know the difference between spirit and matter. They know that it is the conscious soul itself which commits sin and suffers the consequences.

237b-239. Furthermore, a particular momentary, perishable thought is not (the same as) the result (of it existing) at a different time. A present mental state (buddhi) is the doer; another, existing at a different time, experiences (the deed's karmic fruit): indeed one commits sins, another suffers the consequence ! A man of wisdom would ask (at this point): How could the extinction of what has been caused and the emergence of what is uncaused possibly come about ? Therefore the soul itself is both the doer and the enjoyer (or sufferer of consequences) since it (alone) is permanent.

COMMENT: Vādirāja says that if the antaḥkaraṇa, which is non-spiritual and is ultimately no more than a convenient designation of a series of mental states (here labeled buddhis), is the doer and experiencer rather than the Ātman, then the law of karma would become unmanageable. For the mental states which collectively make up the antaḥkaraṇa are *discrete* — the percept of a pot, for example, is both temporally and qualitatively different from that of a piece of cloth — and thus there is no principle of continuity which enables us to contend that the first percept is related to the second. More to the point, there is no basis for asserting a relationship between the mental state of a particular evil desire and the mental state of pain said to be karmically produced by the desire. The law of karma, says our author, would be made a shambles of, for this law is grounded on the assumption that whatever does an action itself reaps the consequences of that action.

It is necessary then that there be a principle of continuity, he says, if the karma-doctrine is to apply. It is necessary to regard one and the same thing as both the doer and the enjoyer. What might that be ? It could be only the jīvātman, he says, for it alone persists. It alone weaves the disparate mental events into a single tapestry. But, of course, if the jīvātman is the actor and enjoyer/sufferer, it would obviously have to be different from the ever-blissful Brahman-Consciousness, and Non-dualism would have to be abandoned.

240-241. Moreover, if the qualities of right (dharma) and wrong (adharma) are postulated only of the mental states, then the destruction of these two (qualities) would doubtlessly ensue because of the destruction of their cause. And therefore the production of new mental states and even the attainment of heaven would be inexplicable. Thus these qualities belong only to the soul.

COMMENT: We have seen that according to Non-dualism activity and enjoyment belong not to the soul or jīvātman, but to the antaḥkaraṇa, and that this antaḥkaraṇa consists of a succession of mental states known as buddhi. Now among these mental states, we are here reminded, are those we characterize as right and wrong, good or evil. Indeed, Non-dualists themselves speak of a buddhi as a "mental state of determination or affirmation"[1] — as, in other words, a state of *willing*.

But these mental states are momentary, we are reminded. Thus, as they perish, so does the good or evil done by them. But since, according to the law of karma, it is precisely the free activity of the antaḥkaraṇa as manifested in its good or evil mental states which *brings about* the corresponding rewards or punishments, these latter are inexplicable. So there is no cause whatever for the future experiences of happiness or sorrow; indeed the attainment of heaven so confidently expected by Non-dualists for an upstanding moral life becomes impossible; for the doer of the good deeds — the various buddhis — which would be expected to land the soul in this temporary land of bliss perish as soon as the good that they do is done.

So again some principle of continuity is essential if right and wrong are to bear their corresponding fruit. This principle *is the soul which is both the doer and the enjoyer, as the karmic law of strict justice requires.*

1. Dasgupta, *Indian Philosophy*, II, p. 75.

242. Moreover, since in that case (i.e., in the event that right and wrong are perpetrated by the mental states) the *fruit* of sin would belong to something different from that which had *committed* the sin, the experience of the torment of hell would have to apply to the soul itself (i.e., to the same entity which has sinned).

COMMENT: If one entity sins and another suffers the fruit, the law of karma is caricatured. Some principle of continuity is required if the law is to be intelligible. This principle is the soul. But since the soul is thereby the sufferer, it is absurd to identify it with Brahman, as Non-dualists do.

Vādirāja's refutation now takes a somewhat different direction; he begins by defining several important terms used by Non-dualists to explain perception:

243. This (soul) has (so you say) its location in the body; the eye (seeing), and so forth, is the stimulus; the antaḥkaraṇa is the mind (manas); the buddhi is but (this mind's momentary) agitation consisting in a thought (or percept).

COMMENT: He says that Non-dualists understand, first, that the soul, which by itself is one with Brahman, is located in and pervades the body; the body is its sphere of influence. He then notes that the senses are for the purpose of stimulating responses within the body-soul complex. Next he asserts that Non-dualism treats the antaḥkaraṇa, or "mind", whose nature we have already learned something of, as functionally indistinguishable from the mental category known as manas. Finally, he defines the buddhi in the manner already familiar to us. He now continues:

244-245. The percept which consists in acute irritation resulting from the contact of one of the senses, the nose, for example, with a fetid taste or smell is no more than this buddhi (you say). But it is always the Ātman (or Self, identical to Brahman), whose nature it is to actually *experience* the affliction, your doctrine says (in effect), while the buddhi is only the impression of the external datum conveyed by the external senses, (in this case, the sense of smell).

COMMENT: Having shown above the absurdity of making

250. How vastly different is Kṛṣṇa, destroying the pains of hell because of the mere mentioning (of His name), from the soul in its relation to the pains of hell after mentioning Him.

COMMENT: In fact the Supreme Lord and the soul have nothing in common, he says. The Lord frees the souls of men who call out to Him, wittingly or unwittingly, while the souls are the freed.

Throughout the next fifteen verses Vādirāja undertakes to show the Lord's sinlessness, a fact which makes the identification of Him and souls, particularly those sinful ones suffering in hell, especially outrageous. He begins with two quotations from Scripture to show the nature of the Lord's activity:

251. One Scriptural passage says, "He is not tainted by evil actions"; and another says, "He does not increase through actions, nor decrease."

COMMENT: These passages, both taken from the *Bṛhadāraṇyaka Upaniṣad,*[1] show the Lord's immunity from karma. He is not capable of growing, as are men, through good actions, for He is already completely fulfilled; and He is not capable of doing evil actions, since He by nature is good. Another way of putting it is that He is capable of neither "good" nor "evil" actions, but only of "perfect" actions; in other words, He is beyond the usual moral distinctions that men make.[2]

252-254. Now (ordinarily) men of the world who instigate action are definitely tainted by evil. But there is no anxiety over Viṣṇu's instigation of action. Look at his wisdom: Since He brings about evil (only) through (the mechanism of the sinner's) prior evil, and not out of spite (for the sinner), He is not tainted by evil — just as (a king) providing the stake for the thief (who is to be executed by it is not); no evil is done by drowning a thief in water, nor is there sorrow over this. So how could wickedness attach itself to Viṣṇu's instigation of activity ?

COMMENT: He says that men ordinarily do evil when they

1. 4.4.23.

2. What is interesting (and problematic) about these two quotations is that whereas in their contexts they refer to the *knower* of Brahman (*brāhmaṇasya*) — of this there can be little doubt — Vādirāja makes them refer to Brahman (Viṣṇu) Himself. He may of course have had a different version of the text from any I have seen.

instigate some action toward another; for their motive is usually attachment or aversion to this person, rather than concern that justice be dispensed. Unlike them is Viṣṇu: He instigates action toward men, it is true; He rewards and He punishes. But his actions are always just and impartial. In the case of the evil-doer, Viṣṇu punishes, to be sure, but only because the sinner has deserved, has even mandated, punishment. Viṣṇu is the doer of evil only in the sense that a king who righteously and lawfully executes a thief is a doer of evil: a genuine evil is indeed done the thief from the thief's perspective, but from a higher, and a truer, perspective, the "evil" turns out to be but the expression of a sovereign and healing justice.

It is interesting that Śaṅkara makes the same argument in his *Commentary on the Brahmasūtras*,[1] but whereas he is talking about the nature of Īśvara, who for Śaṅkara is but a vyāvahārika reality, Vādirāja is of course talking about the nature of an ultimately real Lord.

After comparing the Lord's justice-doing to an earthly king's he now contrasts these two:

255-256. One who is a king over a certain region at a certain time is limited to that (region and time); the punishment of those who do evil within that time is commendable, but not for that reason at another time. But Vyāsa (sūtrakṛt) says (in the *Bhāgavata*) that sentencing by Viṣṇu, the Lord, for wrong-doing is commendable in every region and every world.

COMMENT: The *Bhāgavata Purāṇa*[2] contrasts the limited jurisdiction of a king to the unlimited jurisdiction of God. Echoing this contrast, Vādirāja explains that an earthly monarch has jurisdiction to punish a criminal only during the time he is actually reigning as king and only if the criminal is his legitimate subject. If he punishes under any other circumstances, he himself sins. But there are no restrictions on God; His jurisdiction extends throughout all time and space. Consequently He can do no wrong in punishing the wrongdoer. God is guiltless; if so, He cannot be identical with guilty souls. Still less can He suffer their fate.

1. Cf. Śaṅkara, *Commentary*, I, pp. 358-359 (2.1.34).
2. Book 6, Chapter 3.

257. This same (Viṣṇu) is in that way glorified as King of kings by all who conform to the Vedas. Another passage in Scripture praised "His supreme power."

COMMENT: The *Śvetāśvatara Upaniṣad* speaks of God as "the Supreme Lord of lords."[1] One verse later "His supreme power" is alluded to.

258-259. Everybody agrees that as a rule He would remove men's evil by having them experience the torment of a just retribution in a place like hell, but that in certain cases Viṣṇu — because of (the sinner's) remembrance (of His name) or because of direct realization (of Him) — would remove sins with His power even without (the sinner's) experience (of the usual retribution).

COMMENT: It is sometimes naively assumed that in Hinduism, as opposed to Christianity, there is no room for divine mercy. This is certainly not the case in the Vaiṣṇava cults, as we may easily see from this passage. Viṣṇu's mercy is automatic in two instances: Viṣṇu cannot resist even the most miserable sinner who dies with the divine name on his lips, as we have already seen; such a man not only has his sins removed but achieves liberation for all eternity at death. The other way is by directly realizing God. Such a realization is to be distinguished, Sharma tells us, from "the mental image conjured up by the devotee thro' constant flow of meditative recollection."[2] It is rather a meeting God "face to face," a seeing of His form as it really is. It is an actual and not a figurative seeing. Moreover, it is not open to man by his own efforts. Only by Viṣṇu's dispensation can the devotee realize this supreme achievement. As in the first case, all sins are removed by this direct realization. Were the soul to depart from its body at that moment, it would be eternally liberated.

260-261. Therefore, since by both retribution and power the Lord of the universe removes all sins, of the foolish and the wise (alike), then Lakṣmī's Lord (Viṣṇu), because of His skillful disposition (of sinners), is certainly not (Himself) tainted by evil. On the contrary, He, like

1. 6.7.
2. Sharma, *Philosophy of Śrī Madhvācārya*, p. 318.

the sun, destroys with His innate radiance the deepest darkness.

COMMENT: By "retribution" is meant the normal way of "working out" one's karma. By "power" Vādirāja means the two ways — remembrance of Viṣṇu's name and direct realization — mentioned above: Viṣṇu dispenses with the otherwise ironclad law of karma "with His power" when either of these two situations applies.

One of the two points that Vādirāja makes here is that God, who so wisely and mercifully deals with sinners — as the last four verses have shown — certainly incurs no sin of His own. The other point is that God would not destroy sin if He were Himself sinful. He destroys sin, and makes the complete purification of the sinner a prerequisite for entry into His abode, only because His nature is diametrically opposed to sin of every sort.

So Viṣṇu, the Sinless, is different from sinful souls; and it is utterly absurd to postulate the identity of Him with souls sinning or experiencing the karma of their sins.

262-263. In Him who, uncreated, is not like what is created, who would grant, even without (the retribution associated with) karma, liberation merely because of (a soul's direct) knowledge — where is there something improper ? Since Scripture calls Him "the Lord over all," (He in His) skill, in order to safeguard the authenticity of Scripture, will occasionally exercise a fraction of His power (and nullify karma).

COMMENT: He begins by paraphrasing the scriptural passage, "What is not made is (not characterized) by what is made."[1] God, he says, cannot be faulted for his dismissal of karma in certain cases; it is not the case that God is *unjust* when absolving the karmic debt of some souls but not of others. For He is the master of karma, He is the law's creator and authenticator. He can cancel it when He sees fit. (One is reminded of the New Testament parable of the denarius: the day-long worker can have no bone to pick with his master).

Moreover, Vādirāja continues, it is consistent with Scripture,

1. *Muṇḍaka Upaniṣad* 2.1.1.

which calls God "the Lord over all,"[1] that He dispense with karma on certain occasions. For nothing could as dramatically demonstrate His unique majesty as His over-ruling of this venerated and otherwise inviolable law of the universe.

264. He who effects this (nullification of karma) is "not bound" (by karma), according to Scripture, (even) when He creates, (maintains, and destroys the world). How is there evildoing in this nullification (of karma) if He, after destroying everything, remains stainless (even then) ?

COMMENT: In the *Bhagavadgītā* the Lord says to Arjuna, "Works do not defile Me; nor do I have yearning for their fruit. He who knows Me thus is not bound by works."[2] Now the creation, maintenance, and destruction of the universe are the works of the Lord, and according to the *Gītā* they must be regarded as leaving no karmic traces on the Lord. As the *Bṛhadāraṇyaka Upaniṣad* says, "He does not increase through works, nor decrease."[3] But then, says our author, if the Lord remains sinless even when He destroys the universe at the end of a kalpa, as Scripture assures us, then it is all the more unreasonable to impute sin to the Lord because of His disposition of sinful souls; for any man who was looking for wrongdoing on the part of the Lord would look first to the greater supposed wrong rather than to the lesser. But since Scripture explicitly denies wrongdoing (in the form of karma) to the Lord in the case of the greater, it is absurd to impute Him with it in the case of the lesser.

265. Moreover, the Vedas say, "It conducts the soul to an evil world as a result of its evil." How therefore could the agony of hell which arises from sin characterize the Sinless ?

COMMENT: The *Praśna Upaniṣad* says: "And then udāna [one of the five vital breaths]...conducts the departing soul to the virtuous world, for its virtuous deeds; to the sinful world, for its sinful deeds; and to the world of men, for both."[4] This

1. *Bṛhadāraṇyaka Upaniṣad* 4.4.22, 5.6.1.
2. 4.14. S. Radhakrishnan, *The Bhagavadgītā*, 2d ed., p. 161.
3. 4.4.23. Cf. verse 251.
4. *Praśna Upaniṣad* 3.7. Nikhilananda, *The Upaniṣads*, abridged ed., p. 152.

quotation throws into relief the fact that only the sinful, the evil, experience the pains of hell. And since God is not evil, it is absurd to devise a system, namely Non-dualism, which mandates His suffering there by virtue of His identity with the souls of suffering sinners.

266. Since these two, the Supreme (Brahman) and an individual soul, (although according to you) situated in the very same limiting adjunct (body, antaḥkaraṇa, etc.), are intrinsically different, it is therefore ridiculous to speak of an identity between the two.

COMMENT: Vādirāja concludes that there can no longer be any doubt that Brahman and the spiritual entity existing within and quickening a man's body are intrinsically different. Therefore Non-dualism, which teaches by implication, as Vādirāja is confident he has shown, the contemptible and sacrilegious doctrine of Brahman's identity with souls that sin and suffer, must be rejected once and for all.

XII. REFUTATION OF THE REFLECTION-ANALOGY USED BY NON-DUALISTS TO SHOW BRAHMAN'S IDENTITY WITH THE SOUL

Non-dualists are hard-pressed to explain the apparent multiplicity of souls when in fact there is only, as they believe, the one spiritual principle, Brahman. They do so with the aid of an analogy. Brahman, they say, is like an object which is being reflected in a mirror, while the soul is the reflection of that object. Śaṅkara writes, "...that individual soul is to be considered a mere appearance of the sun in the water..." He continues,

> Hence just as, when one reflected image of the sun trembles, another reflected image does not on that account tremble also; so, when one soul is connected with actions and results of actions, another soul is not on that account connected likewise. There is therefore no confusion of actions and results.[1]

Mahadevan explains the more developed view of the *Vivaraṇa* school of Non-dualism:

> ...the jīva [or soul] is a reflection of intelligence [or Consciousness] present in egoity; and since there is no difference between the prototype [or original] and the reflection, the jīva is non-different from Brahman. The reflected face in a mirror, for example, is not other than the prototype. It is identical with the original face, with certain traits such as facing oneself, being located in the mirror, etc., superimposed thereon.[2]

As was just said, Non-dualists feel that this reflection-analogy is singularly effective for illustrating an apparent duality amid an actual non-duality.

Now for Vādirāja's rebuttal :

267. Now the identity between the Original (Brahman) and Its reflection (the soul) which you hold is not reasonable, for there is the obvious opposition consisting of the state of inner-vs-outer.

1. Śaṅkara, *Commentary*, II, p. 68 (2.3.50).
2. Mahadevan, *Philosophy of Advaita*, p. 220.

COMMENT: He begins the rebuttal by saying that it is unreasonable to declare an identity between the original and its reflection because it is obvious that the reflection is exterior to the object reflected; or as Vādirāja might put it, an object is "interior to itself," while its reflection is "exterior to it." One may speak of an exact resemblance perhaps, but not an *identity*.

268. For to our way of thinking the true nature of the Self (Ātman) for that very reason should consist exclusively of what is within. But to your way of thinking this same (Self) in its entirety becomes (in the analogy) the thing seen outside.[1]

COMMENT: He explains that if the Self, or Brahman, and the soul are related as the original to its reflection, then there is every reason to assume their *difference*, not their identity. For, as stated above, what is inside (i.e., the original) is different from what is outside (i.e., the reflection). Yet what do Non-dualists do ? They in effect say that Brahman which is supposedly the original in the analogy, is also the reflection, "the thing seen outside." They nullify the physical space between the original and its reflection.

269. Even your commentator (on the *Brahmasūtras*, Śaṅkara) says that there is no condition of one being the other because the two are incompatible precisely by reason of the inner-vs-outer relation.

COMMENT: In the opening lines of his celebrated *Commentary on the Brahmasūtras*, Śaṅkara says that "it is wrong to superimpose upon the subject — whose Self is intelligence, and which has for its sphere the notion of the Ego — the object whose sphere is the notion of the Non-Ego, and the attributes of the object, and *vice versa* to superimpose the subject and the attributes of the subject on the object."[2] He then says that the "interior Self" (pratyagātman) "is never an object." Now Śaṅkara's intention is to show, not that an identity between the Original and its reflection is impossible (for that analogy is not in his

1. In our text one syllable failed to print. "Pratya pam" should read "pratyagrūpam."

2. Śaṅkara, *Commentary*, I, p. 3.

mind), but that the *real* Self and the *false* self, the ego, are not the same, since the false self doesn't *really* exist.

Now Vādirāja is not concerned here with the precise context of Śaṅkara's argument. He is interested rather in the *basis* of non-identity in the passage. And he finds it in the inner-vs-outer state characterizing the inner Self, or Ātman, and the outer object, specifically the ego, superimposed on It. For why should Śaṅkara stress the *interiority* of the Ātman if he did not have this relation in mind ? (Actually Śaṅkara never uses the word "exterior" of the object, though from the context he well might have without changing the meaning.)

Vādirāja argues, therefore, that an identity between Brahman and the soul based on the analogy of reflection contradicts the opening lines of Śaṅkara's *Commentary*, where it is said, or rather implied, that what is interior and what is exterior, as is the original with respect to its reflection, cannot be legitimately identified.

270-272a. Since (the impossibility of such an identity is) established by (Śaṅkara's) contradicting words, (which say that) there can be no identity between an original and its reflection, just as (there can't be) between the Self and matter, because they exist in the relation of inner-to-outer, how can you, sir, (dare to) reject this deduction ? If your opposing thesis is allowed, the *Commentary* (of Śaṅkara) would be violated; thus it invalidates (your thesis), for an intelligent man (like Śaṅkara) wouldn't postulate at the very beginning (of his work) a basis (for the non-duality of entities related as outer-to-inner) which didn't apply in every case.

COMMENT: Vādirāja asks how his opponent can dare to contradict the great patriarch of Non-dualism, Śaṅkara. He acknowledges, at least for the sake of argument, that Śaṅkara, whatever else he may be, is an intelligent man and isn't likely to commit the well-known logical fallacy of anaikāntika-hetu,[1] that is to say, of failing to establish an absolute concomitance between what is to be proved (i.e., the non-identity of entities exterior to each other) and the prior existence of the basis for

1. Cf. Dasgupta, *Indian Philosophy*, I, p. 344.

holding it (i.e., the relationship of mutual exteriority). In much less technical language, it would not be expected that Śaṅkara would allow an exception to be made to the law he laid down on page one of his most prestigious work. Yet the identification of an object and its reflection would constitute just such an exception. In that case there is little to fear in this reflection-analogy, for the adversary's chief guru has invalidated it before Dualists had even a chance to!

Nevertheless, you may be sure, Vādirāja will take his turn anyway! He begins:

> **272b-273a.** How could a soft face go into a white copper mirror? If it couldn't, the warmth of a (face's) reflection in hot water should be the property of the face (itself) as well!

COMMENT: If, for example, a face and its reflection are identical, Vādirāja explains, then one of two equally preposterous situations must follow: either the face must pervade the reflection, or the reflection must pervade the face. If the former, then it remains to be explained how a soft face can pass into the hard substance of a copper mirror; if the latter, then it remains to be explained why a face reflected in hot water does not acquire the warmth of the water.

> **273b-274a.** How could a massive elephant enter into the tiny space (of a hand-mirror)? If it could, this (mirror) would drop from the hand because of its weight!

COMMENT: He says that if the Non-dualists are right in identifying original and reflection, then an elephant's reflection in a hand-mirror should send it crashing to the ground, for no man can hold an elephant in his hand!

> **274b-275a.** The actual (flesh-and-blood) figure would belong to what was pervading (the reflecting substance) in precisely that way (i.e., as a reflection), not to something that wasn't. Since not, a *swimmer's* face under water should according to you be (regarded as) the *reverse* (of what everyone knows it to be, i.e., the actual face).

COMMENT: Here Vādirāja further explores the consequences of subsuming the original under the reflection. If, he says, the reflection is the actual figure of the face, then how does one categorize the face of a swimmer under water ? For such a face, although pervading the water, is not a *reflection*. And since it is the reflection which is identical with the real face, it would seem that the Non-dualist would be logically compelled to regard a pervading but *un*reflected face as either an anomaly or a phantom. But either of these alternatives would go contrary to what all men, including Non-dualists, know to be the case.

275b. Musk-perfume would sweeten the mirror (reflecting the girl wearing it) because of pervasion within.

COMMENT: In one of the examples above, Vādirāja showed that if original and reflection are identical, a face should take on the characteristics of the reflecting medium. Here he says that in addition the reflecting medium should take on the characteristics of the face.

276. And therefore no one who is versed in the way of rational thought can agree to speak of an identity between the original and its reflection, for there are (too many) dissimilarities.

COMMENT: In the examples so far, Vādirāja has tried to reduce his opponent's position to absurdity by showing the ridiculous consequences of a mutual sharing of attributes by the (supposedly identical) original and its reflection. He now takes a different tack:

277-280a. Also, as a consequence (of the obvious dissimilarities between original and reflection), anyone saying that the eye (when seeing a reflection) rebounds from contact with a *solid part* of the body and sees (therein) its own (flesh-and-blood) face, is being ridiculous. For if that were so, no percept making the *mirror* appear, by means of the eye's rebounding from this mirror, would even be produced; instead, the face in question would be perceived (merely) as 'that face above the neck' (unframed by the mirror). And thus, by your standards, the reflection would not even exist. So what two could be identical ? in a similar fashion the soul would have vanished.

COMMENT: Vādirāja says that if the face and its reflection

were *really* identical, then, since the actual face is not framed by a mirror, the reflection of the face could not be either. Instead, the reflection's immediate surroundings would have to be identical to the face's. But everyone knows that the reflection appears as framed in the mirror reflecting it and not merely as "that face above the neck" (unframed by the mirror). If it does not, it is not a reflection. Vādirāja contends, therefore, that the only thing the Non-dualist has done by identifying face with reflection is destroyed any basis for the existence of the reflection. And since in the analogy the reflection stands for the soul, in the end the Non-dualist succeeds only in *annihilating* the soul, not in *identifying* it with Brahman.

280b-281a. (Moreover,) why shouldn't the eye not rebound off a rock, if your reasoning is valid ? Why should (it) rebound from water (which is softer than rock) ? Hence this also is absurd.

COMMENT: Vādirāja feels that the Non-dualists' insistence on an identity between the original and its reflection completely subverts the optics of reflection that men live their lives by. If the eye can be said to present the identical original to the man looking at his reflection, then it may be maintained with no more absurdity — and Vādirāja would say with *less* absurdity (since the rock is harder and would better facilitate reflection) — that the man could see his reflection in a rock.

281b-282. And how, according to you, could the eyes of a face turned downward to look at a solar eclipse in a dish designed for the purpose — (how could these eyes), after having rebounded (off the dish), see (simultaneously), after piercing the skull, the fierce brightness (of the sun) at midday ?

COMMENT: In the examples up to this point Vādirāja has been concerned with a face and its own reflection. Here his concern switches; we are asked to consider the face in relation to something else's reflection; namely, that of the sun.

The meaning is this: If the original and its reflection are identical, then the eyes should see both when they look at a given reflection. But everybody knows that doesn't happen. Take the case of someone observing the progress of an eclipse in a device (pātragolaka)[1] which reflects the sun above, which is too bright to be directly looked at. In such a case the eyes, and indeed the observer's face, are inclining downward toward the sun's reflection in the device. But if the reflection of the sun is identical with the actual sun, the eyes would have to be perceiving the latter at the same instant as the former. But the eyes are of course doing no such thing, for the skull of the observer stands between his eyes and the sun above. In order for him to see the sun, he would have to pierce with his eyes his own skull ! One more reason, then, why the Non-dualist reflection-theory is absurd.

283-284a. When there is the cause (the sun being reflected in the device), this contingent effect (the sun's reflection) comes into existence. But (you imply that) this (cause) would perish when it becomes absent (from the reflecting device) — like a blossoming lotus-calyx, or like the melting of tin, lead, and the like through contact with fire.

COMMENT: He here says that, if Non-dualists had their way, when the sun in the reflecting device ceases to be visible there, the sun must needs have perished altogether. For how could it be otherwise, the object being indentical with the now vanished reflection ? So the object would have been destroyed, like the disintegrating sheath of a blossoming lotus or like metal when consumed by fire, just because its reflection in a mirror disappeared ! What could be more absurd than that ?

284b-285a. Moreover, the author of the *Brahmasūtras* announces a *similarity* (between Brahman and a soul, not an identity), by the illustration "sun-resembling, etc." There would be a limited similarity between the original and its reflection, the soul.

COMMENT: Vādirāja is referring to *Brahmasūtra* 3.2.18, "And for this very reason comparisons [of the soul to the Lord] like 'sun-resembling' [are made]." Here he is giving the Dualist version of the reflection-theory,[2] summarized by Madhva

1. "Pātragolaka" means literally "dish-globe" and according to the commentator refers to a device used by an earlier generation to view an eclipse.

2. Dualists do sometimes speak of the soul as a reflection of the Lord,

himself in these words:"...Sūtrakāra, having stated that the self [or soul] is an image of the Lord,...shows that he is quite different from Him. *Śruti* and *smṛti* declare the same thus: 'The selves stand as so many reflections with regard to the different forms of the Lord.' "[1]

Sharma explains further this relationship, as Madhva sees it, between Brahman and the soul:

> Madhava concedes freely that there are points of contact between Jīva [or soul] and Brahman. Their distinction, however great and ineradicable, is yet one of order and degree and not of kind....Some community of nature is certainly there and even with that it is possible to keep the position distinct from the complete merger of the Advaita.[2]

Vādirāja, following his master, affirms a "limited similarity" between Brahman and the soul, original and reflection, but holds that the sūtra in question forbids any identity. He explains further :

> **285b-287a.** The (reflection's) conditioning substance (the mirror, etc.) is the material cause, and the proximity of the face (to the mirror) is the instrumental cause : what is ever brought about on the strength of the seen effect (the reflection) ? How could something sun-like and sun-resembling light up whole regions with its own brightness ? How could Śaṅkara (bhāṣyakṛt) dare to say what the author of the *Sūtras* (Vyāsa) never said ?

COMMENT: Vādirāja says that the original (face) when near a mirror produces a result, and that even the mirror itself produces a result insofar as it is the material stuff of which the reflection is made. Contrasted to these, he then says, is the reflection itself, which is neither the instrumental nor the material cause but is instead the effect of these causes. The point here is that this reflection and the original could not be identical since they function differently, in a sense even antithetically.

but their understanding of what this means is obviously very different from what Non-dualists mean.

1. Madhva, *A Source Book in Indian Philosophy*, eds. Sarvepalli Radhakrishnan and Charles Moore, p. 567.

2. Sharma, *Philosophy of Śrī Madhvācārya*, p. 228.

What Śaṅkara said, commenting on the *Sūtra* quoted just above (3.2.18), was this:

> Because that Self [Ātman] is of the nature of intelligence, devoid of all difference, transcending speech and mind, to be described only by denying of it all other characteristics, therefore the Moksha Sāstras compare it to the images of the sun reflected in the water and the like, meaning thereby that all difference in Brahman is unreal, only due to its limiting conditions. Compare, e.g. out of many, the [following passage]: "As the one luminous sun when entering into relation to many different waters is himself rendered multiform by his limiting adjuncts [reflecting him in the water]; so also the one divine unborn self."[1]

Vādirāja believes that Śaṅkara is going beyond Vyāsa's intent : to hold to such a non-difference would be in effect to hold that the sun's reflection in a pond of water could light up whole regions of the sky just like the actual sun. And surely Vyāsa never meant to imply that !

Vādirāja now explains how we are to take Vyāsa's words:

> **287b-288.** Indeed ordinary people say, "Look at the face-image in the mirror." The expression, "(Look at your) *face* in the mirror," is (heard) neither in colloquial nor in formal speech; if (a locution expressive of identification) *is* (heard), as in the phrase "moon-faced," it too is based on a *resemblance* (of the round face to the moon, not on an actual identity).

COMMENT: This passage is impossible to translate because English-speaking people *do* say, "Look at your face in the mirror.'" With this warning, however, the meaning of the passage is clear. Vyāsa, he is saying, didn't intend, when he spoke of a "resemblance" between the sun and its image, a *literal* resemblance — as one would when speaking of two things having exactly the same natures; but instead intended a *secondary* resemblance — as one does when speaking of two things which are alike in some ways but not in others.

> **289a.** Consider (this): how could a particular sound coming from inside come (also) from outside?

1. Śaṅkara, *Commentary*, II, pp. 157-158 (3.2.18).

COMMENT: Precisely this absurdity would occur if a face identical with its reflection were to speak.

He now explains in what sense speech might be considered as belonging to the reflection:

289b-291a. Just as the sound of a lion is associated with a lion in a sketch because of its similarity to the lion, exactly so the voice of a (human) face is associated with the reflected image of a face because of its likeness to the face. But the face and the face's image could not literally exist together in the same thing. Thus the face's voice would be only figuratively there (in the image).

COMMENT: In other words, speech and roar may be said to characterize image and sketch respectively, but only in a figurative sense.

The ultimate force of this argument may be that it is inconsistent of the Non-dualist to assert an identity between an original and its reflection and *not* assert it between an original and its sketch. Of course, Vādirāja would want to add, it is absurd to assert it in either case.

291b-293a. Since the thing termed *pratimukha* (reflections) is situated *prati* (opposite) the *mukha* (face), then only that sound earlier described (as "coming from inside") deserves to be taken literally. How is the sound of a face — (a sound) sprung up out of the face — traced to some other (origin)? For advice given by this (face) certainly isn't (found) there (in the reflected image) as well — except figuratively.

COMMENT: Here he shows that the very etymology of the Sanskrit term meaning reflection forbids identity and indeed signifies oppositeness. That being so, it is essential to make a distinction between the speech of a face and the "speech" of its reflection: Only the face can be said to be literally speaking.

293b-294. Again, how would what was situated *opposite* the face be *of* (one with) the face itself? For no one, having mounted his own shoulders, starts to dance! Therefore we necessarily speak of the face's image as different from the face (itself).

COMMENT: This humorous image richly evinces the Non-dualists' distortion (via Dualist standards) of reality. If the Non-dualists' reflection-theory is taken seriously, then a man's dancing on his own shoulders, Vādirāja says, is no less feasible a happening than the event validated by their version of bimba-pratibimbavāda, namely, the reflection's speaking. For the supposed dancer and speaker bear the same relationship to their counterparts — the real body and the real face respectively: each is supposedly *identical* with the latter, yet each is physically *separated* from it; moreover, never has such a dancing or speaking been witnessed by anyone. Thus they are equally preposterous, Vādirāja contends, and the Non-dualist reflection-theory which lays the foundation for such monstrosities is itself no less so.

295a. How could these words (of Vyāsa) expressing a difference (between God and soul) speak (of "sun-resemblance" in any way) but colloquially ?

COMMENT: Here he explicitly states what he said implicitly in verses 287b-288: Vyāsa did not intend a perfect similarity between the sun and its reflection — that is to say, between Brahman and soul — but was speaking colloquially, as when people speak of someone's being moon-faced but never mean that the face is like the moon in any but a very limited way.

295b-297a. Moreover, this relation of original to reflection would, because of the (ultimate) *dis*-similarity between the soul and the Supreme Lord, (only further) establish, and not invalidate, difference alone; and (in addition) would reveal, because of (a degree of) likeness, a (limited) affinity between Viṣṇu, the Original, (and the soul), as when (something with) a nature forbidden (to all else) has conceptions common (to other things applied to it) as well.

COMMENT: He begins by saying that once Vyāsa's intent is understood, the passage in question, quite aside from invalidating, actually corroborates the difference between the Lord and souls; for in the popular mind, and indeed in fact, the original is primary, the reflection secondary: the analogy, then, suggests the self-existence of God and the dependency of His creatures upon Him.

Moreover, he continues, we learn from the analogy that we

are "made in His image"; although different in nature from Him, we nevertheless possess certain characteristics which have an affinity to Him. As Sharma says: "The soul of man at its best possesses the characteristics of reality, consciousness, and bliss similar to Brahman."[1] But this similarity, as we have seen, and as we are about to see again in the most vivid terms, is very oblique, and is worlds away from a perfect identity, as Non-dualists in their irreverence would have us believe.

1. Sharma, *Philosophy of Śrī Madhvācārya*, p. 228. Cf. commentary under verses 284b-285a for a different quotation with similar intent.

XIII. HYMN TO DIFFERENCE

Desiring to emphasize this difference between the Lord and souls, Vādirāja now gives his muse free rein. What follows is a rather plodding translation of what in the Sanskrit is a spectacular showpiece of rhythm, alliteration, and pun :

297b-306a.

The Lord is the Begetter, the Nourisher of the jackal; by comparison the soul is the jackal.

He is the Independent One; the soul is dependent on what is other than it.

That One is filled with every delight; this one's delight is slight.

That One is eternally free (from the flux of transmigration); this one is fettered to (the process of) becoming.

He knows all; it knows little.

He is fearless; it is afraid.

He is the Lord of Wealth; it is a beggar.

He is the Supporter; the world (of men) is the supported.[1]

He sleeps on the serpent (Ananta);[2] it is wary of the ground at the edge of an anthill.

He is the God bestriding Garuḍa (Viṣṇu's mount); it's way of life is like Garuḍa's.

He is the revered Abode of the guardians of the regions;[3] it worships the guardians of the regions.

He is the Enjoyer of the sacrifice; it is the sacrificer.

He is the Worshipped; it is but the worshipper.

He is the Defender of the host of celestial sages;[4] it waits on the celestial sages.

1. This is a reference to Viṣṇu's boar-avatār.

2. Ananta is "a serpent with a thousand heads which is the couch and canopy of Viṣṇu whilst sleeping during the intervals of creation" (Dowson, *Dictionary*, p. 293).

3. These are the guardians of the eight points of the compass. Each of these points (the four cardinal and four intermediate points) is presided over by a deity assisted by a fabulous elephant. *Pada* ("abode") could be translated more specifically as "footstep," for the sky, where the guardians live, in Hindu mythology is one of the three "footsteps" of Viṣṇu in His dwarf-incarnation.

4. These sages are highly exalted saints who, after attaining perfection on earth, dwell in the regions of the gods, and are now served, or "waited on," by men offering sacrifices, etc.

That One is imperishable, this one perishable.
He is Unborn, it suffers birth.
He is the Destroyer of the wicked throng; it is the servant of wicked men.
He is by nature the "Great-bodied":[1] its body is despicable.
That One easily raises the mountain ranges;[2] this one cannot even bear the weight of a boulder.
He is playing when He bounds the oceans; it is unable to bound even a brook.
He brings forth the Ganges; its first and last aim is to be bathed in the Ganges.[3]
He is the Master of Veṅkaṭa;[4] it makes religious pilgrimages there.
The Lord is the deliverer (of the soul) when it goes forth (from this world); it murmurs incantations to Him.

COMMENT: Vādirāja now concludes:

306b-307. The attributes of two beings by nature perpetually related in this manner are incommensurate in numberless ways. There would be an identity between these two only if there existed a hare's horn; or if the rope were the snake, or shell were silver.

COMMENT: In other words, if this absolutely obvious truth, the truth of God's difference from his creatures, proves spurious, then we might as well forfeit all reliance on our ability to know the truth; for all we can tell, a hare's horn might exist after all. And if this most obvious of all differences is really not a difference at all, then how can we talk about lesser differences? We cannot: for all we can tell, a rope might as well be a snake, and shell be silver.

How much better for all the world, then, to give up all arrogant grasping after identity with the Supreme God and

1. One of Viṣṇu's many epithets is *mahākāya* ("Great-bodied").

2. In Hindu mythology there are seven mountain ranges dividing the carth into its regions.

3. The Purāṇas say that this sacred river flowed from the toe of Viṣṇu. It is even today regarded by pious Hindus as the river of purification, especially of the dead.

4. Veṅkaṭa, near present-day Madras, is a sacred hill on top of which is famous temple to Viṣṇu-Kṛṣṇa.

admit the obvious: that we are creatures and are infinitely transcended by our Creator.

But what about the identity texts ? the opponent will say.

308. Since countless numbers of trustworthy people say (things like), "the herdsmen's settlement on the Ganges," an intelligent man will certainly recognize as the meaning only what (really) follows from such (a statement).

COMMENT: Vādirāja explains that we have nothing to fear from identity-texts like "That art thou" or "One only, without a second." For men often speak colloquially, as when they speak of a settlement "on the Ganges" and really mean "on the bank of the Ganges." Men of intelligence, he says, have no difficulty in recognizing the actual intent of such statements. They know that settlements don't really sit on rivers ! In the same way they know that souls are not really identical with Brahman even when Scripture may seem to literally indicate that they are.

309. When a statement is (made), what wise person resolves on a meaning which is absurd ? How could the son (spoken of) in Scripture (actually) mount (i.e., copulate with) his sister and mother ?

COMMENT: Here he shows that Scripture contains clear statements, which must surely be recognized even by Non-dualists, of non-literal intent.

His example is from the *Aitareya Brāhmaṇa.* There the story is told of a certain prince who, himself unable to sire even a single son, asks of the great sage Nārada what the worth of a son is. Nārada replies that a son is "a light in the highest heaven"; a son must be had at any cost: "Therefore a son his mother/And his sister mounteth,"[1] if that is the only way the son's son can be conceived. Now Vādirāja singles this passage out as one which is obviously hyperbolic: the passage does not sanction incest, as the literalist must believe; rather it exhorts men to take every reasonable, lawful means to have sons. Vādirāja believes that it is as absurd to take literally the identity-passages in Scripture as it is to take literally this scriptural injunction.

1. 7.13. Arthur B. Keith, trans., *Rigveda Brāhmaṇas*: *The Aitreya and Kauṣītaki Brāhmaṇas of the Rigveda*, p. 300.

XIV. PROOF OF DIFFERENCE THROUGH A CONSIDERATION OF GOD'S OBJECTIVITY AND THE SOUL'S SUBJECTIVITY — REFUTATION OF THE NON-DUALIST VERSION OF BRAHMAN'S "SELF-LUMINOSITY"

Non-dualists maintain that Brahman is self-luminous (svaprakāśa). One of the premier Non-dualist philosophers, Citsukha, has defined this self-luminosity as "immediate, non-objective experience."[1] He means that Brahman cannot be said to know Itself as ordinary consciousnesses do an object. In other words, It is not an object of knowledge; It simply *is* the knowledge: It is, so to speak, the beam of light itself, not the object that the beam illuminates.

In opposition to this doctrine, Vādirāja will maintain that Brahman is an object of both His own and the soul's consciousness. Moreover, He and the soul are subjects in the ordinary sense with respect to this objective knowledge. (Throughout this discussion the terms "subjectivity" and "objectivity" will bear exclusively the meaning derived from this specific context: "subjectness" and "objectness," unfortunately awkward in English, convey the exact meaning.)

Now for the refutation:

310. If (as you say) the subject is not the object, (then) Brahman — attained, seen, heard of, reflected on, meditated on — is different from the consciousness attaining,[2] seeing, hearing, reflecting, meditating.

COMMENT: He refers to the Non-dualist doctrine that, in Ānandabodha's words, "Agency [or subjectivity] and objectives cannot belong to a thing at the same time and with reference to the same act."[3] (Non-dualists feel that this doctrine is essential if Brahman, which is held to be partless, is to exist in a true

1. Cf. Sharma, *Philosophy of Śrī Madhvācārya*, pp. 185-187, 246-247; and Mahadevan, *Philosophy of Advaita*, p. 140.

2. In our text the word "gatam" is obviously a mistake and should read "gantṛ."

3. Mahadevan, *Philosophy of Advaita*, p. 140.

non-dualism with no internal division.) Vādirāja believes that this position logically implies, not non-dualism, but dualism. For there are the two texts — "Indeed, the Self is to be seen, heard of, reflected on, meditated on,"[1] "The knower of Brahman attains the Supreme"[2] — which makes it clear that Brahman (or the Self) is an object, moreover an object in five different ways ("attained, seen, heard of, reflected on, meditated on"); and these same texts also make it clear that the soul is the subject with respect to Brahman: the soul attains, sees, etc. So how, if subject and object cannot be identified, as Non-dualists themselves say, can Brahman and the soul be identical ?

311. If non-difference of subject and object were derived (as you claim) from the identity-texts in Scripture (such as "That are thou"), then an act of knowing belonging to the one known follows from the texts indicating self-luminosity.

COMMENT: If Non-dualists, he says further, press home identity on the basis of the identity-texts, they will contradict the doctrine stated above. For certain other texts that they revere — the so-called "self-luminosity-texts" ("Brahman is consciousness (prajñāna),"[3] "Here this self is self-luminous,"[4] "The self alone is its light"[5]) — make it clear that Brahman is a *subject*. So Brahman, whose objectivity is apparent from an analysis of the two texts first encountered, is also regarded by Non-dualists as a subject, as shown here.

312-314a. If in the first case the argument (for the difference between subject and object) is compelling because of Scripture, then the argument, clearly articulated in five ways, is in the second case like the shafts of the Five-Arrowed (god of love, Kāma): the thief makes your Scripture-wife wayward (i.e., makes the identity-texts give up the meaning assigned them by you). That which in five ways describes Brahman's objectivity — the statement, "Indeed, the Self (is to be seen, heard of, reflected on, meditated on)," and

1. *Bṛhadāraṇyaka Upaniṣad* 2.4.5.
2. *Taittirīya Upaniṣad* 2.1.1.
3. *Aitareya Upaniṣad*, 3.1.3.
4. *Bṛhadāraṇyaka Upaniṣad* 4.3.9, 14.
5. *Ibid.*, 4.3.6. Cf. Mahadevan, *Philosophy of Advaita*, p. 136.

the statement, "The knower of Brahman attains (the Supreme)" — is shown by you in a false light.

COMMENT: He says that if Non-dualists forbid identification of subject and object ("the first instance" — verse 310), identity between Brahman and soul is impossible. For in the verse above ("the second case" — verse 311), Brahman was shown, on the basis of the self-luminosity-texts, to be a knowing subject as well as the object of souls. And that is precisely what the doctrine above said could not be! Thus a soul, the subject, and Brahman, the object of the soul, cannot be identified by the very logic of Non-dualism itself.

The only way out of the dilemma is of course to de-identify Brahman and the soul, is to void the identity-texts of the meaning given them by Non-dualists. Vādirāja depicts the two texts which in the five ways show Brahman's objectivity and His difference from souls as the five flower-tipped arrows of that great infatuator, Kāma, the Hindu Cupid. These texts make scriptural cuckolds of Non-dualists: the identity-texts are made to defy the meaning given them by Non-dualists and take up with other men (Dualists)!

314b-315. The Pure Consciousness of Brahman is regarded (by you) as an "indeterminate perception"; and the capacity to be heard of, reflected on, meditated on, and so forth is situated there in this (Brahman) with reference to a consubstantiality (of the subjective and objective capacities). With this you fit yourself only for the jungle!

COMMENT: Non-dualists argue for Brahman's non-objectivity in spite of Its capacity to be known. Brahman is not known in the ordinary way, they say. It is known by an intuitive perception which involves none of the machinery of ordinary perception. Ordinary perceptions involve knowledge of something not the self. Even when we think of "ourselves," we are not directly cognizing our true selves; instead we are cognizing some *image* of ourselves. All such knowledge involves objectivity. It is something we are looking at, either actually, or as projected onto the inner screen of imagination.

Opposed to objective knowledge, says Non-dualism, is indeterminate knowledge. It does not consist in a "looking at." It is consciousness without being conscious of. "It is a state in which the ultimate pure consciousness returns from its transformations and rests in itself."[1] It is therefore only in this sense that Brahman can be known, they say. Brahman is not known as a thing apart from the knowing consciousness; rather this knowledge of Brahman *is* Brahman. Thus Brahman is not an object.

Vādirāja's initial reaction is not a rebuttal but an exclamation of disgust. "With that reasoning," he says, "you're fit, not for a critical assembly of scholars, but for the jungle, where primitives ill-equipped to reason dwell."

He now explains why the Non-dualist is ill-equipped:

316. The first (scriptural passage), by (announcing) the fact that He is heard of and so forth, sang of the Self (Ātman) as discernible. The latter passage determined that Brahman was discernible and attainable.

COMMENT: First of all the Non-dualist is flying in the face of the obvious meaning of the two texts quoted above. One text, says Vādirāja, mentions "Ātman" as discernible; thus this Ātman is an object with respect to the discerner. The other mentions "Brahman" as both discernible and attainable; thus this Brahman is an object with respect to the one discerning and attaining.

He now gives a common example to illustrate God's (Ātman's, Brahman's) objectivity:

317-318a. Take the case of a man who hears about a village; after reflecting on and contemplating this very (village) while on the road, he in the end, (after coming upon it and) seeing into it, enters it. In that manner the words (of the two texts) derive their sense; and in this way it is agreed that the sense of the two scriptural passages indicates this one's (Brahman's) objectivity.

COMMENT: He says that a man will first (1) hear about a village; he then (2) reflects on it and (3) mulls it over (meditates on it); then he actually (4) sees it, and finally he (5) enters it. Now it is obvious at every stage that the village is an object with respect to the man hearing, reflecting, and so forth. By the very same logic, Brahman is an object with respect to men. Just as the village is an object "five times over," that is to say, with

1. Dasgupta, *Indian Philosophy*, II, p. 22.

respect to the five separate activities of the traveller, so is Brahman with respect to the same five activities of the aspiring saint.

318b-319a. Therefore the Pure Consciousness (supposedly constituting Brahman-knowledge), which in your doctrine is said to refer to an indeterminate knowledge within becomes for you, once (It is) determined to be an object, a lamp on the threshold.

COMMENT: Here he shows again the implicit twofoldness — the simultaneous subjectivity and objectivity — of the Non-dualists' Brahman. Like a lamp placed on the threshold and thereby doing double-duty by lighting two rooms,[1] the One Reality is both "Pure Consciousness" self-luminously perceiving and "Brahman" self-luminously perceived. Once again it is evident that the inner dynamic of Non-dualist doctrine is not consistent with the dogma that the One Reality cannot simultaneously be subject and object.

Having forcefully demonstrated the objectivity of Brahman, Vādirāja now attempts to show more clearly that only a real and separate *subject* could perceive this Brahman:

> **319b-322**. Whoever performs a meritorious action is certainly the same one who enjoys the reward accruing from it: the performer of a sacrifice resulting in this (reward) is the one actually sacrificing, not someone else. (Now) this one's physical (pūrva) body is his lower (pūrva) part, the heaven-body (or spiritual body) his higher part: if the first body is the performer of the sacrifice, at death there would be the cessation of what was produced; if the heaven-body experiences delight (as a consequence of the lower body's sacrifice), there would be the realization of what was unproduced.

Just as everywhere (else) subjectivity belongs to consciousness, so it is in this case too. How did this soul-consciousness, the subject, become the Brahman-Consciousness, the object ?

COMMENT: In order to make possible the identification of Brahman and soul, Non-dualists have argued, let us recall (see verses 237b-239 in particular), that it is not ultimately the ātman,

1. Cf. V.S. Apte, *The Student's Sanskrit-English Dictionary*, p. 305.

or spiritual part within us, which performs an action, but is rather the material part, specifically the unconscious buddhis of the antaḥkaraṇa (mental organ). In this way, they feel, ātman, which is identical to Brahman, is preserved from any involvement in temporal reality, as indeed it must be preserved if non-dualism is to make any sense.

Vādirāja's argument against this position is much as it was in a previous Section (XI). If, as Non-dualism says, the agent were the unconscious, material antaḥkaraṇa — here identified as the "lower part" — and not the soul, then when the antaḥkaraṇa perished at the death of the body, the deeds done by it would die too, and the law of karma would be annulled; thus there would be no justice in this world: sinner and saint would be effectively indistinguishable. If, on the other hand, the soul, or "heaven-body,"[1] or consciousness — in effect they amount to the same thing here — were said to enjoy the consequences of actions done by the lower body, there the law of karma would be thwarted in a different way; for the soul (which) Vādirāja equates with the Non-dualist ātman in this instance) would be reaping the fruits of actions it did not do. It is clear then, he implies, that the *soul* must be regarded as both the doer of actions and the enjoyer of their fruits. How then could the soul be Brahman, Who is the object of the soul's quest ?

> **323-325.** Moreover, you imply that the very Pure Consciousness is an object known in the perception making the oneness visible. Yet the same Pure Consciousness, when indeterminately aware, experiences in accordance with its oneness the subjectivity of realizing, "I am Brahman";[2] for how could the self-luminous (One) be another ? For that reason there was necessarily a subjective aspect to Pure Consciousness. Thus there were *two* Conscious-

1. The "heaven-body" is not strictly speaking the same as the soul; rather it is the coeternal partner of the soul. K. Narain, who believes that Vādirāja was the first Dualist to use such a concept, explains that this body "is necessary for explaining the everlasting enjoyment of the jīva and the permanent presence of its attributes during the state of *mokṣa* [emancipation]; because in the state of *mokṣa* there is no physical organism that may serve as a medium of enjoyment, the ideā of jīva as having form and body is indispensable" (*Mādhva Philosophy*, p. 141).

2. *Bṛhadāraṇyaka Upaniṣad* 1.4.10.

nesses, a subject and an object. Your view of Brahman partook of the (fallacy of the) crow's eye !

COMMENT: By analyzing the Non-dualists' doctrine of Brahman's self-luminosity he shows that, far from transcending the subject-object dichotomy, Pure Consciousness is implicated to an unusual degree. Not only does this supposedly non-dual, uncompounded, aspectless, utterly homogeneous Reality prove to be an object in Non-dualist hands (as we have seen in verses 310-319a); It also proves to be a subject. For the *Bṛhadāraṇyaka* says, "Brahman...in the beginning...knew only Itself—'I am Brahman.' " And therefore, even if the souls *were* one with Brahman, the crucible of Pure Consciousness into which all the liberated souls were poured would nevertheless be a subject knowing "I am Brahman."

Vādirāja then says that the Non-dualist Brahman behaves like the crow's eye; for just as the crow's eye, according to an ancient Indian superstition, moves "from the cavity on one side of the head into that on the other"[1] as convenience dictates, so also do Non-dualists mean one thing on one occasion by the word "Brahman," and another on a different occasion. In other words, even though they claim that Brahman is strictly non-dual, they unscrupulously treat It in one context as object, in another as subject: they treat It as if It were two instead of one. But—

326. Since according to your own doctrine this One (Brahman) could not be (both) subject-consciousness and object-consciousness, then this single snake-of-a-teaching of yours kills all (your other) teachings.

COMMENT: We saw under verse 310 that Non-dualists forbid subjectivity and objectivity to a thing "at the same time and with reference to the same act."[2] But such a teaching, Vādirāja says, has the effect of annulling any possibility of an identity between Brahman and souls. For it is by now perfectly clear that the single act of Brahman-perception can be broken down into two parts: Brahman as object; and the soul, or at least the crucible of souls known as "Pure Consciousness," as subject. And if a subject and its object cannot be perfectly identified, then neither

1. Monier Monier-Williams, *A Sanskrit-English Dictionary*, p. 267.
2. Mahadevan, *Philosophy of Advaita*, p. 136.

can Brahman and the soul; or alternatively, neither can Brahman as object and Brahman as subject ("Pure Consciousness"). Thus this teaching negates rather than affirms the non-duality of the two. It deals death to every teaching associated with it, as a venomous snake deals death to all that approach it. Non-dualism has succeeded once again, then, in refuting itself.

327. So this (Brahman-Consciousness) is definitely attainable by (following) the path rewarded by Knowledge; otherwise the logic presented (above) would be in conflict. Thus the (Brahman-) Consciousness was most certainly an object.

COMMENT: Having disposed of all the adversary's arguments up to this point, Vādirāja asks him to reconsider the rationale presented in the analogy of the village (verse 317). Just as the village is at all phases of our knowledge of it an object of our consciousness, so is Brahman. He is the destination of our quest; when liberated we will directly experience Him as He is described in the Scriptures; and we will experience Him, not in an indeterminate state of awareness transcending subject and object, but as the realized *object* of our greatest desire.

328-329a. And with respect to this (same rationale), the Pure Consciousness is a subject: the mental organ and so forth — different from (this) Consciousness — is a (mere) instrument. For a Consciousness (cetana) hearing (of Brahman) with the ear, reflecting (on Him) with the mind, thus meditating, directly perceiving (Him), is upheld by you as well as me.

COMMENT: Vādirāja says that the same analogy of the village just as securely establishes the subjectivity of whatever hears of and sees Brahman. This seeing consciousness — which he accommodatingly labels "Pure Consciousness" in mock deference to his opponent — is, moreover, to be distinguished from its mental apparatus (manaṣ, buddhi, antaḥkaraṇa, etc.); for even the adversary in the end agrees that it is not the ear or the mental organ (antaḥkaraṇa) which is conscious; rather it is the spiritual Consciousness "behind" these organs which is conscious. In this way he reminds the opponent that it would be wrong for him to point to the antaḥkaraṇa or manas as the sufficient condition of subjectivity (see verse 233 for a refutation of this Non-dualistst ratagem).

He continues:

329b-330b. That which immediately after direct realization attains Brahman by its own merit is none other than this Consciousness. Therefore this sequence of causes (of realization) is situated precisely in this (Consciousness). Otherwise the logic presented (above) would be in conflict.

COMMENT: He says that just as the example of the village shows that the man hearing of it, reflecting on it, etc., was a subject with respect to the village, so must the adversary's "Pure Consciousness" be considered with respect to Brahman.

It follows then from all the above that, even if for the sake of argument it were granted that Brahman and souls are somehow identical, the one Brahman is at one and the same time subject ("Pure Consciousness") and object ("Brahman"), in which case It is dual. For the Non-dualist not to admit at least this much, he would have to negate the perfectly clear sense of the two Scriptural passages declaring Brahman's fivefold cognizability and the cognizing agent's fivefold cognition.

330b-331a. Furthermore you, (though supposedly) liberated, are (actually) reverting to transmigration (nipātyase). For the mental organ's vṛtti, the (actual) seeing (of Brahman), would (according to you) be wholly superimposed, (and would therefore) be inapplicable to (Pure) Consciousness.

COMMENT: Non-dualists say that any act of knowledge is contingent upon a mental operation superimposed on Consciousness and manifesting Consciousness as an object. Then how is the knowledge ushering in Brahman-realization accounted for ? Vādirāja asks. Vyāsa-tīrtha asked the same quesion earlier: "...if the process of knowledge is admitted to be such that the antaḥkaraṇavṛtti [or mental operation] manifests the pure consciousness as limited by objective forms, then the case of final intuition (Brahman-knowledge), where objective characteristics are absent, would be inexplicable."[1] Thus the Non-dualist deludes himself when he speaks of an objectless experience of Brahman. He in fact can expect nothing better at death than further transmigration. And he more than likely will be among

1. Dasgupta, *Indian Philosophy*, IV, p. 236.

those who, "Bewildered by many thoughts, entangled in the meshes of delusion...fall into a foul hell"[1] prior to their next incarnation.

331b. And this (Pure) Consciousness is (according to you) un-mediated by concepts (nirākāra); thus Brahman (Itself) was of necessity the object (of the seeing Consciousness).

COMMENT: Pure consciousness is conceptless, Non-dualists say. It is not a reservoir of concepts through which it looks at, and to a certain extent superimposes these concepts on, the reality perceived. Well, so much the better for Brahman's objectivity ! Vādirāja chimes in. For even granted that the pure intuition of Brahman involves no illusory superimposition, does that remove Brahman's objectivity ? No, it simply makes of Brahman a true object rather than a false object, and therefore, if anything, "more of an object" than before.

332-333a. You say (in effect) that Brahman, attainable by one attaining, is an *object.* And you say that none other (than this Pure Consciousness) is the one attaining; thus without exception It alone is the one attaining, according to what is said (in your doctrine). Thus (we say) objectivity should apply to that (one attained) in liberation; in what way is it *not* entitled to objectivity ?

COMMENT: He says that Brahman must be considered an object; this conclusion is inescapable. Scripture shows it; examples taken from ordinary life when examined in conjunction with Scripture establish it; Non-dualist doctrine affirms it (by implication) in a particularly striking manner, for it makes it clear that Brahman, and not some illusory form superimposed on Brahman, is the object perceived. Just as clear is it that there is a subject experiencing this object. Thus even if Brahman, the object, and Pure Consciousness, the subject, *were* identical, as Non-dualists state, the fact would remain that this One would exist in a dual mode; and this one fact by itself would be enough to scuttle the entire doctrine of the adversary.

1. Radhakrishnan, *The Bhagavadgītā*, p. 339 (16.16).

333b-335a. You don't think that objectivity has any place in the bare act of perception itself. You do agree (however) that objectivity is applicable to that (realization of Brahman, which is) characterized by a different kind of perception. Now by that I conclude that the state of being both subject and object — which by your account is impossible in one and the same being — did not break away even at the Breakaway (or liberation) characterized (supposedly) by the obliteration of objects !

COMMENT: We have seen that Non-dualists deny Brahman any objectivity: liberation does not consist in a soul's seeing Brahman as an object, but as its merging with the Brahman-consciousness in a perpetual identity characterized by self-luminosity ("the bare act of perception itself"). But on the other hand, they speak of a final mental operation ("a special perception") which ushers in this experience. Liberation, they say, should be understood as the "Ātman conditioned by the final *vṛtti* [or mental operation], produced by the hearing, etc., of the Vedānta texts, that destroys the veil of ajñāna [Ignorance]."[1] Now Vādirāja interprets their position as an admission of Brahman's objectivity. For when they say that "there is generated by verbal testimony the unshakable immediate cognition of Brahman,"[2] that is to say nothing more than that Brahman is the *object* of the soul's cognition at the instant of the liberating enlightenment. And of course he finds a contradiction in this. How can Non-dualists, he asks, insist that the soul's relation to Brahman at liberation transcends a subject-object relation when holding simultaneously that the Brahman-realization is ushered in by vṛtti-knowledge ? For vṛtti-knowledge invariably presupposes a subject-object relation. He concludes still again that Non-dualist doctrine inescapably *implies* Brahman's objectivity, even as it baldly *states* that there is no such objectivity.

335b-337a. And there is no identity of consciousnesses distinguished by natures so opposed; your arcane doctrine, which says that everything existing at the time ignorance is destroyed is real, was regarded as ridiculous. Its outcome (phala) was like fruit (phala) off a poison-tree! Ouch!

1. Narain, *Mādhva Refutation*, p. 324.
2. Mahadevan, *Philosophy of Advaita*, p. 272.

COMMENT: Recall that Vādirāja has just shown that Non-dualists, in spite of every attempt to the contrary, inevitably end by treating Brahman as an object and the soul as a subject when describing the moment of liberation. Here he affirms that the Non-dualist doctrine which states that after ignorance is destroyed there remains only that which is ultimately real (pāramārthika) merely further certifies the contradiction of non-duality by the liberation-experience. For it would necessarily follow that subject and object were ultimately real, both alike being essential to the liberation-experience. But if both are real, then they are really different, for according to Non-dualism one and the same entity cannot, as we have seen, be simultaneously subject and object; cannot, in the words of the text, be "distinguished by natures so opposed."

The "poison-tree" refers to "the rule of the poison tree," that is, that "a noxious object [like a poison-tree] should not be destroyed by the producer of it."[1] The Non-dualist violates this rule, for he ends by annulling the noxious doctrine of non-duality with one of his own stratagems.

337b-339a. Certainly the position that one thing could not (simultaneously) act in two ways during a single activity applies equally in every case: since an axe does not chop away at itself, at its very own substance, absolutely nothing should result according to you, for there is a diverseness of activity (in the supposedly unitary Consciousness).

COMMENT: Vādirāja cries out for consistency here. Are you, after dogmatizing about the impossibility of one and the same entity being at once subject and object, now going to make an exception for the liberated Consciousness ? he asks his opponent. It is interesting that Vādirāja here adduces an example to defeat his adversary which could with even greater profit be turned against him by the adversary; for the Dualist does believe that Brahman (*unlike* the axe in the example) is always simultaneously subject and object. In any case, the example works here; for according to Non-dualism it is as absurd to speak of Consciousness as simultaneously acting and acted upon as to imagine an axe being chopped by its own chopping. Yet Consciousness has

1. Monier-Williams, *Sanskrit-English Dictionary*, p. 997.

been shown to be implicated in precisely this way according to the Non-dualists' own doctrine. Obviously, then, they have succeeded only in reducing their own system to absurdity.

339b-340. It is claimed (by you) that an action is what inheres in something other (than the object itself), (while) the object is (merely) what follows from this (action); for the position of (you) illusionists is that this (object) could definitely not be *in* the subject himself, in whom the action resides.

COMMENT: Here he merely restates with slightly more precision the Non-dualist view: that an active subject and the object of his activity are different.

341. That being the case, how could subjectivity and objectivity come together in one place in the case of the one action situated in the (liberated) Self — (the action) consisting of the perception of identity (with Brahman) ?

COMMENT: Here is a clear exception to the rule, he says. For if the soul and Brahman really are one at liberation, subject and object would have to be identical. For the soul, the subject, is engaged precisely in the activity of intuiting Brahman, its object, with Which it is said to be identical.

342. Hence the twofold condition of the Brahman-Consciousness and the soul-consciousness would show the duality of the two and would securely establish difference.

COMMENT: He concludes that according to Non-dualist doctrine the soul's very perception of identity would be (paradoxically) enough to guarantee, not its identity with Brahman, but its difference from Brahman, since related to it as a subject to an object.

343-344a. My position is still further enhanced because of the veracity of Scripture when speaking of difference. How, after disabling your (interpretation of the identity-) texts in Scripture, could my position fail to establish the actual sense (of Scripture) ? Consequently, there is absolutely no fear that because of your texts this (doctrine of the) difference (between God and soul) is untrue.

COMMENT: He says that he can now enlist without any fear

the intent of Scripture to his side. What doubt there may have been at the outset has been removed after analysis of the self-contradictory nature of his opponent's doctrines.

344b-346a. Moreover, how is this truth (of difference), which (we know to) be a truth applicable to final emancipation because of the authenticity of the attaining-attained state at the end, (characterized by an) unmediated knowledge (of Brahman), invalidated ? How is there an identity between one eternally free and one freed at a given moment ? Come now ! Certainly these two, their respective natures, differ — as one born without hearing and one who loses his hearing.

COMMENT: Here he asks how one who is eternally, or by nature free — Brahman — can be identical with what is not — a soul. The failure to see the distinction, at a lower level, between a man deaf from birth, that is, a man who has never experienced hearing, and a man who becomes deaf but who has experienced hearing in the past.

346b-347a. Furthermore my difference by nature invalidates identity. Thus, because of your method, the truth of only the invalidated identity fails to be established, for it is feeble (compared to difference).

COMMENT: He spells out the fact that difference and identity cannot coexist, and since difference has been established, and established by the logic of the adversary's own doctrines, identity must be dropped.

347b. Hence *you* took *your* life with your own arrow.

COMMENT: Evidently we are to assume that Vādirāja's opponent earlier claimed that the Dualist position was indefensible, even self-contradictory (for what precise reason we can do no more than guess). Here Vādirāja is turning the tables on his opponent. He feels he has amply demonstrated that it is Non-dualism, not Dualism, which destroys itself with its own arguments.

348. Furthermore, anyone who wrongs a king and practices treachery against a country is everywhere regarded and described as a ruthless man, and never anything but.

COMMENT: Not only, he says, do Non-dualists hurt themselves;

they also hurt the general public (which is here represented by the king and his country). Vādirāja deplores the victimization of simple, good people by false teachers. He damns the latter as enemies of mankind.

The following statement is an ironic and bitingly sarcastic application of Non-dualist logic:

349-350a. And therefore the eternal Lord (spoken of) in Scripture, in Himself utterly and in every way liberated, is also (identical to) the misery of the whole world non-different from Him : And of course your (theory of) identity should be taught to everyone, but not difference!

COMMENT: Vādirāja is specifically alluding to *Brahma Sūtra* 2.1.14, which Śaṅkara interprets, "The non-difference of them (tadananyatvam) results from such terms as 'origin' and the like."[1] Vādirāja asks us to consider the consequences of such an identity. If Brahman and the world are non-different, then the eternal felicity of Brahman's bliss-consciousness must be identical to the off-again-on-again grief of the world of souls. Now if that happens to be the case, he taunts, then of course the identity-theory is correct and should be promulgated and the difference-theory banished.

He now returns to a straightforward mode of speaking and, as if to atone for the nasty taste lingering from the last verse, rhapsodizes about the doctrine of difference :

350b-351. The protector, the crest-jewel bringing about every goal, the moon swelling the ocean of majesty given by Scripture to the Blessed Lord — this is alone the difference-interpretation of Scripture, (the interpretation) leading to truth; not the interpretation which you give to Scripture.

COMMENT: The "moon" and the "crest-jewel" refer to the difference-interpretation. It swells "the ocean of majesty" of the Lord by accentuating the difference between lowly man and the majestic Deity. Vādirāja calls his interpretation "the protector" in contrast to the interpretation of his adversaries, whom he just called treacherous and ruthless men, "the enemies of mankind" (verse 348).

1. Śaṅkara, *Commentary*, I, p. 320.

352-353. Remember the words of the ancients: "For the sake of a family one member should be cast off...." as is well known, one protects half when the destruction of the whole is impending. It is also known by everyone that when one gives up the whole world, the self (ātmā) is to be protected. Thus the destruction of the self and the destruction of the world (at liberation) are not implied by the statement (in the *Brahmasūtra*).

COMMENT: Vādirāja looks back to Śaṅkara's interpretation of the passage in the *Brahmasūtras* just considered (in verses 349-350a), "Of the effect [the world] it is understood that in reality it is non-different from the cause [Brahman], i.e. has no existence apart from the cause."[1] Now how, Vādirāja counters, can there be any such non-difference ? For everyone accepts the truth of the statement, "for the sake of a family one member should be cast off; for the sake of a village, a family; for the sake of a country, a village; and for the sake of a soul [ātman] the whole world."[2] And it is clear from this passage that the ātman and the world are *not* identical, indeed are related antithetically. There is also the proverb, "When the destruction of the whole is impending, the wise man abandons half [to save the other half]." Like the first one, this passage also strikes a note of difference, of contrast, not of identity.

So the world and the ātman (which Non-dualists equate with Brahman) are not identical. Moreover, each is real; each continues to exist after liberation. No one thinks that either of these two sayings implies destruction, but only separation. Thus the destruction of the world (as it appears to us) and of the ātman (here taken as individual soul) could not have been implied by the *Brahmasūtra*.

He now explains how to take this and other identity-passages:

354-356a. Just as a woman wearing on her ear lobe a golden earring, when seized by a robber would demonstrate her will to live by giving up that for which her head would have been cut off, in the same way this statement (in the

1. Śaṅkara, *Commentary*, I, p. 320.

2. S. C. Nott, trans., *Mahābhārata*, quoted in *The Hindu Tradition*, edited by Ainslee T. Embree, p. 139.

Brahmasūtra) lives with respect to meaning: When a literal meaning (mukhyārtha) similar to the bejeweled earring occurs (i.e., when it would be inappropriate, if not dangerous, to stick with the literal meaning), the Goddess of Speech (Bhāratī) undoubtedly honors only the surrenderer of the (literal) meaning as her protector.

COMMENT: There are times, he says, when we must supply a secondary meaning to passages in Scripture. *Brahmasūtra* 2.1.14, which speaks of Brahman and the world as "not other" is a case in point. To stick to the literal meaning in this instance would be like a woman's refusal to hand over a precious earring when, if kept, it would cost her her life. It goes without saying, of course, that the Non-dualists are like the woman who so refuses.

This passage, incidentally, represents Vādirāja at his poetic best. The pun on *mukhyārtha*—which means both "head-object" (earring) and "literal meaning"—is extraordinarily ingenious.

356b-357a. And the words, "There is no second to Brahman," are like the words, "(This) is *not* a horse." The appropriate position states (instead) that the Brahman is *extremely different* from any second (and not that no second exists).

COMMENT: Lest the Non-dualist use the same argument as the above (354-356a) to justify his own non-literal interpretation of the *duality*-statements, and succeed in squaring them with his identity-statements, Vādirāja here makes an important distinction. It is one thing, he says, to put a difficult statement "into context" (as the Dualists do with identity-statements), but quite another to flagrantly fly in the face of the overall import of the Scriptures, as well as the evidence presented by reason and the senses (as Non-dualists do when they "reinterpret" duality-statements). He holds that to deny the reality of everything besides Brahman is to go directly against the express sense of Scripture. In *Bṛhadāraṇyaka Upaniṣad* 3.4.2, a certain sage Uṣasta Cākrāyaṇa says to Yājñavalkya, "This [Brahman] has been explained by you as one might say 'this is a cow,' 'this is a horse." That is how apparent it is, says Vādirāja, that there are other realities besides Brahman: denying this is like interpreting the statement, "this is a cow," to mean, "this is *not* a cow." Under no circumstances imaginable could such a meaning be legitimately derived from such a statement.

Vādirāja then gives the true (and, he would feel, the *obvious*) meaning of the statement that Brahman is "one only, without a second": nothing can *compare* to Brahman; alhough there is something besides Brahman, there is nothing *beside* Him.

XV. REFUTATION OF ILLUSIONISM

We are well aware by now that Non-dualists consider — and logically must consider (cf. the Introduction) — the world-appearance an illusion.[1] Vādirāja rebuts this theory using a combination of scriptural utterances and logic:

357b-358. This (scriptural) statement concerning Brahman's ("non-secondness") is (like) a cow giving forth its milk, not a crab giving birth (and destroying itself in the process). And since passages in Scripture which make reference to "illusion" do not speak of an illusion which destroys itself, then effort spent to subvert the meaning of Scripture, which teaches that objects (of the world) are real, is wasted.

COMMENT: Vādirāja's commentator tells us that a crab "destroys itself" when it "gives birth to a son." Almost surely this is a reference to the crab's shedding of the old shell it has outgrown; it does indeed appear as if a new, a different crab comes out of the old shell, while the old shell does appear to be the "corpse" of the "mother crab" (karkaṭī). (Actually crabs give birth to many tiny larvae at a time, and the birth of offspring has no connection with molting).

The commentator explains that this self-destroying crab is similar to the Non-dualist interpretation of the "illusion"-texts (like *Śvetāśvatara Upaniṣad* 1.10, which speaks of "viśvamāyā," "the illusion of everything"). If the text really is pointing out the literal, unmitigated illusion of everything besides Brahman, an illusion which is destroyed at liberation — as Non-dualists insist — then it negates (and thereby invalidates) *itself*, for it itself cannot be a real second to Brahman.

Contrasted to the Non-dualist interpretation of such texts is the Dualist. They believe that the world is certainly an illusion,

1. Francis Vadakethala warns that Vādirāja's understanding of Non-dualist illusionism may be too "uncompromisingly negative." He points out the equation of the world appearance (as seen through Non-dualism) with such strongly negative words as *bhrama* and *bhrānti* as evidence of this. He thinks it debatable whether Non-dualists ultimately mean that the world is an illusion or merely that it "is not as real as Brahman" (personal correspondence).

but only in the sense that, for example, a love affair gone sour is an illusion: there is nothing *unreal* about such an affair, but it *was* an illusion for the lovers to feel that the relationship was the key to happiness. The Dualist interpretation of illusion, it should be apparent, does not involve any self-immolation. Such texts as speak of illusion are thus compared, not to a crab, but to a cow giving forth its plentiful milk for the nourishment (edification) of men.

Most notably, this milk exists *in addition to* the cow, whereas the crab's offspring replaces its mother, which is killed in the birth-process. Similarly, in the Dualist account Scripture really exists alongside of, as a second to, Brahman; in the Non-dualist account, however, Scripture immolates itself upon Brahman-realization, for it too is part of *māyā*, which is destroyed at liberation.

359. Moreover, you surpass yourself by greeting what is identical with Brahman by the words, "In those altered conditions (vikāra) the Real is always merely phenomenal." You don't alarm me!

COMMENT: Vādirāja's commentator calls our attention to Sahadeva's eulogy in the *Bhāgavata Purāṇa*: "The Great Deity Sri Krishna... constitutes not only all the celestials but also space, time, and wealth, and other things. The visible universe is wholly pervaded by this Being."[1] These "things," then, are the "altered conditions" of which our author speaks.

Now when Non-dualists read this passage, they are initially confronted with a world which seems to be as real as the Lord himself — certainly anything but illusory. But they get around the problem by saying that the author is speaking only from the conventional (vyāvahārika) point of view; in fact all those things named by the passage are part of the world-illusion.

Vādirāja scoffs at this notion. It is bad enough to call something *apart* from Brahman an illusion but to label as vyāvahārika that which is clearly spoken of as "constituted" by Brahman is the grossest absurdity, especially by Non-dualist standards!

The argument of this section (verses 375b-377) is divided into three parts. The first two are introduced, respectively, in verses

1. Sanyal, *The Srimad-Bhagabatam*, V, Book X, p. 49, (Chapter 74).

357b-358 and in the present verse (359). The argument immediately following logically takes off, then, from verse 358:

360-361. An annulling idea like "This is not silver" is regarded by men of knowledge as relating to (the concept formed from) an absence of silver, (a concept which is) not properly describable as contentless (niṣprakārakatā). Thus the (so-called) indeterminate knowledge of Brahman is not in the least a knowledge which annuls (the world), and because no annulment exists, the truth of (Brahman's) difference (from the world), etc., has not been annulled.

COMMENT: He is here saying that in human experience an illusory perception is replaced by a *corrected perception* of the thing that first caused the illusion, or in other words, "a knowledge that contradicts another knowledge must have a content".[1] For example, one is enabled to say "This is not silver" only after a new impression, that of shell, replaces it. Never has it been heard that an illusion was corrected by a contentless ("pure") perception — whatever that might be.

As we have seen before, the realization of identity with Brahman, a realization which supposedly annuls the "false" world, is for the Non-dualist contentless, indeterminate, trans-ideational. It follows then that this Brahman-knowledge would be incapable of annulling the world. Failing to do that, the world would remain as a second to Brahman, and Non-dualism would have to give way.

362-363a. Moreover, that very knowledge which at the end transcends conceptualization is inferrable (only) from a following concept, and in your state of identity (with Brahman) that (concept) could not be an illusory one. Because of the lack of something to cause the inference, that (concept) is exactly like the hare's horn!

COMMENT: Vādirāja wants to know how the Non-dualist justifies his description of the enlightenment-knowledge as transcending conceptualization. First, since such a knowledge supposedly puts an end to conceptualization for good, then the word used by the Non-dualist to describe the state is unaccountable;

1. Dasgupta, *Indian Philosophy*, IV, p. 229.

for it derives its meaning from a *concept*. Second, since all knowledge following liberation is supposedly the highest (pāramārthika) knowledge, this same concept must be of the highest sort; yet the Non-dualist relegates all concepts to the realm of illusion! Thus the concept of "contentless knowledge" contradicts itself twice over. The concept matches nothing in reality, it is a chimera (hare's horn). So again the mechanics underpinning the "world-illusion" are in a state of bad repair.

363b. Moreover, this (contentless Brahman-knowledge), existing (so you hold) in a realm beyond the power of the senses, cannot be proven (to exist) by observation.

Vādirāja and Dualists in general have a high regard for sense-knowledge. If something is not in any way sensed, there is good reason on that basis alone to be suspicious. If Scripture, inference, and perception are all in agreement as to its non-existence, the case against it is overwhelming.

So the Non-dualist cannot justifiably describe Brahman-knowledge as contentless, trans-ideational, indeterminate ? And failing to do that, he has no right to assume that the world is annulled at liberation; he has every reason to assume that the world, since not annullable, is real.

The next verse and section (364a-372) logically follows from verse 359, the second of the two introductory statements :

364a. In the *Bhāgavata Purāṇa* Śuka says: "Māyā is as iron that moves to and fro."

COMMENT: Here begins the second argument against illusion. Vādirāja begins by quoting from the *Bhāgavata Purāṇa*;[1] the entire paragraph, of which the quoted material in the verse is a fragment, reads :

> He (the Lord) brings about the creation, maintenance, and dissolution of the universe, whatever He desires. Maya with its gunas, of which it is the ground, is not the Master who watches over (all), is (rather) like iron which moves to and fro (under the influence of the magnet). Adoration to you, the (Lode) stone, the overseer of the gunas' movements ![2]

1. 5.18.

2. Sanyal provides a partially inaccurate translation of this same passage (cf. *The Srimad Bhagabatam*, II, Book V, p. 73 (Chapter 18).

Māyā does not mean "Power of Illusion" for Dualists, as it does for Non-dualists, but rather the Lord's inexhaustible power — an ambivalent power both essential to life in the world yet heavy and restrictive.

The *guṇas* in the quotation refer to the usual Sāṅkhya triad of sattva, rajas, and tamas, the ultimate constituents of the created universe. These guṇas are of course real for Dualists and ultimately illusory for Non-dualists.

With this introduction we can now follow our author as he continues:

364b-368a. The equivalence (of iron) with the māyā-generated ignorance — which has taken up its abode in the very souls (of men), troubled like iron goblets (disturbed by a magnet); which is (also) understood to be the ground of the three guṇas as shown by Śuka's words, " of which it is the ground"; (and) which is the cause of the transmigrating flux of souls — arises from a (similar) disturbance of the iron in the metal goblet (when it is near a magnet). At the end (of the passage) he (Śuka) makes a comparison between the Lord of the universe and the lodestone by saying, "Adoration to you, the (Lode) Stone!" Therefore ignorance and the like, abiding far below, are remote (from Him); he (Śuka) said only that my Master, is the *cause* of the turmoil of māyā far removed (from Him), but he did not sing (of Him as) *consisting* of māyā.

We have already seen that Non-Dualists consider Brahman the locus of illusion, or Ignorance. The Non-dualist Vācaspati Miśra considered Brahman the "material cause of the world."[1] Padmapāda, the founder of the prestigious Vivaraṇa school, said outright that "Ignorance resides in Brahman."[2]

Vādirāja here wants to contrast his view — that Brahman wields māyā but in no way consists of it — to that of his opponents: that in one way or another Brahman *constitutes* māyā. Vādirāja says that Brahman is like a powerful magnet while the world (made of māyā) is like iron: Brahman controls the iron (māyā) not by touching it, much less by moving within it, but rather from a great distance. Brahman remains pure; He is in no sense one with this māyā — as He is in the sacrilegious Non-dualist system.

1. Dasgupta, *History of Indian Philosophy* II, p. 11.
2. K. H. Potter, *Presuppositions of Indian Philosophy*, p. 175.

368b-370a. Just as the reflecting medium, a mirror for example, is seen touching the reflection (reflected in it, but) stands at a distance from the original that we call the "face," just so ignorance can abide in the soul but be utterly remote from Brahman, Who is named the "Original" in your creed as well. Hence the *Purāṇa* (smṛtiḥ) is right.

COMMENT: In verses 266-297 we saw Vādirāja rebut the reflection-theory of the Non-dualists. We learned that, for them, "the Jīva [reflection] is false appearance or projection of the Brahman [Original] on the screen of Avidyā (reflector)," and that this Original and its reflection are absolutely non-different. We also saw that Dualists have a reflection-theory of their own. B.N.K. Sharma explains it:

> ... the relation of Bimba-Pratibimbabhāva ["Original-reflection-state"] between God and the souls is a sacred and inviolable relation, which is true for all time and goes to the very core of the Jīva and constitutes his very essence and could never be annulled. Its full significance, missed in Saṁsāra, is realized in Mokṣa. Mokṣa, in fact, is the complete realization of this intrinsic relation of metaphysical dependence and similarity (in some respects) with the Supreme. Pratibimbatva, according to Madhva, is *not a false relation, of which the Jīvas are to be ashamed and should try to shake off*, as in Advaita. It is the truest and most beautiful permanent bond with the Supreme Being and the purpose of Philosophy is its progressive realization, by the Jīva.[1]

While Vādirāja would certainly agree with Sharma's description, he is specifically interested here in showing that, just because one considers the soul (sullied by māyā) the reflection of Brahman, he is not forced to conclude to the identity of the two, and thus the identity of Brahman and māyā. For everyone knows that the reflection of a face in a mirror is not the same as the face itself. That being true, it is not necessary to conclude that the attributes of one would be the same as those of the other. Thus souls (reflections) can be ignorant and God (Original) be free from ignorance, yet the relation of Original-to-reflection can remain intact without logical difficulty.

Thus, he concludes, the *Purāṇa's* passage contrasting the magnet to the iron in no way materially implicates Brahman in māyā.

1. Sharma, *Philosophy of Śrī Madhvācārya*, p. 219.

370b-371. Thus all the scriptural passages dealing with māyā are like passages expressing the fecundity of what is (by nature) powerless. And the experience "I am joined (to māyā)" is perceived only by a soul. Any talk of Ignorance in Brahman, you ignorant fellow, is (but) a measure of your own ignorance of Him.

COMMENT: He says that, because of the dear meaning of the *Purāṇa*-text, passages in Scripture which speak of Brahman in a relation to māyā must be interpreted dualistically and realistically. Vādirāja specifically has in mind the text, "The Great Lord is the māyin."[1] He says that we are to understand from this text that Brahman is the *user* or *wielder* of māyā, and that this māyā isn't illusory, but to the contrary is highly potent and passes on its own fecundity to what it inheres in — a fecundity which all things possess only because of this real enlivening power. The Upaniṣad says, "The Vedas, the sacrifices, the rituals, the observances, the past, the future and what the Vedas declare, all this the maker sends forth out of this, in this the other is confined by māyā";[2] texts like this, Vādirāja says, truly indicate the status of māyā; it is a real, fructifying, yet restricting and sullying power wielded by God and permeating all entities in the universe, most notably souls. It is neither a power of illusion, nor does it in any way manipulate or sully God. Anyone who says so of it is ignorant of the nature of God.

372. And therefore the difference between the Lord and what is (of itself) powerless isn't characterized by (your illusory) māyā, and thus this (difference) is not illusory. How could it be merely phenomenal (vyāvahārikaḥ) ?

COMMENT: With this he concludes the sub-section (beginning at verse 364). He believes that he has shown that māyā, far from being a power of illusion which is grounded on Brahman, is both real and different from Brahman.

The Sanskritist should be warned that in this verse Vādirāja uses the word *māyā* colloquially, that is, as signifying illusion, unreality. Thus when he says here that the difference is not "characterized by māyā," he means that it is not illusory.

1. *Śvetāśvatara Upaniṣad* 4.10.
2. *Ibid.*, 4.9. Radhakrishnan, *The Principal Upanisads*, p. 734.

373-374. Moreover, at the summit of emancipation known as perfect union (sāyujya), (the nature of which) is revealed by its etymology, derived (as it is) from the root *yujir yoge*, there would certainly be a difference between the Lord and the soul, (a difference) characterized by an inseparable unity of the two, abiding in a common abode. How does it happen that what still exists after Ignorance disappears is merely provisional (vyāvahārika) ?

COMMENT: Sharma writes: "The Hindu Scriptures refer to an ascending order of Mukti: Sālokya, Sāmīpya, Sārūpya, and Sāyujya, in which each succeeding stage includes the joy of the preceding one."[1] Narain writes that Sāyujya, "according to Madhva, is the highest and supreme state of emancipation in which the enjoyment and bliss of the liberated soul becomes absolutely similar to that of *Īśvara*. . . ."[2]

The present argument is based on linguistic analysis. Sāyujya, a word consecrated in the Upaniṣads and signifying the highest attainment, comes from the root *yuj*, from which the word *yoga* also comes. *Yuj* means to *yoke* or *join*, to unite; with the prefix *sa*, *unite with*. Now there can be no uniting if there is already an identity, Vādirāja would remind us. Nor does the uniting result somehow in an identity. The *Bṛhadāraṇyaka Upaniṣad* says: "Thereby he wins complete union [sāyujya] with that divinity and residence in the same world with him."[3] How could the soul that has realized Brahman be depicted as residing *with* the Lord if it is identical to Him ? Thus all that can be said is that the soul and the Lord are locked in an inseparable embrace, not that the two are fused together. Therefore the Non-dualist's assertion that duality is merely provisional, ultimately unreal, cannot stand. For what could be more ultimate than Sāyujya, which, as we have just seen, is characterized by duality ?

He now takes a slightly different tack:

375. The words, "Where there is no māyā...," show that the abode of Him who is its Ruler is not characterized by māyā. How can this Lord (Himself) be characterized by māyā ?

1. *Philosophy of Śrī Madhvācārya*, p. 349.
2. *Mādhva Philosophy*, pp. 167-168.
3. 1.5.23. Radhakrishnan, *Principal Upanisads*, p. 182.

COMMENT: The speech referred to appears in the *Bhāgavata Purāṇa.*[1] In it Śuka is describing Vaikuṇṭha, the Hindu counterpart of the Christian heaven. He says:

> *Maya* (illusion) has no access there. How can I describe the beauty of His associates there ? Their complexion is green evincing brilliant lustre; their eyes are expanded and resemble full blown lotus; their clothes are yellow; they possess charming gracefulness and their limbs are soft and tender. All of them have four arms wearing various ornaments set with sparkling rare jems of precious value, and they possess immeasurable effulgence; they are worshipped by the *Suras* (Deities) and *Asuras* (Daityas)."[2]

Vādirāja's purpose is to show that it is obvious from the *Purāṇa* that if the released souls there are no longer dependent on or connected with māyā, then how much more certain we can be that the Lord Himself is not.

The word māyā here carries both Non-dualist and Dualist connotations simultaneously: there is neither illusoriness (Non-dualist) nor impurity (Dualist) in Visṇu's abode.

376-377. Therefore none of the released ones mentioned here was marked by māyā; and all these devotees of Viṣṇu are clearly different from Viṣṇu; and the mutual difference between them on the one hand and the Lord on the other is not something which is illusory (amāyika). Thus a state of merely conventional truth would be far distant from this (abode of Viṣṇu).

COMMENT: He says that from the *Purāṇa*-passage it is obvious that the Lord's devotees are different from the Lord Himself. Nor can it be pleaded by Non-dualists that the description in the text is conventional (vyāvahārika); for māyā, it is clearly stated, has no access to Vaikuṇṭha. Thus it is clear, Vādirāja concludes, that difference extends all the way up to the supreme state: there is difference everywhere, from top to bottom, and no doctrine of illusion is strong enough to refute it.

1. 2.9.
2. Sanyal, *The Srimad Bhagabatam*, I, p. 129.

XVI. THE IMPORTANCE OF SENSE-EXPERIENCE IN ARRIVING AT THE TRUTH OF DIFFERENCE AND THE FALSITY OF IDENTITY

378-379. Furthermore, how can anyone declare that the difference-texts in Scripture which are in agreement with sense-experience can be invalidated, while the identity-texts in opposition to it do the invalidating ? Furnished with a sword, a king-elephant's trunk doesn't kill the enemy; hacked to pieces by the sword it kills the enemy sure enough!

COMMENT: In this ironic passage Vādirāja gives us a way to resolve ambiguities in Scripture. If there is a doubt about its sense, then the doubt should be resolved in accordance with what our senses tell us. Doing so is like outfitting a king-elephant with a sword; such a combination would vanquish any enemy. But if the resolution is at variance with sense-experience, that is like turning the sword against the elephant. There is no success in that.

Yet Non-dualists assert (in effect) just the opposite! Denying their own senses, which tell of a world marked everywhere by mutually distinct particulars, they say that the Scriptures speak of oneness. They might as well say that the way to overcome is to turn the sword against the elephant, so absurd, says Vādirāja, is their view.

He now begins a series of arguments based on the validity of sense-experience:

380-381. Men everywhere determine the meaning of a statement in conformity with sense-experience. But see here! Just when the statement contradicts one's senses, you want to latch on (to its literal meaning)! Accordingly, why wouldn't the statement "...would impregnate by the fire in the being," though indicative of a meaning which is invalid because contradicted by the senses, be literally true ?

COMMENT: Vādirāja reminds the Non-dualists that they too exercise discretion in deciding which texts in Scripture are to be taken literally and which are not. For example, they would regard the statement naming fire as the impregnator of women as a figure of speech not to be taken literally. And how do they decide so ? By deferring to sense-experience, of course. But if they allow sense-experience to determine the intent of such a passage as this, why do they not give sense-experience the upper-hand with respect to certain *other* statements — such as those implying the identity of Brahman with the soul — when *these* run counter to sense-experience ? Why are not the identity-texts ("I am Brahman," etc.) interpreted non-literally, as is the statement, "the male fire pours seed into the female"?[1]

Sharma presents the Dualist position in these words:

> Madhava claims the same latitude in interpreting the monistically worded texts, in conformity with Sākṣi-pratyakṣa [the direct experience of the inner witnessing self] and the numerous other texts which teach the reality of the world and the difference between the human souls and Brahman... The highest deference and most fitting homage we can pay the Scriptures is in trying to find their true import in consistency with the logic of Sākṣyanubhava — instead of being swept off one's feet by the literal sense of such quasi-mystic statements of identity and acosmism.[2]

> **382.** When one has accomplished a journey, upon setting out for home he invariably takes the (same) proven path (he came on). But after accomplishing a journey, you follow on your return home an unreliable (untried) path.

COMMENT: Vādirāja compares sense-experience to a well-traveled, proven path. When one needs to get to a destination — the true meaning of Scripture — he sticks with the dependable path he has traveled before — sense-experience. But the Non-dualist, when seeking this meaning, is like the man who purposely veers off this path; thus he fails to arrive at his destination.

> **383.** What determines whether a soothsayer who (fore) tells the (presence of) some object like a straw which can be established with one's own eyes, is to be celebrated by all or killed ? Its (actual) establishment is the warrant of his words !

1. Muṇḍaka Upanisad 2.1.5. Radhakrishnan, *The Principal Upaniṣads*, p. 681.
2. Sharma, *Philosophy of Śrī Madhvācārya*, pp. 141-42.

COMMENT: This passage is similar in meaning to the previous three verses. The point is again that truth is established when word and experience tally. Here the Scriptures are compared to the prediction of a soothsayer, and sense-experience to the corroboration of the prediction. Needless to say, Non-dualists, in our author's opinion, disregard this basic law of truth-validation.

Nowhere else in this work does Vādirāja commit himself so strongly to the primacy of sense-knowledge. He almost seems to be saying with this example that the truth of Scripture must give way to sense-experience (as when the identity-texts are reinterpreted in accordance with the given datum of difference). In most cases, however, there is not even an apparent contradiction. And, of course, where Scripture speaks of realities *beyond* sense-experience, Scripture is to be strictly adhered to.[1]

384-385a. If corroboration by one's own eyes is said to annul (the truth of) one's speech, then honor only the scriptural passages speaking exclusively of things not experienced; and the words of the omniscient Vyāsa (the legendary compiler of the Scriptures) would not be praised in the three worlds !

COMMENT: Here Vādirāja answers an objection. Non-dualists maintain that any knowledge open to the senses, even if the knowledge in question is mentioned in Scripture, is merely phenomenal, ultimately unreal. All such scriptural knowledge, they say, is anuvādaka, or "merely repetitive" of what our senses establish — and establish falsely (from the ultimate perspective) — independent of Scripture. That is why "corroboration by one's own eyes is said to annul (the truth of) one's speech."

Over and against these anuvādaka statements in Scripture are statements dealing with matters beyond the reach of the senses; for example, the statement, "In the beginning this was only non-being."[2] In this category are most notably the identity-statements, say the Non-dualists; and they of course honor these latter texts alone, a fact that Vādirāja calls to our attention here.

1. Cf. Sharma, *Madhva's Teachings*, pp. 52-58, for a clear presentation of Dualist teaching on the subject of pramāṇas.

2. *Chāndogya Upaniṣad* 3.19.1.

His first rebuttal of their position is this: if the Non-dualists honor only a select few verses in all of Scripture, they dishonor the Scriptures *as a whole*; they in effect are saying that the *omniscient* author of Scripture spoke the truth only a small part of the time; and that is a treacherous view to take.

385b-386a. Tell me: how do the words of one uniquely realized — (words) opposed to an ugly illusionism marking those (seeing an object) — become discardable when dealing with matters experienced only by him (pareṇa) ?

COMMENT: Here he argues that even if self-corroboration did imply annulment, the fact would still remain that Vyāsa spoke often of things beyond our corroboration which presuppose, not the truth of identity and its allied doctrine of illusionism, but difference. For example, most texts dealing with the nature of liberation assume a duality between the soul and the Supreme being. Upon what principle, then, do the Non-dualists discriminate their pet texts from the other "non-repetitive" texts ? By none, says Vādirāja. Thus the doctrines of identity and illusion are mere biases.

386b-387. How is it possible that one who is cherished by all commentators (of Scripture) alike, who precludes with his words the fear that differences attested by the senses are illusory and establishes the true meaning of one passage in the light of other passages, (how is it possible), you foolish man, that he is wrong ?

COMMENT: Vādirāja says that Vyāsa must be considered above reproach. And since he speaks openly of differemce, difference likewise is above reproach.

Again he makes reference, though not specifically, to the identity-texts in Scripture, which he says Vyāsa meant to be understood in the light of everything else in Scripture. Vādirāja's commentator mentions the famous passage beginning "Two birds, companions always united."[1] as an example of the troublesome "identity-texts."

He now concludes:

1. *Muṇḍaka Upaniṣad* 3.1.1.

388. The fact of a narration's being about something that (only) another (Vyāsa) has seen does not thereby invalidate it; conversely, the narration of something seen by oneself is merely enhanced because attuned to the inspired statements (of Vyāsa).

COMMENT: Vyāsa's statements (the statements of the Upaniṣads and *Bhāgavata Purāṇa* in particular) about matters that he has seen are unchallengeable, Vādirāja first says; and most of this material presupposes *difference*. And his statements about matters that ordinary men corroborate, far from invalidated by this corroboration, are only enhanced by it. And of course all such corroboration is of difference, not of identity. So the opponent doesn't have a leg to stand on.

He now shows how inconsistent his opponent is by applying the principle the latter preaches to his own activity:

389-391a. In your way of thinking, the meaning grasped from a mere hearing (of Scripture) is not to be bothered about; a meaning is rather to be meditated on, for this uninterrupted succession of words is alone significant (You say). Moreover the repeated recitation of words in Scripture is approved; and of course the recitation of the nine-fold (illustration of identity) is supremely commendable according to you. Therefore why is a narration (in Scripture) of things experienced (by oneself) said to generate error ?

COMMENT: Vādirāja first lets the opponent know that he is informed of the Non-dualist approach to meditation. To fully grasp the content of the passage it would be helpful to see the distinction that Non-dualists make between directly realizing the truth of something and merely learning about it and thinking about it. Mahadevan writes that the Non-dualist Vācaspati, for example,

> regards *śabda* or verbal testimony as capable of generating only mediate knowledge. It is prasaṅkhyāna (dhyāna) or continued meditation, and not *śravaṇa*, that is the cause of the intuitive experience of Brahman....A bare sentence yields only mediate knowledge. But the sentence whose purport has been inquired into causes immediate experience.[1]

1. Mahadevan, *The Philosophy of Advaita*, p. 58.

Mahadevan goes on to say that Śaṅkara himself in his *Vākyavṛtti* maintained that the identity-texts of the Upaniṣads "are for the sake of the establishment of the immediate experience of Brahman,"[1] and Non-dualists all agree that the identity-statements by themselves are unreal; for it is only the Brahman-experience that they *lead to* which is real.[2]

Vādirāja makes reference in the passage to repeated "recitation" (abhyāsa). It has long been the practice in India to have "a truth conveyed in sacred writings by means of repeating the same word or the same passage."[3] It is this practice in general that he is considering. The specific "nine-fold" abhyāsa that he mentions refers to the nine illustrations and repetitions of the famous statement "Tat tvam asi," "That are thou," spoken by the sage Uddālaka Āruṇi to his son Śvetaketu, in the *Chāndogya Upaniṣad*.[4] The salt pervading the water, the several rivers flowing to the one ocean, and various juices making up the honey are three of the examples the sage uses.

The argument here is that when Non-dualists maintain that what is seen is invalid, they contradict themselves in a particularly striking way. For what is their whole meditative routine — the long repetitions and one-pointed concentration — all about if not *seeing*, and seeing in a supposedly supreme fashion ? Indeed, Vādirāja might have said, if there was no immediate perception (however erroneous) of the truth of the identity-statements themselves, they would not be revered. Personal corroboration in some form or another is essential before a statement will be honored as truth. And yet Non-dualists say that such corroboration is the badge of illusion !

> **391b-393**. Since any (basis for) dispute vanishes because of consent (by everybody) that the two (Scripture and experience) agree, who (is so foolish to) consider non-authoritative the Scriptures which the all-knowing (Lord) set up as an authority so that we might have certainty on

1. *Ibid.*, p. 59.
2. Mahadevan, *The Philosophy of Advaita*: see pp. 60-62 for the Non-dualist explanation of how the ultimately real Brahman-knowledge comes from the ultimately unreal identity-texts.
3. Monier-Williams, *A Sanskrit-English Dictionary*, p. 77.
4. 6.8.7, 6.9.4, 6.10.3, 6.11.3, 6.12.3, 6.13.3, 6.14. 3, 6.16.3, 6.19.3.

all matters spoken of by Vyāsa (sūtrakṛt) himself? Or what man (is foolish enough to) disregard what the Lord has designed to free (us) from the mire of fear over the falsity of things that one experiences for himself?

COMMENT: All the world, he says, agrees that Scripture and direct experience (pratyakṣa) are both honorable and valid means of knowledge. And since both attest difference — Scripture in many cases merely guaranteeing what is already suspected on the basis of direct experience — there is no reason at all to fear the opponent's thesis of identity and illusion.

XVII. SOME ADDITIONAL CONSIDERATIONS NEGATING IDENTITY

394-395. Moreover, your Brahman is qualified by a multitude of attributes — well-being and so forth; Viṣṇu, Brahmā, Śiva, Indra, etc., are qualified by attributes proper to them; certainly sages, and all souls, are qualified in your opinion. Yet there is not a oneness of what is qualified, you believe. So words declaring the identity of these are absurd.

COMMENT: Vādirāja here says that Non-dualists refute their own doctrine by, on the one hand, ascribing attributes — on the basis of Scripture — to all realities and, on the other, holding that the sole Reality, Pure Consciousness, exists in a state of perfect oneness precisely because it is in no sense a "collection" of attributes.

In saying that Non-dualists admit a Brahman qualified by attributes, he may have in mind their concept of Īśvara. Īśvara is considered by Non-dualists to be "omniscient, omnipotent and ...the cause of the origination, sustenance and destruction of the world,"[1] and as such different from human souls. Indeed He is everything the richly theistic fifth and sixth chapters of the *Śvetāśvatara Upaniṣad* say He is — except real. If Vādirāja does have in mind these Non-dualist descriptions of Īśvara, as much a product of vyāvahārika reality as individual souls, then his rebuttal would have been more to the point if he had again refuted the vyāvahārika-doctrine.

But he may just as easily have in mind the Non-dualist description of the "real nature of Brahman."[2] The well-known description of Brahman as "saccidānanda," or "being, consciousness, and bliss" — which Śaṅkara and his school follow — is meant to be more than a statement reflecting a vyāvahārika reality. And Vādirāja may well be saying that, in spite of protests that "the real nature of Brahman [is] unqualified and beyond all change and difference,"[3] Non-dualists do have something *fairly specific*

1. Narain, *Mādhva Refutation*, p. 214.
2. *Ibid.*, p. 211.
3. *Ibid.*, p. 214.

(because specified) in mind when they speak of Brahman. And if that is the case, they have no right to speak of a "Pure Consciousness," or the perfect oneness contingent on Its attributelessness.

396. Furthermore, the identity of the two consciousnesses (i.e., Brahman's and a soul's) which you cherish is taught nowhere in Scripture. And therefore you cannot count on an indirect expression elsewhere as a foreshadowing (of identity).

COMMENT: Vādirāja would be willing to give Non-dualism a hearing if its advocates could muster a quotation expressly and irresistably spelling out the identity of Brahman and souls; if they could, the many ambiguous statements (by which he means the so-called "identity-texts") *might*, he would admit, indicate identity. But instead of identity it is *difference* which the Scriptures expressly declare, so the "shadowy" texts must be interpreted dualistically.

With an example he now contrasts the Dualist and Non-dualist treatment of these disputed texts:

397-399. Nowhere is the word "Ganges" (in the phrase, "the village on the Ganges,") characterizable as a man's horn (nonsensical); rather the (river's) *bank* is well-attested. Therefore the word "I" and so forth (as in "I am Brahman") would indicate the (soul's) inner controller and would not be pronouncing a fiction. And therefore this (doctrine of identity) was excluded from all the scriptural statements. And thus how, you fool, can the difference-texts, unrefuted, free of opposition, fail to invalidate your unscriptural, "identity" ?

COMMENT: The literal sense of the phrase "a village on the Ganges" is meaningless, for villages do not float on rivers. What the phrase "on the Ganges" really means is "on the *bank* of the Ganges." In other words, what has been established by the senses is the clue to the meaning of the phrase.

Now what applies at this common level, Vādirāja is saying, must apply at the level of scriptural interpretation as well. "I am Brahman" is like "the village on the Ganges." Taken literally both statements are absurd ("man's horn"); — obviously they "foreshadow", or indirectly indicate, *something else.* Now it could be that the "I" of the "identity statement" is the "inner guide" (antaryāmī) of the soul. Thus "I am Brahman" becomes "The inner controller is Brahman." On this interpretation the word "I" would not indicate the soul itself, but Brahman residing in and upholding the soul. And how do we arrive at this interpretation ? Because sense-knowledge, inference, and the overall thrust of the Scripture point to its truth.

Vādirāja of course feels that Non-dualists are like fools who, upon hearing of "a village on the Ganges," would expect to find the village sitting atop the river itself. For equally implausible is it that souls and Brahman are identical.

> **400-402a.** Furthermore, Pāṇini[1] has regarded (a word in) the nominative case in a locative sense in order to make an unsuitable meaning in Scripture make sense. Thus he had an answer to your belief: the identity-texts would be saying (in effect), "I am *in* Brahman," "you are *in* That," "All abides *in* Brahman," etc., through an annulment of the literal meaning. Worthy of truth would be the difference of them (Brahman and souls), not (their) identity — slain by a hundred arguments!

COMMENT: Another way of making sense of the identity-texts is to give them a locative sense. There is nothing suspicious about doing this, he says, since Pāṇini, though he never did it with respect to the identity-texts, nevertheless set a precedent by doing it on other occasions. (I have not been able to verify what these occasions were). The resulting meaning is different from that resulting from the equation, as above, of "I" or "You" with the soul's antaryāmī, or inner guide; but it is not contradictory. Brahman in this case must be viewed as the *ground* sustaining us, the reality enveloping and nourishing us. Whereas the first method of reinterpretation put God *within us*, the latter puts *us in Him*, so to speak. So God is not only immanent; He is transcendent as well.

Vādirāja by disposing of his foes' pet proof-texts feels that they are thoroughly bested ("slain by a hundred arguments").

1. Pāṇini is the great Sanskrit grammarian and is considered to speak with the authority of a sage.

The following three verses refer to *Śvetāśvatara Upaniṣad*, Chapter 6, and especially to verse 11, which needs quoting here for clarity's sake:

> The one God hidden in all beings, [is] all-pervading, the inner self of all beings, the ordainer of all deeds, who dwells in all beings, the witness, the knower, the only one, [not ?] devoid of qualities [(a ?) nirguṇaḥ].[1]

Vādirāja explains:

402b-404. Detailing and explaining (God's) qualities (as they relate to His creation), narrating (His) qualities (as they relate to Himself), Śuka and the other sages accordingly hailed this lesson on Viṣṇu's qualities as worthy of high praise. Therefore the text beginning "The one God," having spoken of Viṣṇu's qualities, at its conclusion sung of Him, encompassing the qualities named, as *not* void of qualities (anirguṇa) — as a corrective to wicked men's infatuation with a quality*less* (Brahman).

COMMENT: Chapter Six of the *Śvetāśvatara* is a symphony describing and praising the glorious qualities of a God which in some ways resembles the theistic God of the Judaeo-Christian tradition. Verse 11, however, has historically proven to be an ally to the Non-dualists. The reason is that the verse, as interpreted by them, ends "kevalo nirguṇaś ca," "nirguṇaḥ" meaning "qualityless." Non-dualists of course used the verse to good advantage in support of their non-dualism, for non-dualism presupposes at the very least a qualityless Brahman, or else the qualities themselves would bc seconds.

Now Vādirāja states that the text should read "kevalo *a*nirguṇaś ca" :

405a. The letter *a* preceding (the word *nirguṇa*) has been lopped off the word, as is evident from the foregoing qualities just mentioned.

COMMENT: He believes that there should be the letter *a* before *nirguṇa* and that the text is saying that Brahman is *not* qualityless: *anirguṇa*.[2] He argues that it is unreasonable to suppose that the

1. Radhakrishnan, *The Principal Upaniṣads*, p. 746 (with bracketing added by me).

2. What may look to a non-Sanskritist as an unpardonable interpola-

passage would say that Brahman was qualityless after having *just listed* his qualities.

It is somewhat surprising that Vādirāja should have taken this route to refute his opponents. Other Dualists have been happy to leave the word *nirguṇa* as it stands, and then have explained that the word indicates that God is not constituted of the *three guṇas* sattva, rajas, and tamas.

A more notable Dualist claim of *a*-excision is in regard to the notorious identity-text, "tat tvam asi." The full text reads: "sa ātmātattvamasi." All Hindu theologians prior to Madhva split the text up to read "sa ātmā; tat tvam asi"; but Madhva thought it should read "sa ātmā; *a*tat tvam asi," or "That is the Ātman (Supreme); you are *not* that."

Modern scholarship, incidentally, sides with the Non-dualists' grammatical analysis on both these points.

405b. Thus I am convinced that Madhva's path will be praised by those holding fast to the path of liberation.

406-407a. Furthermore, because of scriptural texts like, "pervading all of it, within and without, Nārāyaṇa abides," you as well as I say that the one consciousness of Brahman pervades all places everlastingly.

COMMENT: He begins a new argument by quoting from the *Mahānārāyaṇa Upaniṣad*,[1] which speaks of God's pervasion everywhere. Both he and his opponents preach the infinity of Brahman, based as it is on numerous scriptural passages.

407b. I affirm that (supreme consciousness) joined to endless powers, and the atom (of consciousness known as the soul).

COMMENT: For the Dualist, God's attributes and powers are not something extrinsic to Him. Without them He would not be God. They go to His very nature. The word "endless" refers both to the number and magnitude of His powers.

Contrasted to God's consciousness, infinite and all pervading, is the soul's which is regarded by all Dualists, in keeping with

tion by Vādirāja is not in fact. For the devanāgarī is such that *kevalo* could be followed, irrespective of the context, just as easily by *anirguṇaś* as by *nirguṇaś*.

1. 11.6.

certain scriptural passages, as no bigger than an atom, and as anything but all-pervading.

408. But according to you there is only that great One separated from powers, unqualified and indivisible. Therefore there is no activity at all by It.

COMMENT: For the Non-dualist there are of course ultimately no souls different from Brahman, no "atoms" of consciousness. Śaṅkara explicitly repudiates the atomicity of souls: he says, for example, that *Śvetāśvatara Upaniṣad* 5.9 — "This living self is to be known as a part of the hundredth part of the point of a hair divided a hundred fold. . . ."[1] — "teaches the soul's small size to depend on its connexion with the qualities of the buddhi, not upon its own Self."[2] By itself, he then says, the soul is none other than the one Brahman, is "altogether undefinable and thence non-existing or rather non-existing in the saṁsāra state."[3] Thus, as Vādirāja here states, "there is only that great One" for the Non-dualist.

Moreover, in contrast to the Dualists' notion of the Supreme, Brahman is unqualified and untouched by powers; for if these powers were real, they would imply real differences; indeed they would subdivide Pure Consciousness Itself. Thus all such powers are the stuff of māyā, far removed from the One Reality.

Non-dualists then conclude that this One is actionless. Agency and action is all a part of māyā. The nature of the One is simply to be purely and transcendentally conscious of ecstasy. As Śaṅkara puts it, "The agentship of the Self...does not form part of its nature...the agentship of the Self is due to its limiting adjuncts."[4]

Vādirāja now challenges:

409a. How could there be activity in the pot-ether through a limiting adjunct like a mere pot ?

COMMENT: Non-dualists account for the appearance of difference, as we have seen before, by the superimposition of limiting adjuncts on the one Brahman. Just as a pot defines space (or

1. Radhakrishnan, *The Principal Upaniṣads*, p. 741.
2. Śaṅkara, *Commentary*, II, p. 44.
3. *Ibid.*, p. 45.
4. Śaṅkara, *Commentary*, II, pp. 53 and 58.

"ether") in the shape of its own potness, though in reality there is no essential difference between the space inside the pot and that outside, so it is with souls and Brahman: souls are the limiting adjuncts superimposed on Brahman, and even though each seems different from Brahman and from all other souls, they are really the same.

Therefore when Vādirāja here asks how there could be activity in the pot-ether, he is really asking how Non-dualists account for activity in souls. For if souls and Brahman are absolutely one, just as pot-ether is one with the ether outside the pot, and furthermore if this Brahman is activityless, then why are the souls active ? The pot-ether analogy suggests only that a limiting adjunct *limits*; it says nothing about how inactivity is miraculously transformed into its opposite.

409b-411. Therefore the sharply distinct (individual) consciousnesses, capable of activity, spoken of as "within" (the body) for the purpose of activating the inert body incapable of activity (by itself), have been radically different from all eternity in order that there be experiences mutually distinct. The inert body's activity comes through the activity of this (consciousness), and in no other way. And therefore these atoms (of consciousness), existing within bodies, are alone the actors.

COMMENT: Vādirāja openly states the Dualist position, not as an argument against Non-dualism, but as a sensible alternative to an already exploded position. We learn (again) that Dualists believe that souls are eternal. We learn unequivocally for the first time how close Dualists are to Plato and his followers with respect to "mind-body dualism": there is an irrevocable distinction between body and soul, no intrinsic connection whatever. Madhva writes: "...the *jīva* is atomic in size....Being in one place, it can vitalize the whole body, just as a lamp can illuminate a room by its light."[1]

Vādirāja feels that his theory logically and neatly makes sense of our immediate experience. *I* have a headache and *you* don't; *he* is laughing and *she* isn't. These obvious experiential differences must be grounded ontologically, say the Dualists. And

1. Dasgupta, *Indian Philosophy*, IV, p. 146.

what better way to do so than to postulate *essential* differences between beings engaged in different activities ? That is to say, what better way than to postulate *essential* differences between beings engaged in different activities ? That is to say, what better way than to postulate an essential difference between souls ?

412-413. Moreover, the activity of a pot or whatever limiting the ether would be provided by *other* consciousnesses in one body or another placing (it) here or there. But there *is* no other activating consciousness acting conjointly with it (in your theory). Thus the example of pot-ether in your analysis has *gone* to pot!

COMMENT: Vādirāja again wants to show how unexplainable human activity is if Non-dualism is accepted. Pots, which in the pot-ether analogy are equated to the soul, do not move themselves, as souls do. They move only when moved by something else (usually people). But in Non-dualism there is no such notion as an external mover. So again the bodily activity we see constantly all around us remains unaccounted for by the pot-ether analogy.

Vādirāja's conclusion consists of a delightful pun on *durghaṭa*, whose primary meaning here is "impossible to accomplish," but which incipiently carries the additional meaning "bad (dur) pot (ghaṭa)."

414. Since a consciousness different from the (all-) pervading consciousness of Brahman must be advanced to account for the body's functioning, then your entire production is contemptible as well.

COMMENT: Not only is the pot-ether analogy ill-conceived, he is saying, but every argument yet put forward by Non-dualists calling for the identity of Brahman and souls is so. For nothing they have said explains or even allows for the immediate fact of bodily activity, or for the equally immediate fact that bodies (and thus presumably the souls within them) are mutually different.

415-416. And the freedom from defilement of the separate natures (at liberation) must be due to the dissolution of the marks (of sin) on the eternally distinct consciousnesses — (they would be) like jewels dislodged from mud, and certainly when that happens one jewel is never seen to be identical with another jewel; and therefore the purified eternal consciousnesses in liberation would be absolutely distinct.

COMMENT: Feeling he has completely disposed of Non-dualism, he here states the true doctrine of difference, which is as obvious with respect to souls in liberation as it is with respect to jewels being pried out of mud.

417-418. Immediately after the cutting of their bonds, Viṣṇu, who cuts the bonds, is as a result experienced at every step as the sustainer, the protector. He would be the Lord of these liberated, at all times just like an exalted king followed by (those whom he had) liberated from slavery. He would not (of course) be the refuge of all the fools (like you Non-dualists).

COMMENT: He is saying in effect that God's lordship is not an anthropomorphism. Rather it is a necessary consequence of the liberation-experience itself. Once liberated, souls cannot help but worship the power which liberated them, as their sovereign. Their experience of dependence upon and gratitude to this sovereign is unending. Thus lordship is natural to God. And lordship of course excludes identity.

He then adds that Non-dualists cannot be saved, for they recognize no Lord, or if they do, they call this lordship vyāvahārika. Thus at death they will either find themselves awaiting another reincarnation (another chance to be Dualist) or plunged into hell.

XVIII. CONCLUSION

Vādirāja concludes now that victory in this debate beyond any doubt belonged to him, for the force of all the opponent's arguments and Scriptural interpretations is annulled by his own doctrine. He explains:

419-420. According to you *true* knowledge is the perfecting, (illusion-) annulling indeterminate (intuition) of Brahman, and is *not* determinate knowledge: no concept (dhī) is true knowledge. (But) then by what standard, according to you, should all the meanings of the sacred books be established in a counsel of sages ? And because (your world-negating, difference-annulling doctrines are) non-authoritative, in a settlement of (the nature of) all things all would indeed be real.

COMMENT: This argument, which we have seen before (verses 25-26a for the first time), is a fit conclusion to the first chapter of the *Nyāyaratnāvalī*. It is the most sweeping, most basic, and the best argument in the Dualists' arsenal. In a sense all their other arguments are superfluous, for whereas the Non-dualists can effectually ignore the Dualists' many piecemeal refutations by copping the vyāvahārika plea, this argument attacks the vyāvahārika doctrine itself head-on. The Non-dualist is embarrassed when forced to confront this charge, for he has no recourse but to admit that the *true* Brahman-intuition is induced by the *false* concepts conveyed by the Scriptures, every word (including the identity-texts) of which is vyāvahārika.

The concluding verse involves, so characteristically, a pun — on the title of the work:

421. The first spotless string of the *Jewel-Necklace of Logical Arguments* acquired by Vādirāja truly adorns the necks of the wise.

COMMENT: He compares the verses he has written to faultless jewels strung together and costituting the first string (chapter) of a five-tiered necklace (the whole work, in five chapters). He compares himself, the writer of the work, to the owner of the necklace. He finally says that just as so splendid a necklace would beautify the wearer's neck, just so these verses enrich you, the fortunate reader !

WHO IS THE VICTOR ? AN ESTIMATE*

Has Vādirāja succeeded anywhere in these arguments in dealing a death-blow to Śaṅkara's Non-dualism ? The argument which has the best chance of doing so, in my estimation, appears in Section XI. I would like to develop the position argued there in more detail and in more modern terms, and then draw some conclusions.

What in each of us, Vādirāja asks there, sins and suffers ? Is it the *antaḥkaraṇa* ? impossible; for material, non-intelligent matter cannot sin — as even the Non-dualist is forced to admit. Furthermore, even if *per impossible* it were somehow the seat of sin, the law of karma would become unintelligible; for the antaḥ-karaṇa is but a series of thought-moments, or buddhis, each lasting only as long as the thought itself: it would flout the karmic law if one thought-moment were made to pay for the sin of an altogether different one.[1] Is the sinner and sufferer, then, the *Ātman*, the spiritual principle limited by the adjuncts of body and antaḥkaraṇa ? If so, then, since the Ātman is identical to Brahman, Brahman itself would have to sin and suffer. And that of course is unacceptable by anyone's standards regardless of what he precisely means by Brahman. What then sins and suffers ? Must it not ultimately be one or the other — either the antaḥkaraṇa or the Ātman ? If the Non-dualist, looking for an answer, were to point to the *jīva* in contradistinction to the Ātman as the sufferer, that would amount to an evasion; for the *jīva*, as he conceives it, is nothing but the Ātman in association with the body and antaḥkaraṇa, or, as M. K. V. Iyer puts it, "Brahman in empirical dress."[2] And since the intelligent or conscious aspect of the jīva *is* the Ātman, it is clear that the jīva's pain is ultimately the Ātman's. The only remaining alternative, it would seem, would

*Appeared as an article "A Death-Blow to Śaṅkara's Non-Dualism? A Dualist Refutation," in *Religious Studies* (Cambridge University), Vol. 12, No. 3, September, 1976), pp. 281-290.

1. The position that Vādirāja is attacking here resembles Nāgasena's in the *Questions of Milinda* (see Lucien Stryk, ed., *World of the Buddha* pp. 89-99).

2. *Advaita Vedānta*, p. 117.

be to hold that the *experience* of pain can exist without an *experiencer*, but this Buddhist answer Śaṅkara himself forcibly rejects.

Let us now look at Śaṅkara's own analysis of pain to see if it withstands Vādirāja's, and in general the Dualist, rebuttal. Śaṅkara writes, "The pain of the individual soul...is not real, but imaginary only, caused by the error consisting in the non-discrimination of (the Self from) the body, senses, and other limiting adjuncts which are due to name and form, the effects of Nescience."[1] In another place he says that "the soul does not really suffer," although as far as the "phenomenal world" goes "we may admit the relation of sufferer and suffering just as it is observed, and need neither object to it nor refute it."[2] All this amounts to saying that the jīva's suffering is merely apparent, not real. The beginningless transmigratory careers of the infinite numbers of jīvas are the stuff of mere seeming: the joy and pain, the rewards and punishments due to karma, are merely apparent, not real. More precisely, they have a conventional (vyāvahārika) reality only, not an ultimately true (pāramārthika) reality.

I do not believe that these considerations invalidate Vādirāja's rebuttal. For the fact still remains that the jīva experiences pain, whether the pain is imaginary or not is irrelevant, for an imagined snake causes as great a fright as a real snake. And what does it mean to say that the jīva does not *really* suffer, but may be said to suffer "as far as the phenomenal world goes" ? I know of no distinction between *suffering* and *seeming to suffer*; who has ever *seemed* to suffer who did not *really* suffer ? Suffering is of its nature a subjective state, and thus to make a distinction between "objective" suffering and "subjective" suffering is invalid, for there is no such thing as "objective" suffering: it is, to use the Indian idiom, a hare's horn. It is invalid, therefore, to hold that the soul does not *really suffer but only seems* to suffer, as Śaṅkara holds. We are in the end left with the fact of suffering and the fact of a sufferer. And since according to Śaṅkara this jīva (the "seeming" sufferer) is really just the Ātman, and since the phrase "seeming suffering" is at best redundant and at worst unintelligible, it is pure legerdemain to hold any view, given Śaṅkara's Non-dualist pre-supposition, but that the Ātman itself *really suffers*.

1. *Commentary*, II, 64.
2. *Ibid.*, I, 379, 381.

This inescapable conclusion is exactly what Vādirāja has been trying to pin on his Non-dualist adversary all along.

I see no legitimate way out for Śaṅkara and Non-dualism. Their only escape turns into a *cul-de-sac*: "imaginary suffering" turns out simply to be suffering. And this suffering, though facilitated by the antaḥkaraṇa, is not the antaḥkaraṇa's; obviously then it is the jīva's, which is to say it is ultimately the Ātman's, which is to say it is Brahman's. So Brahman, whose nature, according to Non-dualism, is pure, undifferentiated Bliss-Consciousness, has turned into a sufferer: the *reductio ad absurdum* is complete.

In summation, it will not help matters to point to the limiting adjuncts (antaḥkaraṇa, buddhi, etc.) as the sufferers; causes of the suffering they may be, but they are not to be confused with the actual subject of the suffering. Nor will it do to say that whereas the jīva suffers, the Ātman does not; for Śaṅkara makes it clear that the jīva is ultimately the same entity as the Ātman. Nor will it do to speak of the jīvātman's suffering as "imaginary," for the reasons just elaborated. Nor again will the Buddhist "solution" suffice. Might there be some *tertium quid* then which suffers? Śaṅkara nowhere advances such a notion for our consideration; what first looks like a halfway-house between Ātman and antaḥkaraṇa, namely jīva, is ultimately identified in the clearest terms with Ātman. Śaṅkara, it is finally clear, has left himself with no *vehicle* for the suffering. It is no wonder he termed suffering "imaginary." Unfortunately for his philosophy, however, he is completely incapable of finding a vehicle even for this "imaginary" suffering. Unless of course it is an "imaginary" person. But such language trails off into the gray twilight of unintelligibility. Or would some call it, as a last resort, the high noon of mystic brilliance? Whatever the case, I do not believe that great mysticism is legitimate warrant for bad philosophy.

It may be, who can tell?, that someday I too will "understand" Śaṅkara, as a few no doubt would say I at present do not. At the moment, however, I am inclined to look at many of those who champion Śaṅkara as themselves failing at that task.[1] But

1. "There is a general belief amongst many that monism of Śaṅkara presents the final phase of Indian thought. . . But the readers of the present volume. . . will realize the strength and uncompromising impressiveness of the dualistic position" (preface by Dasgupta. *Indian Philosophy*, IV, viii).

I say this only of those Śaṅkarians who think that Śaṅkara's philosophy is *rationally* sound. With those who see him as a mystic writing in a philosophical guise I have no quarrel. I can only be pleased at Rudolf Otto's understanding of Śaṅkara when he writes that Śaṅkara's concern was "not metaphysics but a doctrine of salvation."[1] Otto no doubt overstates his case — for Śaṅkara did not separate the two — but it is clear what he is driving at: Śaṅkara's *Brahma-sūtra-bhāṣya,* his major work, ideally should not be read by a philosopher philosophically, but by a mystic mystically. The philosopher (and I am talking about the rational analyst), if he is rigorous, will go away disappointed, while the mystic — and I am really talking about the mystic in each of us — will feel that he has been in communication with someone who has *met* the truth even when he has not understood it. What irony there finally is in all this ! The Dualist, who appears to have better *understood* the truth, gives the impression of not having *met* the truth as directly as the Non-dualist with his untenable metaphysics ! But that is for another day.

I mean by none of the above to imply that the argument developed here, or elsewhere throughout the work, has established the truth of a dualistic theism. That, too, is for another day. But I do maintain, as the title indicates, that it "clears the ground" for a large-scale renewal of philosophical interest in India's extraordinarily rich, and up until now so frequently overlooked, Dualist heritage. At the very least, it forces the Non-dualist to free himself (as Radhakrishnan bravely did) from too trusting an alliance with Śaṅkara and to propound a system as amenable to the demands of the rational intellect as to the phenomenality of the mystical consciousness.

1. *Mysticism East and West*, p. 33 (title of chapter 2).

Appendix

NYĀYARATNĀVALĪ

I (1-2)

श्रीलक्ष्मवक्षसे रूक्षनखशिक्षितरक्षसे ।
स्वपक्षरक्षादीक्षाय नृहर्यक्षाय ते नमः॥ १
त्रिधामा यस्य हृत्सीम्नि कृतधामा निरन्तरम् ।
सुधीश्रियं दिशतु मे समध्वक्षीरसागरः॥ २

II (3-12)

एष सर्वेश्वर इति सर्वस्यैष वशीति च ।
सर्वस्येशान इत्यादौ महिमा श्रूयते हरेः॥ ३
एष नित्यो ब्राह्मणस्य महिमेत्याह काचन ।
सत्यः सो अस्य महिमेत्यस्तौषीत्काचन श्रुतिः॥ ४
स्वाभाविकी ज्ञानबलक्रिया चेत्यपरा जगौ ।
तान्नित्यसत्यमहिमा नित्यं ज्ञानबलक्रियः॥ ५
भगवान्निगमोद्धर्ता धर्ता मन्दरभूभृतः ।
भुवो भर्ता दुष्टदैत्यहर्ता सिद्धो भवत्प्रभुः॥ ६
स्वकार्याय तमेवेशं येऽर्थयन्ते क्षणे क्षणे ।
अतादृशबलज्ञाना ब्रह्मेशानादयः सुराः॥ ७
तस्यानुर्वतिनश्चेति सिद्धमासीद्विवेकिनाम् ।
मात्रापरोऽसि त्वं विष्णो महित्वं नाश्नुवन्ति ते॥ ८
इति श्रुतिश्रुतं विष्णुमहाप्रतिमपौरुषम् ।
नास्ति नारायणसमं न भूतं न भविष्यति॥ ९
स्मृतिरेषा च कृष्णस्य समं कालत्रयेऽपि च ।
निषेधति ततस्तेन कस्यैक्यं स्याद्विचारय॥ १०
महिमा श्रीपतेः सर्वः स्वभावोऽभूच्छ्रुतेर्बलात् ।
अन्यस्य तदभावोऽपि श्रुतिस्मृतिबलादभूत्॥ ११
प्रकृत्यैव च यो नीचो यः प्रकृत्या सदोत्तमः ।
तयोरैक्यं नैव शक्यं वक्तुं कल्पशतैरपि ॥ १२

III (13-32)

अतत्त्वावेदकं सर्वं भेदवाक्यमितीरिते ।
वक्तव्यमद्वितीयत्ववाचा भेदनिषेवने॥ १३

निषिध्यमानभेदस्य स्यात्कथंचिदतत्वता ।
अतत्वावेदकं च स्याद्भेदवाक्यं तदैव हि॥ १४
न चैतद्युज्यते शब्दसामर्थ्यस्य विचारणे ।
आत्मा जडं न जीवो नेत्याकारा नेति नेति वाक्॥ १५
प्रथमांतपदोक्ते न ब्रह्मणा सह सर्वथा ।
नञर्थभूतभेदस्य सामानाधिकरण्यवाक्॥ १६
घटः पटो नेति वाक्ये यथा सर्वैः प्रतीयते ।
घटः पटनिषेधात्मा तथैवात्रापि धीर्भवेत्॥ १७
जगदात्मनि नेत्युक्त त्वत्यंताभाववाग्भवेत् ।
आत्मा जगन्नेति वाक्तु भेदवाक् नात्र संशयः॥ १८
त्वया च वाक्यपूर्त्यर्थमध्याहार्यं मयैव न ।
योग्यं तु प्रतियोग्यत्र मृग्यते द्विः प्रयोगतः॥ १९
सप्तम्यन्तपदेनोक्त भूतले नास्ति गौरिति ।
निषेधे तु नञर्थस्याधारस्तद्भूतलं भवेत्॥ २०
नैवतद्रूपता तस्येत्याहुश्शब्दार्थवेदिनः ।
विलक्षणोक्तेरर्थोऽपि स्यादेवेत्थं विलक्षणः॥ २१
अतस्तवाद्वितीयत्ववाग्द्वितीयं निषेधतु ।
अद्वितीयतयाभातं भेदं न ब्रह्मणि क्षिपेत्॥ २२
तद्ब्रह्म तत्त्वरूपं मे ब्रह्मभेदं वदद्वचः ।
अतत्त्वावेदकं नाभूत्किन्त्वभूत्तत्ववेदकम्॥ २३
द्वितीयं यस्य नेत्युक्त्या नञर्थे ब्रह्मणा सह ।
षष्ठ्यर्थभूतसम्बन्धो भासते न त्वभिन्नता॥ २४
अतस्तवाद्वैतमेव द्वितीयमभवद्बलात् ।
उपस्थितपरित्यागे कारणाभावतः श्रुतिः॥ २५
द्वितीयमिदमेवादौ निषेधेदिति मे मतिः ।
निषिध्यमानद्वैतस्य बोधिका वागियं तव॥ २६
अतत्त्वावेदिकैवासीच्छब्दशक्ति विचारणे ।
नीलमुत्पलमित्युक्त नीलाभिन्नं यथोत्पलम्॥ २७
ईयते नत्वभेदस्याऽप्यभेदस्तेन बोध्यते ।
किन्त्वभेदाधारतैवं सर्वं ब्रह्मेति वाच्यपि॥ २८
सर्वाभिन्नब्रह्मबुद्धिर्भवेन्नत्वेकरूपता ।
अतस्तत्राऽप्येकता न ब्रह्मधर्मतया श्रुता॥ २९
द्वितीयैवाभवत्तांच निषेधत्यद्वितीयवाक् ।
अतत्वावेदिका सर्वा वाक् चैवमभवत्तव॥ ३०

अतो मिथ्यावादिता च भवतामेव शोभते ।
एवंच भेदवाक्यानि भेदतत्त्वप्रमापनात्॥ ३१
विद्वच्छ्लाघ्यानि सत्संसद्योग्यान्यासन्नसंशयः ।
तत्तत्त्ववादिनामेव युक्ताऽभूत्तत्त्ववेदिता॥ ३२

IV (33-46)

अनादिकालमारभ्य सर्गे सर्गे दिने दिने ।
शतशः पण्डितमुखाच्छ्रवणे मननेऽपि च॥ ३३
या भ्रांतिर्न निवर्तेत यावन्मोक्षं पुनः पुनः ।
सर्वार्थेषु च सार्वज्ञाद्योगीन्द्रेऽप्यनुवर्तते॥ ३४
व्यावहारिकमानानि दद्युर्भ्रान्ति किलेदृशीम् ।
एवं च सर्वजगतामनिवर्त्यं महाभ्रमम्॥ ३५
कुर्वतां वेदशास्त्राणां महावंचकता भवेत् ।
प्रातिभासिकमानं तु किंचित्किंचित्क्वचित्क्वचित्॥ ३६
कदाचिद्भ्रामयेत्तस्य दोषे सत्येव नान्यथा ।
तत्पामराणामेवैतदपकारि न योगिनाम्॥ ३७
महावंचकता तस्य ततो नात्यन्त (नीच) तोचिता ।
भेदभेदिपदार्थानां साधकस्य स्थले स्थले॥ ३८
चोदनारूपतः सर्वयागानां बोधकस्य च ।
वेदादेरुक्तविधया दीर्घभ्रान्तिकरस्य तु॥ ३९
व्यावहारिकमानत्ववाचाऽप्यत्यंतनीचता ।
आगता न गुणश्रैष्ठ्यमतोऽप्येतदसङ्गतम्॥ ४०
व्यवहारस्य निर्वाहकरी या तु दशाखिलैः ।
सत्यस्यैवोच्यते सैव दशेयं चेद्भवेदपि॥ ४१
बाधितार्थत्वसाम्ये तु बाधदूरत्वमात्रतः ।
नास्या विशेषः कोऽपि स्यात्किंतु स्यादुक्तदूषणम्॥ ४२
रजतार्थी भ्रमे जाते तदैव तदपेक्षया ।
तत्र गत्वा बाधकं च तत्काले प्रतिपद्यते॥ ४३
तदनर्थी भ्रमे जातेऽप्युपेक्ष्य स्वगृहं गतः ।
बाधं तु नैव जानीते को विशेषस्तयोर्वद॥ ४४
अनिवर्त्यं महाभ्रान्तिजनकोन्मादरोगवान् ।
सर्वोपकारिवेदादेर्हीनादपि च हीनताम्॥ ४५
यो ब्रूते वैदिकच्छद्मी हन्ति मातरमेव सः ।
विश्वापकारकरणं तस्य लीलेति मे मतिः॥ ४६

V (47-66)

किं च कृष्णः किल ब्रह्मरुद्राद्युत्कृष्टचेतनः ।
अपकृष्टाश्चेतनाश्च ब्रह्माद्यास्तत एव यत्।। ४७
सिद्धास्तज्जीवपरयोर्विरुद्धाऽभूच्चिदेव हि ।
चिन्मात्रौपाधिकं नीचोच्चत्वं चिन्नाश एव हि।। ४८
नश्येन्नापरथा तस्मात् नित्या जीवेशयोर्भिदा ।
विष्णोः सर्वोत्तमत्वं च चित्स्वभावनिबन्धनम्।। ४९
निराबाधं च नित्यं च कथं नाभूद्विचार्यतां ।
ब्रह्मेशाद्यानतैषीको रामः किल महाबलः।। ५०
तृणास्त्रेण रिपुं जिग्ये वयं च तदनुव्रताः।
जयेमहि तृणेनैव सदसि प्रतिवादिनः।। ५१
यद्धस्तस्पर्शमात्रेण तृणं च ब्रह्मपूर्वकैः ।
नतं बभूव तं देवं को वा देवोऽतिवर्तते।। ५२
एवं च रामदेवस्य जीवात्यन्तविभिन्नतां ।
देवेशत्वं च संसत्सु को वा तेन न साधयेत्।। ५३
पश्य नामबलं विष्णोस्तद्धि लिङ्गानुशासनम् ।
यदीदमवजानासि कुप्येत्तर्हि शिवस्तव।। ५४
त्वं वासुदेवो भगवानवतीर्णो जगत्पतिः ।
इति प्रस्तोभितो बालैर्मेने स्वात्मानमच्युतम्।। ५५
कदाचित्पौंड्रको नाम काशिराजः प्रतापवान् ।
वासुदेवोऽहमित्यज्ञो दूतं कृष्णाय प्राहिणोत्।। ५६
कत्थनं तदुपाकर्ण्य पौण्ड्रकस्याल्पमेधसः ।
उच्चकैरुग्रसेनाद्याः सभ्याः प्रजहसुस्तदा।। ५७
इति भागवते स्पष्टं सोऽहंभावो ह्यनेकधा ।
यतो विनिन्दितस्तस्मात्को वा तं भावयेद्बुधः।। ५८
अच्युतोऽहमनन्तोऽहं गोविन्दोऽहं सनातनः ।
इति मायावादिनां या भावना नित्यकर्मणि।। ५९
अहमेवाच्युतोऽस्मीति वासुदेवोऽहमित्यपि ।
या भावना पौण्ड्रकस्य को विशेषोऽनयोर्वद।। ६०
वंचनं किल तज्ज्ञानं बालानां भाषितं किल ।
दैत्यः किलाधिकारी च यः कृत्रिमचतुर्भुजः।। ६१
रथस्थहेमगरुडारूढो यश्च पथि व्रजेत् ।
अज्ञोऽल्पमेधाः स किल कत्थनं किल तद्वचः।। ६२

सभ्यानामपहास्यं चेत्याह निन्दां पदे पदे ।
यदि तत्वज्ञानमिदं तर्हि निन्दां शुकोऽसकृत्।। ६३
कुतश्चकार योगीन्द्रो महासंसदि योगिनाम् ।
ज्ञानिनोऽस्य शिरः कस्माच्छुतदेवगृहातिथिः।। ६४
चिच्छेद भगवान्कृष्णः कुपितो दूतवार्तया ।
शुकस्य सूत्रकारस्य राज्ञो राजसभासदाम्।। ६५
कृष्णस्य चाप्रियं ज्ञानं मिथ्याज्ञानं न संशयः ।
दासोऽहमिति यज्ज्ञानं तत्त्वज्ञानं तदेव तत्।। ६६

VI (67-124a)

प्रतिकर्मव्यवस्थाया मायिनां हृदयंगमा ।
व्यावहारिकतापक्षं प्रतिक्षिप्य तयैव तु।। ६७
प्रपंचपारमार्थ्यं च तयैव प्रतिपाद्य हि ।
अन्ते तामेव या हन्ति सा कृतिः कैर्नमान्यते।। ६८
यत्तत्तद्वस्तुविभ्रांतावधिष्ठानं तदेव यः ।
तत्तद्भ्रम इति प्राह स प्रष्टव्यः सभान्तरे।। ६९
एवं चेच्छुक्तिरूप्ये च शुक्त्यवच्छिन्न चिद्धिया ।
अधिष्ठानचिदेषैव भ्रमेऽप्यस्तु द्वयी गतिः।। ७०
कस्मात्तं भांतमित्यस्याः सङ्कोचश्च श्रुतेः कुतः ।
अधिष्ठानस्य चाविद्यावरणं न हि दूषणम्।। ७१
विक्षेपशक्तितो भ्रान्तार्थोल्लेखोऽपि न दूषणम् ।
यद्येवमेव सर्वत्राप्यस्त्वित्यङ्गीकृतं त्वया।। ७२
तांस्तान्भ्रमांस्तु जीवेषु केनोपायेन नेष्यसि ।
उपाध्युपहितैरंशैस्तैरस्यैक्याप्त्यसंभवात्।। ७३
यद्घटोपहितोंशोऽसौ वृत्तिग्रस्तोऽपरस्तव ।
यदि वृत्त्या भ्रमी सोऽपि तर्हि सर्वत्र विभ्रमः।। ७४
(सैवा) सर्वोऽस्तु किमपूर्वैतद्भ्रमकल्पनया फलम् ।
भान्तं तमनुभातीति श्रुतिः सूर्यं प्रशंसतु।। ७५
न चायमपि पक्षस्ते शोभतेऽक्षार्थसङ्गमात् ।
भवन्ती घटधीर्यस्माद्घटसत्तामपेक्षते।। ७६
श्रुतियुक्ती समुल्लंघ्य भ्रान्तिः सा(न्तिसा)क्ष्येव तत्र चेत् ।
घटेऽपि तद्वदेवास्तु द्वेधा साध्यं न किंचन।। ७७
नचैतदपि युक्तं ते दृश्येवारोपवादिनः ।
दृश्यानां घटपूर्वाणां यस्साक्ष्यंतर्बहिर्हिते।। ७८

यदि रूप्यभ्रमादौ च दृष्टं पक्षं त्यजन्निह ।
अधिष्ठानचितं तत्तद्भ्रान्ति वदसि तच्च न॥ ७६
अधिष्ठानस्यावरकाज्ञानमध्यस्तवस्तुषु ।
उपादानं तव मते तन्नाशे कारणक्षयात्॥ ८०
वस्तुनाशोऽप्यवश्यं स्यात्तद्घटो नेति धीर्भवेत् ।
घटोऽस्तीति भ्रमस्त्री या द्वेधा सा विधवाऽप्यभूत्॥ ८१
यद्येवमपि पूर्वेषां मतं रक्षितुमिच्छसि ।
तथाऽपि तस्य शिक्षैव भवेत्पश्याद्य कौशलम्॥ ८२
घटाधिष्ठानचैतन्यं घटारोपस्तदा किल ।
निवर्तेत यदाऽज्ञानं चैतन्यावरकं स्वतः॥ ८३
अज्ञाननाशपक्षेऽस्मिन्कार्यनाशो भवेदिति ।
प्रागुक्तदोषे सत्येव चान्यो दोषोऽपि कीर्त्यते॥ ८४
दोषरूपे तवाज्ञाने भ्रमकारणतोचिता ।
न तु भ्रमविरोधित्वरूपदिव्यगुणात्मता॥ ८५
किंचावरणविक्षेपशक्तिद्वययुतैव या ।
अविद्याख्यपिशाची सा कथं विद्यागुणं भजेत्॥ ८६
तस्मात्स्वप्रतिकर्माख्यदुःस्थावस्थानवस्थधीः ।
अज्ञानोपादानमतं विसस्मार गुरुस्तव॥ ८७
प्रमाणाधिष्ठानचितो वैकल्यादावृतत्वतः ।
अज्ञानाख्येन दोषेण जडाग्रहणमिष्यते॥ ८८
न तु दोषान्तरं तत्रेत्याहुस्त्वत्पूर्वसूरयः ।
अधिष्ठानावरकता जडोपादानताऽपि च॥ ८६
एकस्यैव यतस्तस्मात्कार्यनाशो भवेद्ध्रुवम् ।
अतो दोषान्तरस्यापि सम्भवादेव कीर्तनम्॥ ६०
अज्ञानस्य निवृत्तिश्च वृत्त्या प्रत्यक्षरूपया ।
सा निर्दोषार्थसंयोगसापेक्षेति च ते मतम्॥ ६१
असन्निकृष्टप्रत्यक्षं रजतादि भ्रमेपरं ।
अन्यत्रार्थेन संयुक्तमिन्द्रियं करणं त्विति॥ ६२
भित्तिव्यवहितार्थस्याज्ञानात्सर्वस्य सम्मतम् ।
अर्थे सत्येव संयोगो दृष्टो नापरथा क्वचित्॥ ६३
कस्माद्वा नाक्षसंयोगि शुक्तिरूप्यं विचारय ।
एवं चारोपतः पूर्वं विद्यमानं घटादिकम्॥ ६४
अनारोपितमेवासीत्तवापि च ममापि च ।
अभूदनारोपितत्वादबाध्यं च तदात्मवत्॥ ६५

व्यावहारिकता तस्मात्कस्य वा स्याद्विचारय ।
इदानीं बाधितभ्रान्त्या या सत्तोल्लिखिता भवेत्॥ ९६
प्रातिभासिकसत्ता सा दीर्घभ्रान्त्यैव ते मते ।
या सत्तोल्लिख्यते सा हि व्यावहारिकतोच्यते॥ ९७
आरोपात्प्राक्तु या सत्ता ब्रह्मसत्तोपमैव सा ।
प्रतिकर्मव्यवस्था या भवद्भिरुररीकृता॥ ९८
चित्रं सैवाभवत्पश्य प्रत्यर्थिमतसाधिका ।
अतः सभायां हास्यं ते मतमासीन्न संशयः॥ ९९
व्यासोऽपि भगवानाह द्रोग्धुर्वै परतो भयम् ।
विश्वस्मै द्रुह्यतः पश्य स्वत एव भयं तव॥ १००
कैमुत्यात्तद्द्वयं च स्यात् व्यासेन च निरूपितम् ।
चैतन्यं न घटारोपः प्रागर्थं यदपेक्षते॥ १०१
वृत्तिस्तु न घटारोपः प्राक्तु यत् साप्यपेक्षते ।
अतो द्वेधाऽपि नैवाभूदारोपाद्यं मते तव॥ १०२
व्यावहारिकतावादस्तस्माद्देशांतरं गतः ।
घटाधिष्ठानचैतन्ये घटोल्लेखो भवेद्यदि॥ १०३
हृदिस्थजीवचैतन्ये व्यवहारस्तदा कुतः ।
ऐक्याच्चेत्सर्वजीवानां सदा स्याद्व्यवहर्तृता॥ १०४
अथान्तःकरणे चक्षुःसहायेन बहिर्गते ।
केदारान्तस्थजलवदर्थाकारविवेकवान्॥ १०५
घटादिवृत्तिरूपेण परिणामो यदा भवेत् ।
तदाऽस्याः प्रतिबिम्बः स्याद्देहान्तस्थचितो बलात्॥ १०६
सा चिद्घटचितैकत्वमत्या तज्ज्ञानमेव च ।
एवं चेदनुमित्यादिज्ञाने तज्ज्ञानता कथम्॥ १०७
न ह्ययं प्रक्रिया तत्राऽप्यस्ति युष्मन्मतेऽपि च ।
परोक्षवृत्त्यैव तत्र यदि स्याज्ज्ञानमात्मनः॥ १०८
आवश्यक्या तदाऽत्राऽपि वृत्त्यैव द्रष्टृता भवेत् ।
बकबन्धस्य निर्बन्धमिमं व्यर्थं परित्यज॥ १०९
भान्तं तमनु भातीति श्रुतिस्त्वत्र यथा न ते ।
तथाऽत्राऽपि भवेन्नासौ दीप्तिमन्तमुपैतु च॥ ११०
अनुसृत्य हि भानन्तु भिन्नयोरेव शोभते ।
सूर्यप्रकरणे चाऽस्मिन्श्रमायान्यकथोद्यमः॥ १११
अस्यांच त्रिक्षणस्थायिवृत्तौ चित्प्रतिबिम्बता ।
तस्या नाशक्षणे नष्टा पुनरायात्कथं हृदि॥ ११२

किंचाऽविद्याविनाशेऽपि कथमेकत्वमेतयोः ।
यतो वृत्तिघटाख्योपाधिद्वयोपहितौ हि तौ॥ ११३
उपाधिभेदे सति तु भेदोऽवश्यं तवैव हि ।
यदि वृत्तिगता चिच्च घटं पश्येत्स्वशक्तितः॥ ११४
तर्ह्यारोपातिरिक्तोऽपि सम्बन्धोऽभूत्तयोर्बलात् ।
एवं चाबद्धशकलमालाभिः किं प्रयोजनम्॥ ११५
आवश्यकी वृत्तिरेव किं न स्यात्तत्तदर्थधीः ।
तयोः फलबलादेव सम्बन्धोऽप्यस्तु कश्चन॥ ११६
दृष्टकार्यानुसारेण कस्य कस्य न कल्पना ।
अस्वच्छदेहान्तरितचैतन्यं घटसन्निधौ॥ ११७
बहिः परिणमद्वृत्तौ कथं स्यात्प्रतिबिम्बितम् ।
हस्तेनान्तरितादर्शे यन्मुखप्रतिबिम्बनम्॥ ११८
नेक्षते क्वापि कस्यापि तद्देहान्तरितोऽपि न ।
न चेद्देहान्तरं श्लिष्यद्देहान्तः संस्थितैव चित्॥ ११९
तस्यापरोक्षवृत्तौ च फलिता तद्वदेव हि ।
तद्दृष्टमर्थं जानातु किमबद्धान्तरे भयम्॥ १२०
यतोऽन्यद्दर्पणेऽप्यन्यवक्त्रप्रतिकृतिर्भवेत् ।
ततो भिन्नचितोः कैमुत्येन स्यात्प्रतिबिम्बनम्॥ १२१
किंचाधिष्ठानचैतन्यमन्योन्यात्मकतां घटे ।
अध्यस्य तं घटं पश्येन्नोचेत्कुप्येद् गुरुस्तव॥ १२२
गौरोऽहमितिवत्तस्माद्घटोऽहमिति धीर्भवेत् ।
देहान्तस्थितजीवोऽपि घटोऽहमिति पश्यतु॥ १२३
घटं जानाम्यहमिति कस्माद्व्यवहरत्यसौ ।

VII (124b-145)

अज्ञानापगमे तत्तदधिष्ठानचितोऽखिलाः॥ १२४
तत्तदर्थभ्रमाश्च स्युरज्ञानावरणे च ताः ।
नार्थानुल्लिखितुं शक्तास्तच्चानादित एव ताः॥ १२५
आवृत्य तिष्ठतीत्याहुस्तेषामित्थमभून्मतम् ।
चैतन्यावरकाज्ञानविक्षेपाख्याः स्वभावतः॥ १२६
विरुद्धाकारतो वर्तमानस्य जगतः पुरा ।
विवर्तो ह्यतदाकारपरिणामात्मकोऽभवत्॥ १२७
तच्चाधिष्ठानचैतन्यमज्ञानावरणात्तदा ।
तानर्थान्नोल्लिखेदेव वैकल्येन जडाग्रहम्॥ १२८

यस्माद्ग्रन्थकृदेवाह प्रतिकर्मव्यवस्थितौ ।
विषयाणां विवेकाय तन्नाशोऽप्याप्यपेक्षते।। १२९
तस्मादविद्यावरणे सति तच्चिन्न तद्भ्रमः ।
तच्चावरणमज्ञानमुपादानतया चिति।। १३०
एवं चाभ्रमसिद्धत्वं सर्वस्य जगतोऽपि च ।
तदैव सर्वथा वाच्यं ततः सृष्टौ न तद्भ्रमः।। १३१
भवन्न्यायबलादेव न भवेत्किं विचारय ।
अज्ञानोपादानमतादारोपितमतं गतम्।। १३२
आरोपशोधने चास्य नोपादानमतं भवेत् ।
वृत्त्याऽज्ञाननिवृत्तौ हि चित्यारोपो भवेत्तव।। १३३
यन्निवृत्तौ च यत्कार्यं सर्वैश्च परिदृश्यते ।
तदुपादानतां तस्य को वदेत्कोविदः सुधीः।। १३४
तस्मादविद्याकार्यत्वादप्यासीन्न मृषा जगत् ।
आरोपितत्वादपि च नासीज्जगदिदं मृषा।। १३५
एकं संधित्सतस्तस्मादपरं च्यवते तव ।
ज्ञानातपोऽपि न तपेद्दृढमूलतरोः शिखाम्।। १३६
दुर्घटत्वमविद्यायाः केवलं भूषणं न ते ।
पूर्वोत्तरविरुद्धायास्त्वद्विधायाश्च भूषणम्।। १३७
अविद्याकार्यमप्येतद्भवेदाविद्यकं परम् ।
मृषात्वं तस्य केन स्यात्किं चाण्डालीशिशुर्मृषा।। १३८
नचेदज्ञानसम्बन्धा ब्रह्मापि स्यान्मृषा तव ।
आरोपाभावतो ब्रह्म सच्चेत्तेनैव सज्जगत्।। १३९
अविद्या ज्ञाननाश्याचेन्नाश्यनाशकताभिधः ।
विरोधोऽपि तयोर्भूयान्मिथ्यात्वं केन वा भवेत्।। १४०
प्रकाशनाश्यतमसा किं मृषात्वमपेक्ष्यते ।
यत्प्राक्सतो नाश्यतैव दृष्टा घटपटादिके।। १४१
तस्मान्नाश्यस्य सत्तैव युक्ता स्यान्न त्वसत्यता ।
यदारोपं विनैवास्ति न तस्योपायकोटिभिः।। १४२
नास्तिता शक्यते वक्तुं नोचेत्स्याद्ब्रह्मनास्तिता ।
तस्मादबद्धमालाया नान्तोऽस्ति भवतो मते।। १४३
अनुवादोप्यबद्धानां दोषायेत्युपरम्यते ।
स्पष्टत्वाद् ग्रन्थविस्तारभयाच्चोपरमाम्यहम्।। १४४
सोऽहंभावस्यैव निन्दा यतो भागवते कृता ।
ततोऽपि भेदः शङ्कां ते हुङ्कारेणैव वारयेत्।। १४५

VIII (146-167)

दृग्दृश्ययोगायोगेन यद्यध्यासो निगद्यते ।
तर्ह्यध्यासमते योगाभावेऽपि ज्ञेयतास्ति किम्।। १४६
उताध्यासाध्यस्तभाव एव योगो विवक्षितः ।
आद्ये रूप्यभ्रमे ज्ञेयं रज्जुसर्पादिकं भवेत्।। १४७
घटदृश्येव दृश्यः स्यात् पटादिरपि ते मते ।
यदज्ञानस्य यत्कार्यं तस्य ज्ञानं तदेव चेत्।। १४८
तर्हि शुक्तेरपि ज्ञेयं शुक्तिरूप्यं भवेत्तव ।
अज्ञानं वा कथं ज्ञेयं स्वज्ञानस्य भवेद्वद।। १४९
कथं च चरमज्ञाने ज्ञेयत्वं ब्रह्मणो भवेत् ।
यदज्ञानस्य यत्कार्यं तस्य ज्ञेयं तदेव चेत्।। १५०
यदज्ञानस्य यत्कार्यं तस्य ज्ञानं च तद्भवेत् ।
भूलग्नमृत्तिकाकार्ये घटे भूज्ञेयता भवेत्।। १५१
ज्ञानत्वाभावतो नो चेत्तर्हि ज्ञानस्वभावतः ।
ज्ञेयता च भवेत्काचित्किमनेन प्रयोजनम्।। १५२
अज्ञानस्य स्वभावोऽपि कार्येऽप्यज्ञेयतामपि ।
तस्मिन्काले क्षिपेदेव न तु तत्र विनिक्षिपेत्।। १५३
वृत्तिस्त्वज्ञानमुच्छिद्य घटादौ ज्ञेयतामपि ।
बलात्सम्पादयेत्तस्माज्ज्ञानतामपि साऽर्हति।। १५४
मुखमस्तीति किं ब्रूषे दशहस्तां हरीतकीम् ।
अज्ञानक्षेपणाशक्ते स्वार्थस्योल्लेखनाक्षमे।। १५५
ज्ञानता यदि चैतन्ये घटादौ च कुतो न सा ।
अज्ञाननाशे त्वन्येन कृते सति तदेव च।। १५६
यदि ज्ञानं भवेत्तर्हि यदज्ञानस्य नाशकम् ।
तदेव ज्ञानतामर्हेत् ज्ञेयोऽसौ तर्ह्यमुं लिखेत्।। १५७
दीपशक्त्या तमोघ्नस्य किं घटस्यापि दीपता ।
त्वत्प्रांचोऽपि यतः प्राहुर्ज्ञानमज्ञाननाशकम्।। १५८
ज्ञानस्वभावादेवेत्थं ज्ञानं ज्ञेयं निरुच्यताम् ।
अज्ञानशक्त्या ज्ञेयत्वज्ञानत्वोक्तिस्त्वसङ्गता।। १५९
अतिप्रसङ्गभङ्गाय निर्वाहं चेच्चिकीर्षसि ।
मायालुप्त्यै तवाप्यावश्यकवृत्तौ स चिंत्यताम्।। १६०
गृहोपगतशुद्धोदपानायैव मतिं कुरु ।
दूरे मरीचिकातोयपानायाशा त्वियं वृथा।। १६१

यदक्षयोगजा या धीस्तस्या ज्ञेयं तदुच्यताम् ।
विशेष्यमेव सर्वं च मुख्यं ज्ञेयं विदुर्बुधाः।। १६२
रूप्यत्वेनापि यच्छुक्तिं ज्ञात्वा तत्र प्रवर्तते ।
रूप्योल्लेखस्तु रूप्यत्वाकारधीयोग्यताभिधात्।। १६३
प्रधानरूप्यसादृश्यादित्याहुः पूर्वसूरयः ।
तच्च स्वरूपसत्तत्तद्भ्रमेषु नियतत्वतः।। १६४
तादृशाकारघटकं प्राग्धीस्तस्य तु नेष्यते ।
प्रागज्ञातादेव यथा तत्तदिन्द्रिययोगतः।। १६५
तत्तदर्थोल्लेखिनी स्यात्प्रमा तद्वत् भ्रमोऽप्ययम् ।
यदिच्छादिकरी या धीस्तस्याज्ञेयं तदेव वा।। १६६
यद्वा स्वरूपसंबन्धविशेषः सम्भविष्यति ।
दृष्टालाभे त्वदृष्टं च कार्यं तत्कलयेत्किल।। १६७

IX (168-175)

द्वितीयेऽध्यासशब्देन मिथ्याज्ञानमुदीर्यते ।
तस्य ज्ञानस्य यज्ज्ञेयं तदध्यस्तं विदुर्बुधाः।। १६८
एतावताऽपि ज्ञानत्वं ज्ञेयत्वं चाभवत्परम् ।
केन वा ज्ञानतैकस्य ज्ञेयतान्यस्य केन वा।। १६९
इति प्रश्नस्य पक्षेऽस्मिन्नपि किं स्यात्तवोत्तरम् ।
ज्ञानज्ञेयत्वमात्रं तु वृत्तिज्ञाने तु वर्तते।। १७०
यदि कश्चित्फलबलात्सम्बन्धस्तत्र कल्प्यते ।
सर्वस्य सम्मतायां मे वृत्तावेवास्तु कल्पना।। १७१
न चेच्चरमवृत्तौ ते ब्रह्म ज्ञेयं कथं भवेत् ।
चक्षुषा घटविज्ञानं ममाभूदिति लौकिकाः।। १७२
वदन्ति घटचैतन्ये घटधीत्वप्रथैव न ।
अधिष्ठानोल्लेखशून्या भ्रान्तिः क्वाऽपि न दृश्यते।। १७३
स्वावेद्यब्रह्मचैतन्यं कथं विभ्रभ्रमो वद ।
तद्दृष्टशिशुरक्षार्थं यत्नः सर्वस्य शोभते।। १७४
पिचण्डिलवधूगर्भशिशोरर्थे यतेत कः ।
अतोऽपि भेदरत्नस्य नास्ति तस्करतो भयम्।। १७५

X (176-230)

सरस्वत्यास्तटे राजन्नृषयः सत्रमासत ।
वितर्कः समभूत्तेषां त्रिष्वधीशेषु को महान्।। १७६

तच्छ्रुत्वामुनयः सर्वे विस्मिताश्छिन्नसंशयाः ।
भूयांसं श्रद्दधुर्विष्णुं यतः शान्तिर्यतोऽभयम्।। १७७
इति स्मृतेः सर्वजीवराशितोऽत्यन्तभिन्नता ।
सिद्धा त्रयाणां देवानां तेषां च समतैकता।। १७८
नास्त्येव किन्तु तेष्वेको महानस्ति स को भवेत् ।
इति प्रश्नकृतां वाक्यकौशलादैक्यवादिनाम्।। १७९
समत्ववादिनाञ्चैव गर्भस्रावान्मतं गतम् ।
यदि तत्राऽपि सन्देहस्तर्हि तन्निश्चयोद्यमम्।। १८०
कुर्युस्तमुल्लङ्घ्य येयं महत्वस्यैव चोदना ।
साऽनङ्गीकारनिहतं करोत्येव मतद्वयम्।। १८१
त्रयाणाञ्च मिथोऽत्यन्तभेदमेकस्य चोच्चताम् ।
योग्यस्त्यर्षिमतत्वञ्च प्रश्नोऽयं साधयत्यहो।। १८२
त्रयाणां निकटं गत्वा तत्तत्सामर्थ्यशोधने ।
गरीयसी यस्य शक्तिः स एवोच्चो भविष्यति।। १८३
इति मत्वा भृगुं शक्तिं प्रत्यक्षेणैव वीक्षितुम् ।
सम्प्रेष्य निश्चयस्यान्ते चक्रुः किल महर्षयः।। १८४
स्वसामर्थ्यपरीक्षायै योऽभ्यागात्तन्मनीषितम् ।
अज्ञात्वा कुपितौ देवौ ब्रह्मशङ्करनामकौ।। १८५
सार्वज्ञ्याख्यब्रह्मधर्मवैधुर्यान्नीचतोचितौ ।
सर्वज्ञाग्रेसरो विष्णुः सर्वदा सर्वहृद्गतम्।। १८६
पश्यन्नसह्यमप्यंहः सेहेऽस्य द्रोहिणो मुनेः ।
अतः स सर्वजीवोच्चो रुद्राच्च ब्रह्मणोऽपि च।। १८७
महानिति विनिश्चित्य तमेव शरणं गताः ।
इत्याहोत्तरवाक्यं च तस्मान्मैत्रेयवागपि।। १८८
विरोधाऽऽख्यभिदामेव त्रयाणां प्रतिषेधति ।
विस्मर्ता निश्चितस्यास्य तत्वस्य स कथं मुनिः।। १८९
यस्त्विमं मुनिराद्धान्तं मिथ्यावादं वदेद्बुधः ।
व्यावहारिकतावाण्या स प्रष्टव्यः सभान्तरे।। १९०
मुनिमार्गमिमं कस्मात्त्यजसीति विवेकिभिः ।
यद्यैक्यश्रुतिसामर्थ्यात्तद्विरुद्धं जिहीर्षसि।। १९१
तर्हि श्रुतीनां द्रष्टारो वसिष्ठाद्या महर्षयः ।
नवश्रुतिमिमां केऽपि नाविदन्निति मे मतिः।। १९२
वेदव्यासोऽपि वेदार्थं किं न वेत्ति स सूत्रकृत् ।
सञ्जग्राह कथामेतां यश्च भागवते प्रभुः।। १९३

वेदश्च वेदव्यासश्च वेदद्रष्टार एव च ।
यं भावं न क्वचित्प्रोचुस्तं भवान्कथमूचिवान्॥ १९४
न हि ते वंचकाः शिष्टाः येन तत्वमिदं तव ।
न ब्रूयुर्नापि वेत्तारः तत्वस्यास्य महर्षयः॥ १९५
कृष्णश्रैष्ठ्यविरोधाप्तौ तद्व्याख्या जनमोहिनी ।
इत्युत्तरं च तत्रैव किन्नाह भगवान्शुकः॥ १९६
किं चासङ्गश्रुतेः सत्वाद्यतो वाच इति श्रुतेः ।
सत्वाच्च ब्रह्मचिन्मात्रमैक्यं न श्रुतिसङ्गवत्॥ १९७
तवाखण्डार्थवादस्य सत्वाच्चैक्यश्रुतिर्नहि ।
अतः कस्य विरोधेन श्रुतेरर्थं जिहीर्षसि॥ १९८
भेदश्रुतिसहायेयं स्मृतिरैक्यमवैदिकम् ।
बहिष्कृत्य महर्षीणां मतमेव प्रमापयेत्॥ १९९
किं च श्रुतिविरोधस्ते यदि स्याद् व्यावहारिकः ।
तदा स्मृतेर्न भीतिः स्यात् स्वार्थं च परमार्थतः॥ २००
वदेदेव श्रुतिः सत्यो विरोधो न हि ते मते ।
व्यावहारिकभेदो मे यथा ते न भयङ्करः॥ २०१
तथा स्मृतेश्च न भयं विरोधाद् व्यावहारिकात् ।
यद्ययं परमार्थः स्यात् तर्ह्यैक्यश्रुतिमेव सः॥ २०२
विरुणद्धि तदाऽप्यैक्यस्यैवाभावात्स्मृतेर्न भीः ।
यदि सङ्गविशेषस्य निषेध्री सा श्रुतिर्भवेत्॥ २०३
तदा भेदविशेषस्य निषेध्री स्यात्तवश्रुतिः ।
किं चैक्यभेदागमयोः परस्परविरोधतः॥ २०४
व्यासङ्गे सति वागेषा कस्मात्स्वार्थं न साधयेत् ।
परमार्थैक्ययोगेन विरोधो बलवान्यदि॥ २०५
अतादृग्भेदयोगेन दुर्बलोऽपि कथं न सः ।
प्रतियोगिनि सामर्थ्यं प्राबल्ये कारणं यदि॥ २०६
तर्हि भेदोऽपि सत्योऽस्तु तद्बलेन बलीयसा ।
भेदस्मृतेर्विरोधेन तवैक्यस्याऽनुयोगिनः॥ २०७
व्यर्थो भवेत्सत्यतैव भेदश्रुतिसहायिनी ।
विशिष्टा च विचाराख्यशिष्टाचारसमेधिता॥ २०८
स्मृतिः साधयति स्वार्थं व्यावहारिकतां क्षिपेत् ।
उभयोः सत्यताऽयोगे भेद एवास्तु सन्मम॥ २०९
सत्यं भिदेति शपथं कुर्वती श्रुतिरस्ति हि ।
ऐक्यस्य सत्यतावाणी तवाऽपि न ममाऽपि न॥ २१०

यदि सत्यब्रह्मरूपमैक्यं सत्यं भवेत्तव ।
तर्ह्यार्थिकार्थसत्ता सा चोदनार्थः कथं वद॥ २११
मुख्यार्थभेदसत्ताऽग्रे तिष्ठेत्केन मुखेन सा ।
बहुव्रीहौ च तद्योग एव स्यान्न तदेकता॥ २१२
किञ्च श्रुतेरबाध्योऽर्थः सत्यः स्यान्न तु बाधितः ।
यथाश्रुतैक्यवाक्यार्थं प्रत्यक्षादिविरोधतः॥ २१३
त्वमेव बाधितं ब्रूषे कथं तस्याद्य सत्यता ।
मुख्यवृत्तेरलाभे वाग्ज्ञातिवाक्यान्तराश्रिताम्॥ २१४
अमुख्यवृत्तिमाश्रित्य ज्ञातिभिः सह मोदते ।
न गोत्रकलहं कुर्यान्न च सर्वं जगत्क्षिपेत्॥ २१५
व्यावहारिकशब्दोऽयं स्वकपोलेन कल्पितः ।
अपौरुषेयवेदोक्तौ महापुरुषनिर्मिते॥ २१६
पुराणे च कथं योज्यः स्वमताग्रहतः परम् ।
अनर्घ्यरत्नमालायां कः काचमपि योजयेत्॥ २१७
यद्गोत्रेष्वज्ञ जातोऽसि तान्गोत्रस्य प्रवर्तकान् ।
ऋषीन्वृथावजानंस्त्वं कुलघ्नो नात्र संशयः॥ २१८
इत्थं सारस्वता विप्राः नृणां संशयनुत्तये ।
पुरुषस्य पदाम्भोजसेवया तद्गतिं गताः॥ २१९
फलश्लोकममुं पश्य नृणां संशयनाशिनी ।
महापुरुषसेवेयं किल तद्गतिदायिनी॥ २२०
इति स्तुताध्यायकथां कथं तां व्यावहारिकीम् ।
वदेत्कः पण्डितो विद्वत्सभामध्ये दुराग्रहात्॥ २२१
किं चानया निगूढोक्त्या स्पष्टं कस्मान्न कथ्यते ।
अतत्वावेदकत्वं हि व्यावहारिकता मता॥ २२२
एवं चेदैक्यवाक्यस्य विरोधाच्छ्रुतयोऽखिलाः ।
कर्मकाण्डस्थिताश्चैव ब्रह्मकाण्डस्थिताश्च याः॥ २२३
नित्यनैमित्तिकं कर्म बोधयन्त्यः स्थले स्थले ।
भेदादिकं साधयन्त्यः सन्ति सन्तोषदाः सताम्॥ २२४
अतत्वावेदकाः सर्वास्ता इत्येव सभान्तरे ।
कुतो वा नोच्यते वेदस्याप्रामाण्यं यदि स्फुटम्॥ २२५
वक्तुं भीतोऽसि तर्हि स्याच्छद्मना वेदनिन्दनात् ।
दोषद्वयं तथैवाज्ञ वंचनं चाधिकं सताम्॥ २२६
श्रुत्योर्मिथो विरोधे च यद्येका मानतां त्यजेत् ।
तर्हि बह्वीः कुतो हंसि तव श्रुतिरकल्पका॥ २२७

अर्हदमानतां नोचेत्स्वानुकूलं वचः श्रुतौ ।
मानयन्नितरान्वेदराशीन्सर्वानमानयन्॥ २२८
कुतो न युज्यते बौद्धः केन वा युज्यते भवान् ।
अतः शङ्कापिशाचीयं नानेया बुधसंसदि॥ २२९
तस्मात्सर्वज्ञमुनिभिर्निर्णीतोच्चत्वधर्मवान् ।
निर्णीतनीचभावेभ्यो जीवेभ्योऽभूद्धरिः पृथक्॥ २३०

XI (231-266)

यद्यैक्यं जीवपरयोस्तर्हि जीवः स्वपाप्मना ।
नरके पच्यमानः सन् यद्दुःखमनुभोक्ष्यति॥ २३१
तस्य कर्तुश्च भोक्तुश्च प्रेरणाय सदा हृदि ।
निवसन् भगवांश्च स्यात्तेन दुःखेन दुःखवान्॥ २३२
जीवस्यैवोचितं पापं जडस्य तु न पातकम् ।
प्रायश्चित्तं नराणां वा शराणां वा विचारय॥ २३३
देहांतःकरणादेश्च न पापाश्रयता तव ।
सुप्तौ सर्वलये पापाधाराभावप्रसङ्गतः॥ २३४
तस्यापि च लये सुप्तेर्लयः स्यान्निर्निमित्तकः ।
सर्वोत्पत्तेर्निमित्तं यत्कर्मप्राहुर्विचक्षणाः॥ २३५
प्रतिबिम्बे पक्षपाति तवाज्ञानं च पातकम् ।
तज्जं दुःखाख्यसंसारं जीव एव विशेद्ध्रुवम्॥ २३६
धर्माधर्मौ कस्य गुणाविति बालान्विचारय ।
क्षणभंगुरधीरेषा नास्ति कालान्तरे फलम्॥ २३७
कर्त्रीदानीन्तना बुद्धिर्भोक्त्री कालान्तरेऽपरा ।
एकः पापानि कुरुते फलं भुङ्क्तेऽपरः किल॥ २३८
कृतहान्यकृतप्राप्ती को वा प्राप्तो वदेद्बुधः ।
तस्मात्कर्ता च जीवोऽयं भोक्ता चाऽयं यतः स्थिरः॥ २३९
किञ्च बुद्धेरेव गुणौ धर्माधर्मौ मतौ यदि ।
तर्हि कारणनाशेन तयोर्नाशो भवेद्ध्रुवम्॥ २४०
अतो बुद्ध्यन्तरोत्पत्तिः स्वर्गादेः प्राप्तिरेव च ।
निर्निमित्ता भवेत्तस्माज्जीवस्यैव हि तौ गुणौ॥ २४१
एवं च पापिनोऽन्यस्य यतः पापफलं भवेत् ।
अतो जीवस्यैव युक्ता नारकासुखभोक्तृता॥ २४२
देहाधिकरणं यस्य करणं चक्षुरादिकम् ।
मनोन्तःकरणं बुद्धिर्धीरूपा सैव विक्रिया॥ २४३

दुष्टगन्धरसादीनां घ्राणादीन्द्रियसङ्गमात् ।
या धीः सा यातनारूपा बुद्धिर्दुःखकरी परम्।। २४४
दुःखानुभवरूपस्तु सर्वत्रात्मेति ते मतम् ।
बुद्धिस्तु बाह्यकरणैः बाह्यार्थानुभवः किल।। २४५
तस्मान्नारकदुःखौघसाक्षात्काराख्यभोगवान् ।
जीव एव भवेन्नोचेत्सिद्धान्तस्यान्तकृद्भवान्।। २४६
यस्य स्मरणमात्रेण नरकाच्च तरेन्नरः ।
तस्य दिक्पालपालस्य नैव स्यान्नारकी व्यथा।। २४७
पतितः स्खलितो मग्नः सन्दष्टस्तप्त आहतः ।
हरिरित्यवशेनाह पुमान्नार्हति यातनाम्।। २४८
इत्यादिस्मृतिभिः कृष्णनामकीर्तनमात्रकृत् ।
भक्तोऽपि यातनां नार्हेत्किं पुनः स महाप्रभुः।। २४९
क्व कृष्णः कीर्तनादेव नरकक्लेशनाशनः ।
क्व जीवः कीर्तनादस्य नरकक्लेशभाजनः।। २५०
न कर्मणा लिप्यतेऽसौ पापकेनेति हि श्रुतिः ।
न कर्मणा वर्धते नो कनीयानिति चापरा।। २५१
लोके कारयितारश्च लिप्यंते पातकैः किल ।
हरेः कारयितुश्चांऽहो नाभूत्पश्यास्य कौशलम्।। २५२
यत्पूर्वपाप्मना पापं कारयेन्नतु वैरतः ।
तत्पापलेपवान्नासौ चोरशूलप्रदातृवत्।। २५३
अप्सुमज्जयतश्चोरं न पापं नापि चासुखम् ।
तथा हरेः कारयितुः कुतः स्यादशुभागमः।। २५४
यस्मिन्काले यत्र देशे यो राजा तस्य केवलम् ।
तत्कालपापिनां शिक्षा श्लाध्या न तु ततोऽन्यदा।। २५५
हरेस्तु सर्वदेशेषु सर्वलोकेषु च प्रभोः ।
पूर्वाघफलदत्वच यच्छ्लाघ्यं प्राह सूत्रकृत्।। २५६
राजाधिराजस्तेनासौ कीर्त्यते सर्ववैदिकैः ।
पराऽस्य शक्तिरित्यस्तौत्तथा तमपरा श्रुतिः।। २५७
नरकादौ दुःखफलं भोजयित्वैव पातकम् ।
प्रायः स नाशयेन्नॄणां क्वचिच्च स्मरणादिना।। २५८
अपरोक्षज्ञानतश्च बलाद्भोगं विनैव च ।
पापानि नाशयेद्विष्णुरिति सर्वस्य सम्मतम्।। २५९
एवं च सर्वपापानि फलेन च बलेन च ।
अज्ञानिनां ज्ञानिनां च यतो नाशयति प्रभुः।। २६०

अतो न कौशलेनैव पापालेपो रमापतेः ।
किंत्वन्धतमसं भास्वानिव हन्ति स्वतेजसा॥ २६१
कृतेन योऽकृतो नास्ति तं मोक्षं ज्ञानमात्रतः ।
विनैव कर्म यो दद्यात्तस्यासाध्यं किमस्ति तत्॥ २६२
श्रुतिप्रामाण्यरक्षार्थं क्वचित्कौशलमाश्रयेत् ।
किं चिच्छक्ति यतः सर्वस्येशान इति च श्रुतिः॥ २६३
कर्तास्य जन्मादिषु यो न बध्यत इति श्रुतेः ।
संहृत्य निखिलं यस्य न लेपः क्वास्य पातकम्॥ २६४
पापेन पापलोकं स नयतीति च वेदवाक् ।
तत्पापजा नारकार्तिरपापस्य कथं भवेत्॥ २६५
एकोपाधिगतावेव यज्जीवपरमाविमौ ।
विलक्षणस्वभावौ तत्तयोरैक्यकथा वृथा॥ २६६

XII (267-297a)

बिंबस्य प्रतिबिम्बैक्यमपि युक्तिसहं न ते ।
प्रत्यक्पराग्भावरूपविरोधस्य स्फुटत्वतः॥ २६७
अस्मदर्थो ह्यात्मतत्वं प्रत्यग्रूपं च तत्किल ।
युष्मदर्थस्तु विषयः पराग्रूपः स चाखिलः॥ २६८
तयोः प्रत्यक्पराग्भावमात्रेणैव विरुद्धयोः ।
नेतरेतरभावोऽस्तीत्याह भाष्यकृदेव ते॥ २६९
अतः प्रत्यक्पराग्भावान्न बिम्बप्रतिबिम्बयोः ।
ऐक्यं स्यादात्मजडयोरिवेति प्रतिवादिना॥ २७०
साधिते सति तद्युक्तिं प्रत्याख्याति कथं भवान् ।
विपक्षे तव दूष्यं स्याद्भाष्यमित्यस्ति बाधकम्॥ २७१
नह्यनैकान्तिकं हेतुमादावेव वदेत्सुधीः ।
कथं मृदुमुखं कांस्यदर्पणस्यान्तरं विशेत्॥ २७२
न चेन्मुखेऽपि दाहस्स्यात्तप्ताम्बु प्रतिबिम्बिते ।
कथं स्थूलगजस्य स्यात्सूक्ष्मोपाधौ प्रवेशनम॥ २७३
यदि स्यात्तर्हि भारेण करात्स पतितो भवेत् ।
प्रविष्टस्य तथैव स्यादाकारो नत्वतादृशः॥ २७४
जले स्नातुर्मुखं नोचेद्विपरीतं भवेत्तव ।
दर्पणं सुरभीकुर्यात्कस्तूर्यतः प्रवेशतः॥ २७५
अतो विसदृशत्वाच्च न बिंबप्रतिबिम्बयोः ।
एकता वक्तुमुचिता न्यायसंचारवेदिना॥ २७६

निबिडावयवासङ्गात्पराधृत्य मुखं स्वकम् ।
पश्येन्नयनमित्याह कश्चित्तच्च न युक्तिमत्।। २७७
तर्हि दर्पणतस्तस्मात्परावृत्तेन चक्षुषा ।
दर्पणोल्लेखिनी बुद्धिर्नैवोत्पाद्येति मे मतिः।। २७८
किन्तु कण्ठोपरि मुखमित्यवेक्ष्येत तन्मुखम् ।
एवं च प्रतिबिम्बस्यैवाभावोऽपि भवेत्तव।। २७९
अतः कयोरेकतास्याज्जीवोऽप्यस्तङ्गतो भवेत् ।
न परा ववृते कस्माच्छिलातो नयनं तव।। २८०
जलात्कुतो निवर्तेत ततोऽपीदमसङ्गतम् ।
अवाङ्मुखस्य ग्रस्तार्कं पश्यतः पात्रगोलके।। २८१
निवृत्तमपि ते चक्षुः कथं निर्भिद्य मस्तकम् ।
मध्यन्दिनगतं सूर्यं पश्येदत्युग्रदीधितिम्।। २८२
नैमित्तिकमिदं कार्यं निमित्ते सति जायते ।
तदभावे पुनर्नश्येत्पद्मकोशविकासवत्।। २८३
यथा वा त्रपुसीसादेर्द्रवत्वं वह्निसङ्गमात् ।
सूत्रकृच्चोपमामाह सूर्यकादिनिदर्शनात्।। २८४
प्रतिबिम्बस्य जीवस्य तद्बिम्बाल्पोपमा भवेत् ।
अस्योपाधिरुपादानं प्रत्यासत्तिर्मुखस्य च।। २८५
निमित्तं दृष्टकार्यस्य बलार्तिक किं न कल्प्यते ।
किं सूर्यवत्सूर्यकोऽपि स्वभासा भासयेद्दिशः।। २८६
यत्सूत्रकारानुदितं तत्को वा भाष्यकृद्वदेत् ।
पश्यादर्शे मुखच्छायामित्येवाहुर्हि लौकिकाः।। २८७
दर्पणे मुखमित्युक्तिर्न लोके नाऽप्यलौकिके ।
अस्ति चेत्साऽपि सादृश्यान्मुखचन्द्रादिवाक्यवत्।। २८८
कथं प्रतीचः शब्दोऽयं पराचः स्याद्विचारय ।
यथा चित्रस्य सिंहस्य सिंहसाम्येन सिंहवाक्।। २८९
तथा प्रतिमुखस्यापि मुखसाम्यान्मुखत्ववाक् ।
न हि प्रतिमुखत्वं च मुखत्वं चैकवस्तुनि।। २९०
मुख्यं स्यात्तेन मुखवागेव तत्रौपचारिकी ।
मुखं प्रति स्थितं वस्तु यतः प्रतिमुखं स्मृतम्।। २९१
अतस्तादृशशब्दोऽसावेव मुख्यत्वमर्हति ।
मुखशब्दो मुखे रूढः कथमन्यत्र नीयते।। २९२
विनोपचारं नह्यस्य तत्राप्यस्त्यनुशासनम् ।
मुखं प्रति स्थितत्वं च मुखस्यैव कथं भवेत्।। २९३

न हि स्वस्कन्धमारुह्य स्वयमेव प्रनृत्यति ।
अतो मुखात्पृथग्भूतं वाच्यं प्रतिमुखं बलात्॥ २९४
भिन्नवाचकशब्दोऽयं विना गौण्या कथं वदेत् ।
तद्बिम्बप्रतिबिम्बत्वमपि जीवपरेशयोः॥ २९५
वैसादृश्याद्भेदमेव साधयेन्नतु बाधयेत् ।
बोधयेद्वा प्रतिकृतेर्बिंबहर्यनुगामिताम्॥ २९६
विरुद्धप्रकृतिर्यद्वत्समप्रत्ययवत्यपि ।

XIII (297b-309)

क्रोष्टुः स्रष्टा स पोष्टेशः क्रोष्टा जीवस्तथैव च॥ २९७
सस्वतन्त्रोऽन्यतन्त्रोऽयं जीवः पूर्णसुखो ह्यसौ ।
अयमल्पसुखो नित्यमुक्तौऽसौ बन्धभूरयम्॥ २९८
स सर्वज्ञोऽयमल्पज्ञः सोऽभयोऽयं भयातुरः ।
स लक्ष्मीशो दरिद्रोऽयं स धर्ता धार्यते जगत्॥ २९९
स सर्पशयनः सोऽयं वल्मीकोपान्तभूभयः ।
स देवो गरुडारूढः सोऽयं गारुडजीवनः॥ ३००
स दिक्पालार्चितपदः सोऽयं दिक्पालपूजकः ।
स यज्ञभुगयं यज्वा स पूज्यः पूजको ह्ययम्॥ ३०१
स देवर्षिगणत्राता सोऽयं देवर्षितर्पकः ।
अमर्त्योऽसावयं मर्त्यः सोऽजन्मी जन्मवानयम्॥ ३०२
स दुष्टकुलसंहारी सोऽयं दुर्जनसेवकः ।
सोप्राकृतमहाकायः सोऽयं निन्द्यकलेवरः॥ ३०३
शैलोद्धरणशीलोऽसौ शिलाभारासहो ह्ययम् ।
स सिन्धुबन्धनक्रीडः कुल्याबन्धाक्षमो ह्ययम्॥ ३०४
स गङ्गाजनकः सोऽयं गङ्गास्नानपरायणः ।
स वेंकटपतिः सोऽयं तद्यात्राकरणव्रती॥ ३०५
स प्रभुर्निर्गमोद्धर्ता सोऽयं तन्मन्त्रजापकः ।
इत्थं प्रकृत्या यौ नित्यं विरुद्धशतधर्मिणौ॥ ३०६
तयोरैक्यं तदैव स्याच्छशशृङ्गं भवेद्यदि ।
रज्जुसर्पो भवेच्छुक्ती रजतं वा यदा भवेत्॥ ३०७
गङ्गायां घोष इत्याप्तशतैरप्युदिते सति ।
तस्यानुकूलमेवार्थं कलयेद्धि विचक्षणः॥ ३०८
वाक्यमस्तीत्ययोग्यार्थे मतिं कः कुरुते सुधीः ।
अधिरोहति किं पुत्रः स्वसारं मातरं श्रुतेः॥ ३०९

XIV (310-357a)

कर्ता कर्म न चेद्ब्रह्म गम्यं दृश्यं मतं श्रुतम् ।
ध्यातं गातं द्रष्टृमन्तृश्रोतृध्यातृचितः पृथक्॥ ३१०

यद्यैक्यश्रुतिसाचिव्यादभेदः कर्तृकर्मणोः ।
तर्हि चेत्स्वप्रकाशत्वश्रुत्या वेद्यस्य वेत्तृता॥ ३११

तत्र श्रुतेर्बलवती युक्तिश्चेदत्र पञ्चधा ।
स्पष्टं निरूपिता युक्तिः पंचबाणशरोपमा॥ ३१२

तव श्रुतिस्त्रियं चोरः कुरुते स्वैरचारिणीम् ।
आत्मा वा इति वाग्ब्रह्मविदाप्नोतीति वाक्च ते॥ ३१३

ब्रह्मणः कर्मतामाह पंचधा या प्रपंचिता ।
दृश्यते ब्रह्मचिन्मात्रं निर्विकल्पकधीर्हि सा॥ ३१४

ततः श्रोतव्यमन्तव्यध्येयत्वादि च तद्गतम् ।
सामानाधिकरण्याय तेनारण्याय शोभसे॥ ३१५

दृश्यमात्मानमेवाद्या श्रोतव्यादितया जगौ ।
दृश्यं ब्रह्मैव गम्यं च वागन्त्या निर्णिनाय हि॥ ३१६

यं ग्रामं शृणुयान्मत्वा ध्यात्वा मार्गे तमेव च ।
मध्ये पश्यन् विशत्यन्ते तेन युक्तिं युनक्ति वाक्॥ ३१७

एवं च श्रुतियुक्तिभ्यां कर्मतैकस्य सम्मता ।
तत्त्वन्मतोदितं मध्ये निर्विकल्पकगोचरम्॥ ३१८

चिन्मात्रं देहलीदीपायते कर्मविनिर्णये ।
यः पुण्यकर्ता तज्जन्यफलभोक्ता स एव हि॥ ३१९

तद्धेतुयागकर्ता च यजमानो न चापरः ।
पूर्वदेहोऽस्य पूर्वांगं स्वर्देहोऽस्याङ्गमुत्तरम्॥ ३२०

प्राग्देहो यज्ञकर्ता चेत्कृतहानिर्भवेन्मृतौ ।
स्वर्देहो भोगभोक्ता चेदकृताभ्यागमो भवेत्॥ ३२१

यथा सर्वत्र कर्तृत्वं चितस्तद्वदिहापि च ।
कर्त्री जीवचिदेवाभूत् सा कर्म ब्रह्मचित्कथम्॥ ३२२

किं चैक्याध्यक्षधीवेद्यं कर्म चिन्मात्रमेव ते ।
ब्रह्माहमस्मीति दृशिकर्तृतां चैकतोचितम्॥ ३२३

चिन्मात्रमेव भजते निर्विकल्पकसंविदि ।
किमन्यः स्वप्रकाशः स्यात्ततश्चिन्मात्रकर्तृता॥ ३२४

बलादभूत् तेन चितावभूतां कर्मकर्तृते ।
ततः काकाक्षितामाप तव ब्रह्मनिरीक्षणम्॥ ३२५

यत्कर्तृ चित्कर्मचिच्च नैकेयं ते मते भवेत् ।
तत्सर्वप्रक्रियां हन्ति तवैका प्रक्रियोरगी।। ३२६
एवं ज्ञानफलीभूतगत्या गम्यं तदेव हि ।
उक्तन्यायो न चेत्कुप्येत्तत्कर्मचिदभूद् ध्रुवम्।। ३२७
अत्र कर्तृ च चिन्मात्रं चितोऽन्यन्मनआदिकम् ।
करणं कर्णतः शृण्वन्मन्वानो मनसा तथा।। ३२८
ध्यायन् पश्यंश्चेतनो हि तवापि च ममापि च ।
दर्शनानन्तरं यद्धि ब्रह्माप्नोति फलात्मना।। ३२९
सा चिद्धि तेन तद्धेतुमालेयं तद्गतैव हि ।
न्यायः कुप्येन्नचेदुक्तो मुक्तोऽपि त्वं निपात्यसे।। ३३०
मनोवृत्तिर्हि दृक्सर्वारोपः स्यान्नोचितश्चितः ।
निराकारा च सा चित् तद्ब्रह्म कर्मबलादभूत्।। ३३१
गत्या गम्यं हि ते ब्रह्म कर्मैवात्रापरा गतिः ।
न तेऽपि तेन सर्वत्र गतिः सैवोक्तवर्त्मना।। ३३२
मुक्तौ तत्कर्मतामर्हेत्तन्नार्हेत्कुत्र कर्मताम् ।
स्वरूपवेदनायां हि कर्मतां त्वं न मन्यसे।। ३३३
वेदनांतरवेद्यस्य कर्मता सम्मतैव तत् ।
एवं च कर्तृकर्मत्वमेकत्रानुचितं तव।। ३३४
कर्मक्षयाख्यमुक्तौ च नामुंचदिति मे मतिः ।
विरुद्धधर्मवैशिष्टचवत्योश्चित्योश्च नैकता।। ३३५
अविद्याध्वंसकालीनं समस्तं च न मायिकम् ।
इति यस्य रहस्यं हि तस्य हास्यमभून्मतम्।। ३३६
फलं च विषवृक्षस्य फलकल्पमभूदहो ।
एकक्रियायामेवैकं कारकद्वयरूपवत्।। ३३७
न भवेदिति या युक्तिः सा सर्वत्र समैव हि ।
यत्कुठारः स्व (स) स्वरूपं स्वयमेव छिनत्ति न।। ३३८
अतः क्रियाया वैजात्यान्न किंचिदपि ते फलम् ।
परस्मिन्समवेताया क्रि (तंतत्क्रि) या तत्फलशालि यत्।। ३३९
तत्कर्मेत्युच्यते तच्च क्रियायाः समवायिनि ।
स्वस्मिन्कर्तरि नैव स्यादिति युक्तिर्हि मायिनाम्।। ३४०
अतः कर्तृत्वकर्मत्वे कथमेकत्र सङ्गते ।
भवेतामैक्यधीरूपस्वनिष्ठैकक्रियां प्रति।। ३४१
अतो ब्रह्मचितो जीवचितश्च द्विप्रकारता ।
तयोर्द्वितां दिशेत्सा च तद्भेदं साधयेद्ध्रुवम्।। ३४२

किं भेदेऽपि श्रुतेः सत्वाद्युक्तिर्बलवती मम ।
कथं न साधयेत्स्वार्थं व्यर्थीकृत्य भवच्छ्रुतिम्॥ ३४३
तत एव न भेदोऽयमसत्यस्त्वच्छ्रुतेर्भिया ।
किं चापरोक्षज्ञानांते गन्तृगम्यत्वयुक्तितः॥ ३४४
महामुक्तौ च यत्सत्ता तत्सत्ता केन बाध्यते ।
कथं कदाचिन्मुक्तस्य नित्यमुक्तस्य चैकता॥ ३४५
हन्तोभौ तौ च धर्मौ तौ भिन्तोऽकर्णास्तिकर्णवत् ।
अपि चैक्यनिषेधात्मा भेदो मे तेन तेऽध्वना॥ ३४६
निषेध्यैक्यस्यैव सत्ता न युक्ता दुर्बलं हि तत् ।
अतस्तवैव बाणेन प्राणत्यागोऽभवत्तव॥ ३४७
किं च राज्ञो द्रोहकर्ता राष्ट्रस्य द्रोहकृच्च यः ।
स एव रूक्षः सर्वत्र शिक्ष्यो दृष्टो न चापरः॥ ३४८
एवं च श्रौतनित्येशसर्वसर्वस्वमोचकम् ।
शोचकं तदनन्यस्य सर्वस्य जगतोऽपि च॥ ३४९
तवैक्यमेव शिक्ष्यं स्यान्न तु भेदोऽखिलस्य च ।
रक्षकः सर्वमर्यादानिर्वाहकशिरोमणिः॥ ३५०
भगवच्छ्रौतमाहात्म्यवार्धिवर्धनचन्द्रमाः ।
तत्सत्यार्था श्रुतिर्भेदश्रुतिरेव न ते श्रुतिः॥ ३५१
त्यजेदेकं कुलस्यार्थे इति प्राचां वचः स्मर ।
सर्वनाशे समुत्पन्ने सत्यर्धं रक्षते किल॥ ३५२
दत्वाऽपि पृथिवीं सर्वामात्मा रक्ष्योऽखिलैः किल ।
तत्स्वनाशजगन्नाशौ वाक्योक्तेर्नाभिसंहितौ॥ ३५३
यथा चोरगृहीता स्त्री स्वशिरच्छेदकारणम् ।
दत्वा सुवर्णताटङ्कं कर्णपत्रधरा सती॥ ३५४
जिजीविषेत्तथैषा वाक् केनाप्यर्थेन जीवति ।
रत्नताटङ्कसदृशमुख्यार्थे सति भारती॥ ३५५
अर्थदातारमेवेयं भर्तारं भजते ध्रुवम् ।
ब्रह्म द्वितीयं नैवेति वाक् चाश्वो नेतिवाक्यवत्॥ ३५६
द्वितीयादतिभिन्नं तद्ब्रह्माह पदसम्पदा ।

XV (357b-377)

तद्दुग्धदोग्ध्री गौरेषा प्रक्षिपन्ती न कर्कटी॥ ३५७
यन्मिथ्यात्वश्रुतिश्चाह न मिथ्यात्वं स्वनाशकम् ।
तत्सत्यार्थश्रुतेरर्थव्यत्यासाय श्रमो वृथा॥ ३५८

त्वं चामीषु विकारेषु सन्सदा व्यावहारिकः ।
इत्युक्तेर्ब्रह्मसाम्याप्त्या व्यत्यासेऽपि न मेऽस्ति भीः।। ३५९
निष्प्रकारकतानर्हरूप्याभावादिगोचरा ।
नेदं रजतमित्याद्या बाधिका धीर्विदां मता।। ३६०
तन्निर्विकल्पकब्रह्मप्रमा बाधप्रमैव न ।
बाधाभावाच्च भेदादेः सत्यताभूदबाधिता।। ३६१
या चान्ते निर्विकल्पा धीः सा चोत्तरविकल्पतः ।
अनुमेया तवैक्ये च नासौ स्याद्भ्रमरूपवान्।। ३६२
अतोऽनुमापकाभावात्सैवाभूच्छशशृङ्गवत् ।
अध्यक्षाच्च न सा सिध्येदतीन्द्रियशरीरिणी।। ३६३
माया यथाऽयो भ्रमत इति भागवते शुकः ।
कांस्यपात्रसदृक्कृच्छ्रजीवेष्वेव कृतास्पदे।। ३६४
यदाश्रयेति प्रागुक्तत्रिगुणाश्रयतोचिते ।
मायापदोदिताज्ञाने जीवानां भवकारणे।। ३६५
अयसः कांस्यपात्रान्तर्भ्रमतः समतोदिता ।
ग्रावणे नमस्त इत्यन्ते सोऽयस्कांतशिलोपमाम्।। ३६६
जगतामीश्वरे प्राह तेनाज्ञानादि दूरगम् ।
अधोभागे विदूरस्थमायाभ्रमणकारणम्।। ३६७
मम स्वामिनमेवाह न तु मायामयं जगौ ।
यथोपाधिर्दर्पणादिप्रतिबिम्बस्पृगीक्ष्यते।। ३६८
मुखाख्यबिम्बाद्दूरस्थस्तथाऽज्ञानं च जीवगम् ।
भवेत्तवापि राद्धान्ते बिंबाख्यब्रह्मणस्तु तत्।। ३६९
अतिदूरस्थितं च स्यादतो युक्तिमती स्मृतिः ।
तन्मायित्वश्रुतिः सर्वा निर्माये धनितोक्तिवत्।। ३७०
योज्याहमिति चाध्यक्षं जैवप्रत्यक्षमेव तत् ।
ब्रह्माज्ञानकथाप्यज्ञ तत्स्वाज्ञानानुमापिका।। ३७१
निर्मायभगवद्भेदस्तन्मायाकल्पितोऽपि न ।
एवं चामायिकः सोऽग्रं कथं स्याद्व्यावहारिकः।। ३७२
युजिर्योग इतिख्यातधातूत्थफलबोधिते(तः) ।
सायुज्याख्यमहामोक्षेऽप्येकस्थानस्थयोर्द्वयोः।। ३७३
योगाविनाभूतभेदः स्यादेवेश्वरजीवयोः ।
योऽविद्यास्तमयेऽप्यस्ति स कथं व्यावहारिकः।। ३७४
न यत्र मायेति वाणी यस्य स्थानीममायिकाम् ।
ब्रूते तस्याः पतिः सोऽयं कथं मायामयः प्रभुः।। ३७५

अतस्तत्र श्रुताः सर्वमुक्ताश्चासन्नमायिकाः ।
हरेरनुव्रताः सर्वेऽप्यपरे च हरेः किल।। ३७६
प्रभुणा च मिथश्चैषां भेदो यः सोऽप्यमायिकः ।
व्यावहारिकता तस्मादस्माद्दूरं गता भवेत्।। ३७७

XVI (378-393)

किं च प्रत्यक्षसचिवा बाध्या भेदश्रुतिः किल ।
बाधकं तद्विरुद्धैक्यवाक्यमित्यपि को वदेत्।। ३७८
शस्त्रानुबद्धो हस्तीन्द्रहस्तः शत्रोर्न मारकः ।
शस्त्रेण शकलीभूतः शत्रूणां मारकः किल।। ३७९
उक्तवाक्यार्थनिर्णीत्यै प्रत्यक्षानुसृतिर्नृणाम् ।
त्वं तु हन्ताक्षरोधेऽपि वाक्यार्थे निर्णिनीषसि।। ३८०
एवं सत्यग्निना सिंचेदिति वाक्यं प्रमापकम् ।
कुतो माभूदक्षरुद्धतदसिद्धार्थबोधकम्।। ३८१
गताध्वनि पुनर्गच्छन्मार्गं निश्चिनुतेऽखिलः ।
कदध्वीकुरुषे त्वं तु गताध्वनि पुनर्गतौ।। ३८२
स्वाक्षसिद्धतृणाद्यर्थं वदन् शाकुनिकोऽखिलैः ।
किं मान्यते हन्यते वा तत्सिद्धिर्भूषणं गिराम्।। ३८३
स्वाक्षसिद्धिः स्ववाक्यस्य यदि दूषणमुच्यते ।
तर्हि स्वादृष्टमेवार्थं वदन्तीं मानय श्रुतिम्।। ३८४
सर्वज्ञव्यासवाक्यं च श्लोक्यं न स्याज्जगत्त्रये ।
परेण दृष्ट एवार्थे तद्भ्रांतित्ववारिका।। ३८५
परमाप्ततमस्योक्तिर्व्यर्थीभवति किं वद ।
भेदेऽक्षसिद्धभ्रांतित्वशङ्कां श्रुत्या निवारयन्।। ३८६
श्रुतेः श्रुत्यन्तरात्सत्वं तत्सहायेन साधयन् ।
कथं वा दूष्यते मन्द यः पोष्योऽखिलवादिभिः।। ३८७
परदृष्टार्थकथनमपि तस्मान्न दूषणम् ।
स्वदृष्टा च कथा त्वाप्तवाक्यत्वादतिभूषणम्।। ३८८
श्रवणादेव दृष्टोऽर्थो यतनार्हो न ते मते ।
ध्यानार्हश्च स एवार्थः सार्था चेयं परंपरा।। ३८९
उक्तस्यैव पुनश्चोक्तौ योऽभ्यासः सोऽभ्युपेयते ।
नवकृत्वश्च योऽभ्यासः सोऽपि श्लाघ्यतमो हि ते।। ३९०
दृष्टार्थकथनं तस्मात्कस्माद्दोषाय कथ्यते ।
मिथस्तयोर्हि संवादाद्विवादापगमो यतः।। ३९१

सर्वज्ञः सूत्रकृत्स्वोक्तसर्वार्थप्रत्ययाय याम् ।
प्रमाणीकुरुते कस्ताममानीकुरुते श्रुतिम्।। ३९२
स्वदृष्टार्थेष्वसत्यत्वशङ्कापङ्कापनुत्तये ।
यामीशोऽपेक्षते को वा मानवस्तामुपेक्षते।। ३९३

XVII (394-418)

किंच ब्रह्म विशिष्टं ते वृद्धयाद्यैर्गुणसंचयैः ।
विष्णुब्रह्मशिवेन्द्राद्या विशिष्टाः स्वोचितैर्गुणैः।। ३९४
मुनयः सर्वजीवाश्च विशिष्टा एव ते मते ।
शिष्टैक्यं च ते नास्ति तदेषामैक्यवाग्वृथा।। ३९५
तवेष्टन्तु चितोरैक्यं श्रुतौ न श्रूयते क्वचित् ।
अतस्तच्छाययान्यत्र लक्षणाश्रयणं च न।। ३९६
न हि गङ्गापदाल्लक्ष्यं नृभृङ्गं क्वापि कथ्यते ।
किन्तु प्रामाणिकं तीरं तथान्तर्यामिलक्षकम्।। ३९७
अहमादिपदं स्याद्धि नत्वप्रामाणिकं वदेत् ।
अतः सर्वश्रुतिभ्योऽपि बहिर्भूतमभूदिदम्।। ३९८
एवं चाश्रौतमैक्यं ते भेदश्रुतिरबाधिता ।
कथं न बाधते मन्द प्रतिद्वन्द्वविवर्जिता।। ३९९
किंचायोग्यार्थघटनां श्रुतौ कर्तुं हि पाणिनिः ।
सप्तसु प्रथमामाह तत्प्रत्याह मतं तव।। ४००
अहं ब्रह्मणि तस्मिंस्त्वं सर्वं ब्रह्मणि वर्तते ।
इत्याद्यैक्यं वदेदैक्यवाक्यं मुख्यार्थबाधतः।। ४०१
तद्भेदः सत्यतामर्हेन्नैक्यं युक्तिशतैर्मृतम् ।
गुणानुबाद शंसन्तो गुणानुकथनं तथा।। ४०२
हरेर्गुणानुवादं च श्लोक्यमाहुः शुकादयः ।
तस्मादेको देव इति श्रुतिरुक्त्वा हरेर्गुणान्।। ४०३
तदन्ते दुर्मतप्राप्तनिर्गुणत्वजिहीर्षया ।
समुच्चितं गुणैरुक्तैस्तमेवानिर्गुणं जगौ।। ४०४
अपूर्वोऽयं पदच्छेदो यत्पूर्वं चोदिता गुणाः ।
मुक्त्यध्वनीनैस्तच्छलाध्यो मध्वस्याध्वेति मे मतिः।। ४०५
किंचैकं ब्रह्मचैतन्यं व्याप्तं सर्वत्र सर्वदा ।
अन्तर्बहिश्च तत्सर्वं व्याप्य नारायणः स्थितः।। ४०६
इत्यादिश्रुतितो वाच्यं त्वयापि च मयापि च ।
अनन्तशक्तियुक्तं तदणु चाङ्गीकृतं मया।। ४०७

त्वया तु शक्तिविधुरमखण्डं महदेव तत् ।
अच्छेद्यं चोच्यते तस्मात्तस्य संचरणं न हि।। ४०८
किं स्याद्घटाभ्रसंचारो घटाद्यैरप्युपाधिभिः ।
अतः संचरणार्हाणि चैतन्यानि पृथक् पृथक्।। ४०९
अन्तः संचरणानर्हजडदेहप्रवृत्तये ।
वाच्यानि नानाभोगाय भिन्नभिन्नान्यनादितः।। ४१०
तत्संचारेण संचारो जडदेहस्य नान्यथा ।
अतस्तान्येव देहांतः क्रियावन्ति ह्यणूनि च।। ४११
अभ्रोपाधिघटादीनां संचारोप्यन्यचेतनैः ।
इतस्ततः स्थापने स्याद्देहे देहे न चापरः।। ४१२
प्रवर्तकश्चेतनोऽस्ति सह तेन प्रवृत्तिमान् ।
तद्घटाकाशदृष्टान्तो दुर्घटस्ते विचारणे।। ४१३
देहप्रवृत्तये व्याप्तब्रह्मचिद्भिन्नचिद्यतः ।
बलाद्वाच्या तेन शोच्या सर्वापि प्रक्रिया तव।। ४१४
अनादितोऽपि भिन्नानां चितां लिंगस्य भंगतः ।
स्वस्वाकारस्य शुद्धिः स्यात्पङ्कादुत्क्षिप्तरत्नवत्।। ४१५
रत्नान्तरैकता रत्ने नैव दृष्टा तदापि हि ।
अतः शुद्धानन्तचितो मुक्तौ च स्युः पृथक् पृथक्।। ४१६
तद्बन्धच्छेदको विष्णुर्बन्धोच्छित्तेरनन्तरम् ।
अप्यन्नदाता ज्ञेयः स गोप्ता तेन पदे पदे।। ४१७
बन्धमुक्तानुगस्तुत्यराजादिरिव सर्वदा ।
मुक्तानामप्यधीशोऽस्तु मास्तु मूढाखिलक्षयः।। ४१८

XVIII (419-421)

प्रमा तु निर्विकल्पा ते साधिका बाधिका न सा ।
सविकल्पा च सर्वा धीर्न प्रमा तत्तवाखिलाः।। ४१९
शास्त्रार्थाः केन मानेन साध्याः स्युर्बुधसंसदि ।
अप्रमाणाच्च सर्वार्थसिद्धौ सर्वद्धि भवेद्धि सत्।। ४२०
वादिराजार्जितन्यायरत्नावल्याः सरोऽमलः ।
प्रथमः सुधियां कंठालंकारं कुरुतेतराम्।। ४२१

SELECT BIBLIOGRAPHY

A. Linguistic:

Apte, V. S. *The Student's Sanskrit-English Dictionary*, Delhi: Motilal Banarsidass, 1965.

Gonda, Jan. *A Concise Elementary Grammar of the Sanskrit Language*. Translated from the German by Gordon B. Ford, Jr. Alabama Linguistic and Philological Series, No. 11. University, Alabama: University of Alabama Press, 1966.

Grassmann, Hermann. *Wörterbuch zum Rig-Veda*. Wiesbaden: Otto Harrassowitz, 1964.

Jacob, Colonel G. A. *A Concordance to the Principal Upaniṣads and Bhagavadgītā*. Delhi: Motilal Banarsidass, 1963.

MacDonell, Arthur Anthony. *A Practical Sanskrit Dictionary*. London: Oxford University Press, 1954. (First published in 1929).). (Orig. ed. 1929; reprint).

Monier-Williams, Monier. *A Sanskrit-English Dictionary*. New Ed. Oxford: Clarendon Press, 1956. (Reprint of the New Edition first published in 1899).

Perry, Edward Delavan. *A Sanskrit Primer*. 4th ed. New York: Columbia University Press, 1936.

Whitney, William Dwight. *A Sanskrit Grammar*. 5th ed. Leipzig: Breitkopf & Hartel, 1924.

Whitney, William Dwight. *The Roots, Verb-forms, and Primary Derivatives of the Sanskrit Language*. American Oriental Series, Vol. 30. New Haven: American Oriental Society, 1945.

B. Philosophical, Theological, and Religious:

Betty, L. Stafford. "A Death-Blow to Śaṅkara's Non-Dualism ? A Dualist Refutation." *Religious Studies*, 12 (September, 1976), 281-290.

Betty, L. Stafford. "Towards a Reconciliation of Mysticism and Dualism." *Religious Studies*, (due to appear soon).

Bishop, Donald H., ed. *Indian Thought: An Introduction*. New York: John Wiley & Sons, 1975.

Bloomfield, Maurice, trans. *Hymns of the Atharva-Veda Together with Extracts from the Ritual Books and the Com-mentaries.* New York: Greenwood Press, 1969. (First published 1897).

Bose, Abinash Chandra. *Hymns from the Vedas: Original Text and English Translation with Introduction and Notes.* Bombay: Asia Publishing House, 1966.

Dasgupta, Surendranath. *A History of Indian Philosophy.* 4 vols. Cambridge: Cambridge University Press, 1922-49.

Deutsch, Eliot and Van Buitenen, J. A. B. *A Source Book of Advaita Vedānta.* Honolulu: University of Hawaii Press, 1971.

Devaraja, N. K. *An Introduction to Śaṅkara's Theory of Knowledge.* Delhi: Motilal Banarsidass, 1962.

Dowson, John. *A Classical Dictionary of Hindu Mythology and Religion, Geography, History, and Literature.* 7th ed. Trubner's Oriental Series. London: Routledge & Kegan Paul Ltd., 1950.

Dutt, M. N. trans. *The Rāmāyaṇa.* 3 vols. Calcutta: Deva Press, 1893.

Edwards, Paul, ed. *The Encyclopedia of Philosophy.* 8 vols. New York: Macmillan, 1967.

Embree, Ainslie T., ed. *The Hindu Tradition.* New York: Random House, 1966.

Griffith, Ralph T. H. *The Hymns of the Ṛgveda Translated with a Popular Commentary.* 2 vols. The Chowkhamba Sanskrit Studies, Vol. XXXV. Varanasi-1 (India): Chowkhamba Sanskrit Series Office, 1971.

Herman, A. L. *An Introduction to Indian Thought.* Englewood Cliffs, N. J.: Prentice-Hall, Inc., 1976.

Hiriyaṇna, M. *The Essentials of Indian Philosophy.* London: George Allen & Unwin Ltd., 1949.

Iyer, M. K. Venkatarama. *Advaita Vedānta According to Śaṁkara.* Bombay: Asia Publishing House, 1964.

Jung, C. G. *Psychological Types* from *The Collected Works of C. G. Jung.* Bollingen Series XX, Vol. VI. Princeton: Princeton University Press, 1971.

Keith, Arthur Berriedale. *The Religion and Philosophy of the Veda and Upaniṣads*, Vol. II. Westport, Conn.: Greenwood Press, 1971. (First published 1925).

Keith, Arthur Berriedale, trans. *Rigveda Brāhmanas:*

The Aitareya and Kauṣītaki Brāhmanas of the Rigveda. Harvard Oriental Series, Vol. 25. Delhi: Motilal Banarsidass, 1971. (First published 1920).

Kirk, James A. *Stories of the Hindus: An Introduction Through Texts and Interpretation.* New York: The Macmillan Company, 1972.

Limaye, V. P. and Vadekar, R. D., eds. *Eighteen Principal Upaniṣads* (Sanskrit). Poona: Vaidika Samsodhana Mandala, 1958.

Madhva. *The Upaniṣads with the Commentary of Madhvācārya.* Part I: *Īśa, Kena, Kaṭha, Praśna, Muṇḍaka and Māṇḍūkya.* Translated by Srisa Candra Vasu. The Sacred Books of the Hindus. Allahabad: The Panini Office, 1909.

Madhva. *Vedānta-sūtras with the Commentary of Śrī Madhwācārya.* Translated by S. Subba Rao. Anthologized in Sarvepalli Radhakrishnan and Charles A. Moore, eds., *A Source Book in Indian Philosophy.* Princeton: Princeton University Press, 1957.

Mahadevan, T. M. P. *The Philosophy of Advaita.* Rev. ed. Madras: Ganesh & Co. (Madras) Private Ltd., 1957.

Mazumdar, Shudha. *Ramayana.* Calcutta: Orient Longmans, 1958.

Muller, F. Max, trans. *Vedic Hymns.* Part I: *Hymns to the Maruts, Rudra, Vāyu, and Vāta.* Sacred Books of the East Series, Vol. XXXII. Delhi: Motilal Banarsidass, 1967. (First published 1891).

Murti, T. R. V. *The Central Philosophy of Buddhism: A Study of the Mādhyamika System.* London, George Allen & Unwin Ltd., 1960.

Narain, K. *A Critique of Mādhva Refutation of the Śāṁkara School of Vedānta.* Allahabad: Udayana Publications, 1964.

Narain, K. *An Outline of Mādhva Philosophy.* Allahabad: Udayana Publications, 1962.

Nikhilananda, Swami. *The Upaniṣads.* Abridged ed. (Harper Torchbooks). New York: Harper & Row, 1964.

Oldenberg, Hermann, trans. *Vedic Hymns.* Part II: *Hymns to Agni* (Mandalas I-V). The Sacred Books of the East, Vol. XLVI. Delhi: Motilal Banarsidass, 1967. (First published 1897).

Otto, Rudolph. *Mysticism East and West: A Comparative Analysis of the Nature of Mysticism.* Translated by Bertha L. Bracey and Richenda C. Payne. New York: Collier Books, 1962. (First published 1932).

Pereira, José, ed. *Hindu Theology: A Reader.* New York: Doubleday & Company, Inc., 1976.

Potter, Karl H. *Presuppositions of India's Philosophies.* Englewood Cliffs, N. J.: Prentice-Hall, Inc., 1963.

Prabhavananda, Swami, trans. *The Wisdom of God (Srimad Bhagavatam).* New York: Capricorn Books, 1968. (First published 1943).

Radhakrishnan, Sarvepalli and Moore, Charles A., eds. *A Source Book in Indian Philosophy.* Princeton: Princeton University Press, 1957.

Radhakrishnan, Sarvepalli, trans. *The Bhagavadgītā.* 2nd ed. London: George Allen & Unwin Ltd., 1949.

Radhakrishnan, Sarvepalli. *Indian Philosophy.* 2nd ed. 2 vols. London: George Allen & Unwin Ltd., 1929.

Radhakrishnan, Sarvepalli, ed. and trans. *The Principal Upaniṣads.* Muirhead Library of Philosophy. London: George Allen & Unwin Ltd., 1953.

Ramachandran, T. P. *Dvaita Vedānta.* New Delhi: Arnold Heinemann, 1976.

Śaṅkara. *The Vedānta Sūtras of Bādarāyaṇa with the Commentary by Śaṅkara.* Translated by George Thibaut. 2 vols. The Sacred Books of the East, Vols. XXXIV, XXXVII. New York: Dover Publications, Inc., 1962. (Fist published 1890-96).

Sanyal, J. M., trans. *The Srimad-Bhagabatam.* 2nd ed. 5 vols. Calcutta: Oriental Publishing Company (undated).

Sastri, Ananta Krishna. *Śrīnyāyāmṛtādvaitasiddhi.* Calcutta Sanskrit Series, No. 9, Part I. Calcutta, 1934.

Shankara. *Crest-Jewel of Discrimination with a Garland of Questions and Answers.* Translated and edited by Swami Prabhavananda and Christopher Isherwood. New York: New American Library, 1970. (First published 1947).

Sharma, B. N. K. *A History of the Dvaita School of Vedānta and Its Literature.* 2 vols. Bombay: Booksellers' Publishing Co., 1960-61.

Sharma, B. N. K. *The Brahmasūtras and Their Principal*

Commentaries (*A Critical Exposition*), Vols. I & II. Bharatiya Vidya Series No. 31. Bombay: Bharatiya Vidya Bhavan, 1974.

Sharma, B. N. K. *Madhva's Teachings in His Own Words*. Bhavan's Book University. Bombay: Bharatiya Vidya Bhavan, 1961.

Sharma, B. N. K. *Philosophy of Śrī Madhvācārya*. Bombay: Bharatiya Vidya Bhavan, 1962.

Sharma, Chandradhar. *A Critical Survey of Indian Philosophy*. London: Rider & Company, 1960.

Siauve, Suzanne, trans. *La Voie vers la Connaissance de Dieu (Brahma-Jijñāsa) śelon l'Anuvyākhyāna de Madhva*. Pondicherry: Institut Français d' Indologie, 1957.

Smart, Ninian. *Doctrine and Argument in Indian Philosophy*. Muirhead Library of Philosophy. London: George Allen & Unwin, Ltd., 1964.

Smart, Ninian. "Interpretation and Mystical Experience." *Religious Studies*, 1 (1965), 75-87.

Stace, Walter T. *Mysticism and Philosophy*. London: Macmillan & Company Ltd., 1961.

Stace, Walter T. *The Teachings of the Mystics*. New York· New American Library, 1960.

Stryk, Lucien, ed. *World of the Buddha: A Reader*. Garden City, N. Y.: Anchor Books, 1969. (First published 1968).

Subramaniam, Kamala. *Mahabharata*. Bombay: Bharatiya Vidya Bhavan, 1971.

Vādirāja. *Nyāyaratnāvalī* (Sanskrit). Udipi: Prabhākara Press, 1935.

Van Buitenen, J. A. B., trans. & ed. *The Mahābhārata*. Vol. I: *The Book of the Beginning*. Chicago: University of Chicago Press, 1973.

Zaehner, R. C. *The Bhagavad-Gītā with a Commentary Based on Original Sources*. London: Oxford University Press, 1969.

Zaehner, R. C. *Mysticism Sacred and Profane*. New York: Oxford University Press, 1961.

Zimmer, Heinrich. *Philosophies of India*. Edited by Joseph Campbell. Bollingen Series XXVI. Princeton: Princeton University Press, 1969.

GLOSSARY-INDEX (BY VERSE NUMBER) OF KEY SANSKRIT TERMS IN THE NYĀYARATNĀVALĪ

akarṇāstakarṇavat "as one born without hearing and one who loses his hearing" (346)
akalpaka not conforming (227)
akṛta uncreated, unproduced (262, 321); something uncaused (239)
akṣa eye, sensual perception, perception (76, 94, 162, etc.)
akṣaruddha contradicted by the senses (381)
akṣarodha contradiction of one's senses (380)
akṣasiddha attested by the senses (386)
akhaṇḍa partless, unqualified (said of Brahman) (198, 408)
agni fire (381)
aghaphaladatva "sentencing for wrongdoing" (256)
acchedya indivisible (408)
acyuta the Imperishable (Viṣṇu) (55, 59, 60)
ajanmin the Unborn (God) (302)
ajña stupid, ignorant (one) (usually used in direct address) (56, 62, etc.)
ajñāna ignorance, Ignorance (generating the world-illusion) (80, 83, 84, 85, 87, 88, 91, 93, 124, 125, 126, 128, 130, 132, 133, 139, 148, 149, 150, 151, 153, 154, 155, 156, 157, 158, 159, 236, 365, 367, 369, 371)
ajñeyatā unintelligibility, "unknowableness" (153)
aṇu atom (of consciousness known as the soul) (407, 411)
atat(t)vatā unreality (14)
atat(t)vāvedaka untrue and unrevelatory (13, 14, 27, 30, 222, 225)
atidūrasthita "utterly remote (from Brahman)." (370)
atiprasaṅga undue extension, overinclusiveness (160)
atibhinna extremely different (357)
atibhūṣaṇa something valued highly because in close agreement with or attuned to (something else) (388)
atirikta redundant (115)
atīndriya beyond the power of the senses (363)
adṛṣṭa not seen, something not seen (167)
advitīyatva non-secondness (13, 22)
advitīyavāc non-secondness text (30)
advaita Non-dualism, non-duality (25)
adharma wrong deeds (237, 240)
adhikaraṇa location (243)
adhiṣṭhāna substrate, substratum, ground (69, 70, 71, 80, 89, 173)
adhiṣṭhānacit Substrate-Consciousness (79, 88, 124)
adhiṣṭhānacaitanya Substrate-Consciousness (83, 103, 122, 128)
adhīśa lord (176, 418)

adhobhāga (region) existing below, lower region (367)
adhyakṣa perception; perceptible, observable, making visible (323, 363, 371)
adhyasta superimposed (168)
adhyāsa superimposition (146, 168)
adhyāsādhyasta superimposing and superimposed (147)
adhyāhārya ellipsis (19)
anāropita not superimposed (95)
anāropitatva condition of not being superimposed (95)
anirguṇa not devoid of attributes (404)
anukathana narration (402)
anubhava experience (245)
anumāpaka (something) causing an inference (363)
anumiti inference (107)
anumeya inferrable (362)
anuvāda explanation, reiteration with illustration, rehearsal (144, 402, etc.)
anuśāsana advice, instruction (293)
anaikāntikahetu a basis which doesn't apply in every case, arbitrarily applied norm or justification (272)
anta (anta) (case) ending (16, 20)
antaḥkaraṇa inner mental organ (105, 234, 243)
antaryāmin inner controller (the essential "I" of a person) (397)
annadātṛ sustainer (417)
anyatantra dependent on another (298)
anyonyātmakatā sharing of nature (122)
apagama disappearance; vanishing (124, 394)
apanutti removal, freeing from (393)
aparokṣajñāna direct realization (of Viṣṇu) (259)
aparokṣavṛtti "perceptual vṛtti," vṛtti constituting perceptual knowledge (120)
apūrva preceded by (the letter) *a* (405)
apauruṣeya not coming from men, "utterly transcendent" (216)
apramāṇa non-authoritative (420)
aprāmāṇika unauthoritative, fictional, invalid (398)
aprāmāṇya quality of being unauthoritative, lacking authority (225)
abaddha disconnected, absurd, absurdity (115, etc.)
abādhita not annulled, unrefuted (361, 399)
abādhya not annullable, indissoluble, unsublatable (95, 234, 243)
abhāva non-existence, absence (11, 46, etc.)
abhinnatā non-difference (24)
abheda non-difference, something non-different (28, 311)
abhyāgama arrival, realization (321)
abhyāsa repeated recitation (usually of words in Scripture) (390)
abhrama non-illusoriness (131)
abhropādhighaṭa not limiting the ether (412)
amānatā non-normativeness, invalidation (228)
amāyika not illusory, not characterized by māyā (372, 375, 377)
ayas iron (364, 366)
ayaskāṁtaśilā lodestone (366)
ayoga disagreement, variance, inappropriateness (146, 209, etc.)

artha meaning (21, 309); object, thing (72, 76, 91, etc.)
arthadātṛ "surrenderer of the (literal) meaning" (356)
avidyā ignorance, beginningless ignorance, Ignorance (71, 86, 113, 135, 137, 138, 140, 336, 374)
avidya unknowable (174, etc.)
avaidika unscriptural (199)
aśakta inability, powerlessness (155)
aśva horse (356)
asaṅgata illogical, absurd (159, etc.)
asaṅgaśruti the scriptural passage "(This Supreme Being is) unattached" (197)
asatyatā unreality (142)
asatyatva falsity, unreality (393)
astamaya perishing, disappearance (374)

ākāra figure, shape, form, appearance (105, 127, etc.)
āgama "Upaniṣadic statements" (204); approach, attachment (254)
āgraha grasping, comprehending
āgrahaṇa grasping, comprehending, comprehension (88)
ātmaka having as its nature, consisting in (127)
ātmatat(t)va true nature of the Self (Ātman) (268)
ātman Self (identical to Brahman, according to Non-Dualism) (15, 18, 95, 245, 270, 313, 316)
ādarśa mirror (118, 287)
ādhāra location (20); basis, suport (234)
ādhāratā quality of being the ground, basis, or location (28)
āptatama one who has achieved the highest, one uniquely liberated (said of Vyāsa) (386)
āptavākya inspired statement (388)
āpti gain, arising, onset (196); greeting (359)
āropa superimposition (78, 83, 94, 98, 101, 102, 115, 133, 139, 142)
āropita superimposed (132)
āropitatva state of being superimposed (135)
ārti pain, agony (265)
ārthika pertaining to the real or genuine meaning (of a word or text) (211)
ālepa (act of) tainting (261)
āvaraka veiling, concealing (128)
āvarakatā a veiling or concealing (of Brahman-Consciousness by Ignorance) (89)
āvaraṇa a veiling or concealing (by Ignorance) (71, 86, 125, 128, 130)
āvidyaka made of Ignorance, ignorant (138)
āvṛtatva veiling, concealing (by Ignorance) (88)
āśraya ground, basis, abode (365)
āśrayatā foundation, basis, seat (234, 265)
āsaṅga association, contact (277)

itaretarabhāva "condition of one being the other" (269)
indra (the god) Indra (394)
indriya the senses, sense organ, eye (92, 165, 244)

īśa Supreme Lord (Viṣṇu) (49, 297, 349, 393); Śiva (50)
īśāna ruler, Lord (Viṣṇu) (3, 263); Śiva (7)
īśvara Lord (Viṣṇu) (367, 374)

ukta statement, saying, expression, word (18, 2, etc.)
ukti statement, saying, expression, assertion, word (27, 159, etc.)
ugrasena Ugrasena, member of Kṛṣṇa's court (57)
uccatā supremacy (182)
uccatva supremacy (230)
uttamatva supremacy (49)
utpatti arising, production, happening (235, 241)
utpala lotus (27)
uddhartṛ rescuer, deliverer (6, 306)
udyama undertaking, continued effort (111)
upacāra figurative application, metaphor (293)
upamā comparison, similarity; like, similar (98, 284, etc.)
upahita conditioned by (113)
upādāna material cause (of the world's illusory appearance) (80, 87, 132, 133, 285)
upādānatā condition of being a material cause (89, 130, 134)
upādhi limiting adjunct, thing which limits distortingly (73, 113, 114, 266, 409, 412); (limiting) space (273); conditioning substance, reflecting medium (mirror) (285, 368)
upāya means, device, strategem (73, 142, etc.)
uragī snake (326)
ullaṅghya spurned, transgressed (181)
ullikhita made known, made visible, manifested (96)
ullekha appearance, manifestation, shining forth (103, 163, etc.)
ullekhana shining forth, manifesting (155)
ullekhin manifesting, making shine forth (166)

ṛṣi sage, seer (176, 184, 218)

eka one, one thing, the One, etc. (169, etc.)
ekatā oneness, identity (29, 178, 212, etc.)
ekatva oneness, identity (107, 113, etc.)
ekasthānastha abiding in a common abode (373)

aikya identity, oneness (10, 104, 179, 197, 199, 203, etc.); identical (12)
aikyavāc identity-text(s) in Scripture (395)
aikyavākya identity-text(s) in Scripture, non-duality statement(s) (213, 378, 401)
aikyaśruti identity-text(s) in Scripture (191, 198, 202, 311)

aupacārika figurative, metaphorical (291)

kathana telling, narration (388, 391)
kathā discussion, speech (111, 221, etc.)

kadadhvin unreliable path, deplorable course (382)
kaṇṭhoparimukha "face above the neck" (279)
karaṇa cause, causing, making (92, etc.); stimulus (243); instrument (328)
karkaṭī female crab (257)
karṇapat (t) ra ear lobe (354)
kartṛ doer, agent, one who acts (232, 238, etc.)
kartṛkarma subject and object (311)
kartṛcit subject-consciousness (326)
kartṛtā "doership", subjectivity (323, 324, etc.)
kartṛtva "doership", subjectivity (322)
karma action (s), observance (s) (224, 251); moral consequences of actions which in turn give rise to conditions both fortunate and unfortunate (235, 262); object (310, 319, 322, etc.)
karmakāṇḍa the part of Scripture which relates to ceremony and sacrifices (223)
karmacit object-consciousness (326)
karmatā "objectness," objectivity, a thing's being an object (of an experiencing subject) (314, 318, etc.)
kalevara body (303)
kalpanā hypothesis, invention, rationale, mechanism, bringing about (75, 117, 171)
kastūri musk-perfume (275)
kāṁsyapātra brass goblet (364, 366)
kākākṣitā "crow's eye-ness," partaking of the "crow's eye" fallacy (325)
kāca glass, "rhinestones" (217)
kāraṇa basis, cause (25, 80, 240, 354, etc.); principle (206)
kāraṇatā ability to cause or produce (85)
kārayitṛ "a man who instigates action" (252)
kārya occupation (7); object (84, 90); product, effect (117, 134, etc.)
kāryatva state of being an effect (135)
kāla time (10, 255, etc.)
kāśi Kāśi (Benares) (56)
kīrtana mention, report, pronouncing (90, 249, etc.)
kula throng, multitude (303); family (352)
kṛta something done or caused (239); done, made; one who does or makes (145, 179, etc.); created (262)
kṛti procedure, methodology (68)
kṛṣṇa Kṛṣṇa (10, 47, 56, 65, 66, 196, 249, 250)
kṛṣṇaśraiṣṭhya Kṛṣṇa's sovereignty (196)
kedāra field (under irrigation) (105)
kaimutya *a fortiori*, the relation "how much more" (101, 121)
kauṣala skill, wisdom (82, 179, etc.)
kriyā activity (5, 337, etc.)
kroṣṭṛ jackal (297)
kleśa pain, suffering (250)
kśepaṇa throwing off, jettisoning (155)
kṣaya destruction (80); refuge, abode (418)
kṣīrasāgara milk-ocean (2)

gaṅgā Ganges River (305, 308, 397)
gaja elephant (273)
gata gone to, situated in (114, etc.); perished (180, etc.); fled (132, etc.)
gatādhvan one who has accomplished a journey (382)
gati state, condition (70); path, way (327); one attaining (332)
gantṛgamyatva attaining-attained state (at liberation) (344)
garuḍa the great bird Garuḍa (Viṣṇu's mount) (62, 300)
garbhasrāva miscarriage (180)
girḥ words, speech (383)
guṇa basic element or constituent (of matter) (40, 85, 365)
guṇānuvāda explanation of (God's) attributes (402, 403)
guru guru, teacher (87, 122, etc.)
gṛhopagataśuddhoda "pure water obtained at home" (161)
go cow (20, 357)
gotra clan, family (218)
gotrakalaha family quarrel (215)
goptṛ protector, preserver (417)
govinda Govinda (Viṣṇu-Kṛṣṇa) (59)
gauṇa secondary, colloquial (as opposed to formal) (295)
grantha a work, treatise (144)
g(r)anthakṛt author (129)
grastārka solar eclipse (281)
grāvan (lode) stone (366)

ghaṭa pot, jar, jug (17, 74, 76 77, 78, 81, 83, 94, 101, 102, 103, 106, 107, 113, etc.)
ghaṭākāśa pot-ether (413)
ghaṭābhra pot-ether (409)
ghoṣa herdsmen's settlement (308)

cakṣus eye, eyes (105, 172, etc.)
caturbhuja four-armed (Viṣṇu) (61)
candramas moon (351)
caramajñana Final Knowledge (of Brahman) (150)
caramavṛtti final vṛtti (issuing in knowledge of identity with Brahman) (172)
cāṇḍāliśiśu untouchable's child (138)
cit consciousness, (Pure) Consciousness (48, 49, 70, 106, 107, 112, 114, 119, 121, 130, 133, 310, 322, 325, 328, 330, 331, 335, 342, 396, 414, 415, 416)
citra sketch (289)
cinmātra Pure Consciousness (48, 197, 314, 319, 323, 324, 328)
cetana intelligence, consciousness (47, 329, 412, 413)
caitanya consciousness, (Pure) Consciousness (101, 104, 117, 126, 156, 173. 174, 406, 409); also see "adhiṣṭhānacaitanya"
codanā precept, sacred precept, injunction (39, 181, 211)
cora thief (253, 254, 313, 354)
coraśūlapradātṛvat "providing the stake for the thief" (253)

chadman veiling, pretense, disguise (226)

chāyā foreshadowing (396)
chinnasaṁśaya one whose doubts are dispelled (177)
cheda a lopping off (405)

jagat world (18, 35, 127, etc.)
jagat(t)raya the three worlds, all reality (385)
jagatpati Lord of the world (55)
jaḍa matter, material thing(s) (15, 88, 89, 128, 233, 270)
jaḍadeha inert (physical) body (410, 411)
janamohin delusion of men (196)
janma creation (264)
janmavat creature, (one) undergoing birth (302)
jala water (105, 275, 281)
jīva soul, human soul (15, 48, 49, 53, 73, 104, etc.)
jīvaga abiding in the soul (369)
jīvacit soul-consciousness (322)
jīvana way of life, livelihood (300)
jñāti kinsman (214, 215)
jñāna knowledge, true knowledge, wisdom, knowing (5, 7, 61, 63, 66, 107, etc.)
jñānajñeyatva condition of knowing and being known (170)
jñānatā condition of knowing, capacity to know, knowledge (107)
jñānatva same as jñānatā (152, etc.)
jñānin knower, sage (64, 260)
jñeya known, to be known (147, etc.)
jñeyatā condition of being known, capability of being known, "knowability" (146, etc.)
jñeyatva same as jñeyatā (150, etc.)

taṭa riverbank (176)
tat(t)va truth (23, 31, etc.)
tat(t)vajñāna true, valid knowledge (66)
tat(t)vavādin truth-speaker (Dualist) (32)
tat(t)vavedaka true and revelatory (23)
tat(t)vaveditā knower of the truth (32)
tamas darkness (141, 261)
tāṭaṅka earring (354)
tīra bank (of a river) (397)
tṛṇa straw, any insignificant object or matter (383)
tṛṇāstra weapon of straw, straw arrow (51)
tejas radiance (261)
trikṣana "three instants," an instant (112)
triguṇa the three guṇas, or basic constituents of matter (365)
tridhāman triple-gloried (Viṣṇu) (2)

daridra beggar (299)
darpaṇa mirror (272, 275, 278, 288, 368)
darśana (direct) realization (of Brahman) (329)
dāhas warmth, heat (273)

dikpāla guardian of one of regions of the universe (301)
dikpālapāla "the Support of those who support the regions (of the universe)" (Viṣṇu) (247)
diś region, place (286)
dīdhita brightness (282)
dīpa lamp (158, 319)
dīpatā lamp-like capacity (158)
duḥkha pain, suffering, affliction (231, 232, 236)
dugdhadogdhrī (cow) giving forth milk (357)
durāgraha perverse obstinacy (221)
durghaṭatva unintelligibility (137)
durjana wicked man (303)
dūratva remoteness, distance (42)
dūṣaṇa (falsifying) objection, corruption, vitiation, refutation, annulling, falsification (42, 71, 72, 383, etc.)
dṛgdṛśyayoga relation of the one seeing to the thing seen (146)
dṛḍhamūlataroḥ sikhām "top of a firmly rooted tree" (136)
dṛś witnesser, one who sees (77); seeing, act of seeing or perceiving (148, 331)
dṛśi seeing, realizing (323)
dṛśya visible, seen, thing seen (148, etc.)
dṛṣṭa perceived, seen (117, etc.)
dṛṣṭānta example (413)
dṛṣṭārtha a thing experienced, object seen (391)
deva god (52, 178, 185, 300, 403, etc.)
devarṣi celestial sage (302)
deveśatva sovereignty over the gods (53)
deśa place, region (255, etc.)
deha body (106, 117, etc.)
dehalīdīpa "lamp on the threshold" (319)
dehānta within the body (119, 123, 411)
dehāntara inside the body (119)
daitya demon, demon-descended (6, 61)
doṣa distortion, defect (coextensive with and generated by Ignorance) (37, 84, 85, 88, 89, 90); fault, error (144, etc.)
dravatva melting (284)
draṣṭṛ visionary, seer (192, 310)
draṣṭṛtā perception, vision (109)
drogdhṛ foe (100)
droha injury, wrong, treachery (348)
drohin one who is hostile (187)
dvitā duality (342)
dvitīya a second (22, 24, 25, 351, etc.)
dviprakāratā condition in which two things are different in nature; two fold condition (342)
dvaita Dualism, duality (26)

dhanitā fecundity (370)
dhartṛ supporter (6, 299)

dharma essential attribute, nature (186, 230, 335, etc.); right action (237, 240)
dharmatā quality of being an attribute (29)
dharmin having an attribute or nature (306)
dhātu verbal root (373)
dhyātṛ meditator, meditating (310)
dhyāna meditation
dhvaṁsa destruction (336)

nañartha negative meaning, meaning of "not" (16, 24); negated object (20)
nayana eye (277, etc.)
naraka hell (231, 247, 250, 258)
navakṛtvas nine-fold (illustration of identity in Scripture) (390)
navaśruti novel (interpretation of) Scripture (192)
nāmabala efficacy or power of (reciting) a name (54)
nārakaduḥkhaughasākṣātkāra "the direct perception of the stream of torment found in hell" (246)
nārāyaṇa Nārāyaṇa (Viṣṇu) (9, 406)
nāśa destruction, cessation, ruin (48, 80, 81, 84, 90 etc.)
nāśaka destroying, destruction (157, etc.)
nāśin destroying, removing, one who destroys (220)
nāśya destroyed, that which is destroyed (142, etc.)
nāśyatā destruction (141)
nāśyanāśakatā the relation destroyed-versus-destroying (140)
nāstitā unreality, non-existence (143)
nigama the Vedas (6)
nityakarman continuing, day-to-day (spiritual) exercise (59)
nidarśana example, illustration (284)
nindā censure, blame (63, 145, etc.)
nimitta cause, caused (235, 283, 286, etc.)
nirākāra formless, "unmediated by concepts" (331)
nirgama going forth, departure (306)
nirguṇatva "qualitylessness," state of being devoid of attributes (404)
nirṇīti ascertaining, determining (380)
nirdoṣa defectless (91)
nirnimitta causeless, inexplicable (241)
nirnimittaka causeless, inexplicable (235)
nirmāya powerless (ness) (370, 372)
nirvāha success, accomplishment (160)
nirvikalpa (ka) indeterminate (knowledge) not dependent on or derived from the senses (314, 318, 361, 362, 419)
nirvikalpakasaṁvid indeterminate (objectless) awareness (324)
niścaya examination, inquiry, ascertainment, determination (180, 184)
niṣe(d)dhṛ restrainer, injunction (203, 204)
niṣedha negation, invalidation (17, 20, 346, etc.)
niṣprakārakatā being without distinction or specification, contentless state (360)
nivṛtta rebounded (282)
nivṛtti removal, turning back, ceasing (91, 133)

nīcatā depravity, lowness (40, 186, etc.)
nṛśṛnga "man's horn" (something never encountered in reality) (397)
nṛharyakṣa Man-Lion (Viṣṇu) (1)
neti neti "not this, not this" (15)
naimittika caused (283)
nyāya logic, rationale, logical argument (132, 327, etc.)
nyāyaratnāvalī *The Jewel-Necklace of Logical Arguments* (the title of the present work) (421)
nyāyasaṁcāra rational thought (276)

pakṣa view, position, side, opinion, doctrine (1, 67, 79, etc.)
paṅka mud (415)
pañcabāṇa five-arrowed (god of love, Kāma) (312)
paṭa piece of cloth (17, 141, etc.)
paṇḍita learned teacher (33, 221, etc.)
pati Ruler (375)
pada word (16, 20, 397, etc.); position (357); abode (301)
padāmbhoja lotus-like feet (219)
padārtha meaning of a word (38)
padmakośa lotus-calyx (283)
para highest (Supreme Being) (231)
paraṁparā uniterrupted succession (of words) (389)
parama the Supreme (266)
paramārtha ultimately real or true (202, 205)
paramārthatas "in an ultimately real way" (200)
parāñc outside, outer (268, 289)
parāvṛtta rebounding from (278)
parīkṣā test, trial (185)
pariṇama undergoing transformation (118)
pariṇāma modification, transformation (106, 127)
parityāga abandoning, abandonment (25)
pareśa Supreme Lord (295)
parokṣavṛtti "mediate vṛtti," vṛtti constituting non-perceptual knowledge (108)
pāṇini Pāṇini (the great Sanskrit grammarian) (400)
pātaka that which causes to fall, cause of sin, sinner (233, 236, etc.)
pātragolaka literally "dish-globe"; dish designed for viewing a solar eclipse (281)
pāpa sin, evil (233, 234, etc.)
pāpaphala fruit or wages of sin (242)
pāpin sinner (242, 255)
pāpman sin, wickedness, evil (231, 253)
pāramārthya ultimate, true reality (68)
picaṇḍilavadhūgarbha "womb of a round-bellied wife" (175)
piśācī malignant demoness (86, 229)
pumān man (248)
pūjaka worshipper (301)
puṇyakartṛ one who performs a meritorious action (319)

purāṇa the Purāṇas (217)
puruṣa (Supreme) Spirit (Viṣṇu) (219)
pūrvadeha lower (physical) body (320)
pṛthak pṛthak absolutely different, sharply distinct, entirely separate (409, 416)
pṛthivī world (353)
poṣṭṛ nourisher (297)
pauṇḍraka (pauṁḍraka) Pauṇḍraka, the foolish king of Benares (56, 57, 60)
pauruṣa human deeds (9)
prakaraṇa treatment, matter (111)
prakṛti nature (12, 297, 306)
prakriyā activity (108); teaching, production (326, 414)
pratikarman retaliation, opposition (67, 98)
pratikarmavyavasthā retaliatory formula, method of refuting the opposition (67, 98)
pratikarmavyavasthiti retaliatory formula, method of refuting the opposition (129)
pratikṛti counterpart, likeness, reflection (121, 296)
pratidvandva opposition (399)
pratibimba reflection (106, 236, 267, 270, 276, 279, 285, 368)
pratibimbatā state of being reflected (112)
pratibimbana act of being reflected, reflection (118, 121)
pratibimbita reflected (118, 273)
pratimukha reflected image of a face (290, 291, 294)
pratiyogin appropriate correlative (19); adversary, something antagonistic (206)
prativādin adversary, one who opposes or contradicts (51, 270, etc.)
pratyakparāgbhāva state of inner-vs.-outer, inner-vs.-outer relation (267, 269, 270)
pratyakṣa experience, sense perception, perceptual knowledge, the eyes (92, 184, 213, 371, 378); thing perceived (91)
pratyakṣānusṛti conformity with sense-experience (380)
pratyañc within, inward (268, 289)
pratyaya certainty (392)
pratyarthin adversary, opposition (99)
pratyāsatti proximity (285)
prathamā nominative (case) (16, 400)
prathā origin (173)
pradhāna substrate, substratum, ground (164)
prapañca (prapaṁca) world-appearance, phenomenal world (68)
prabhu Lord (6, 256, 260, etc.)
pramā true, right knowledge (166, 418)
pramāṇa means of valid knowledge (88)
pramāpaka literally true (381)
pramāpanā certainty (31)
prayojana purpose, aim, use, gain, (115, 152, etc.)
pravartaka founder (218)
praviṣṭa that which pervades, pervading (274)

pravṛtti activating, functioning (410)
praveśa pervasion, entering into (275)
praveśana pervasion, entering into (273)
praśna inquiry (170, 179, etc.)
prāgdeha first (physical) body (321)
prāṇatyāga abandonment of life, suicide (347)
prātibhāsika purely delusive (33, 221, etc.)
prāpti attainment, gaining (241); arriving at, emergence (239)
prābalya superiority of force, ascendency (206)
prāmāṇika founded on authority, well-attested (397)
prāmāṇya authenticity, validity (263)
prāyascitta atonement, expiation, amends (for sin) (233)
preraṇa incitement, urging into motion (232)

phala reward, merit, retribution (220, 258, 260, 329); result, effect, resultant, outcome (116, 171, etc.)
phalabhoktṛ one who enjoys merit (319)
phalita producing results (120)

bandhamukta "liberated from slavery" (418)
bandhocchitti cutting of bonds (at liberation) (417)
bala strength, force, power (5, 7, 116, etc.)
bahuvrīhi possessive adjectival compound (as in "having no second") (212)
bāṇa arrow (347)
bādha annulment, cancellation, removal (42, 44, 361, 401)
bādhaka annuling, removing, invalidating (43, 271, 378)
bādhika annuling, removing (360, 419)
bādhita annulled, sublated, invalidated, (96, 213, 214)
bādhya annullable, annulled, invalidated (378)
bāhyakaraṇa external senses (245)
bāhyārtha external object or datum (245)
bimba the original (of a reflection), the actual thing reflected (as opposed to its "pratibimba" or reflection) (267, 270, 276, 285, 296, 368)
bimbapratibimbatva relation of original to reflection (295)
buddhi understanding (29); a particular mental state of momentary duration, a percept (238, 240, 241, 243, 244, 245, 278)
budha sensible man, wise person (58, 162, etc.)
bodhaka revealing, manifesting, indicative of (381, etc.)
bauddha Buddhist (229)
brahmakāṇḍa the part of Scripture which relates to Brahman (Upaniṣads) (223)
brahmacit Brahman-Consciousness (322, etc.)
brahmacaitanya consciousness of Brahman, Brahman-Consciousness (406)
brahman Brahmā (7, 47, 50, 52, 185, 187, 384); Brahman (16, 22, 23, 24, 28, 29, 98, 139, 143, 150, 172, 174, 186, 197, 211, 310, 314, 316, 322, 323, 325, 329, 331, 332, 342, 356, 357, 359, 361, 369, 371, 384, 401, 406, 414)
brahmavid knower of Brahman (313)
brahmasāmya identical with Brahman (359)

brahmāhamasmi "I am Brahman" (323)

bhakta worshipper, worshipping (249)
bhaṅga breaking down, dissolution (160, 415)
bhagavat Blessed One (Viṣṇu) (6, 55, 65, 232, 351, 372)
bhaya fear, dread (100, 101, 120, etc.)
bhartṛ bearer (6); protector (356)
bhava becoming, transmigrating flux (of souls) (365)
bhāgavata *Bhāgavata Purāṇa* (58, 145, 364)
bhāna shining, appearance (111)
bhānta (bhāṁta) shining (71, 75, 110)
bhāra weight (274, 304)
bhāratī Goddess of Speech (Bhāratī) (355)
bhāva nature, being, existence, state (230); sentiment, meaning (58, 145, etc.)
bhāvanā sentiment, fancy (60)
bhāṣya Śaṅkara's commentary on the *Brahmasūtra* (271)
bhāsyakṛt writer of a commentary on the *Brahmasūtra* (referring to Śaṅkara) (355)
bhāsvat sun (261)
bhitti flaw (93)
bhidā difference, separation (49, 189, 210)
bhinna different, something different (111, 121, etc.)
bhinnatā difference (178)
bhū earth (6)
bhūtala earth (20)
bhūlagnamṛttikā "clay adhering to earth" (151)
bhuṣaṇa ornament, decoration (137); fulfilment, warrant (383)
bhṛgu Bhṛgu, one of the great seers of old (184)
bheda difference (13, 14, 16, 22, 201, 204, etc.); something different (18)
bhedavākya declaration of a difference, statement affirming the difference (of God from all souls and all things from each other) (13, 14, 31)
bhedaśruti difference-text(s) in Scripture (199, 208, 378, 399); difference (interpretation of) Scripture (351)
bhoktṛ one who experiences, one who enjoys (232, 238, 239)
bhoktṛtā an experiencing, experience (242)
bhoga experience (259, 410); delight (321)
bhogavat experiencing, enjoying (246)
bhrama illusion, error (43, 44, 69, 70, etc.)
bhramaṇa turmoil, staggering (367)
bhramī illusion (74)
bhrānti (bhrāṁti) error, illusion (34, 35, 77, 79, etc.)
bhrāntitva (bhrāṁtitva) state of error, illusionism, illusoriness (389, 386)

mati opinion, doctrine, belief, perception (26, 46, etc.)
madhva Madhva, founder of the Dualist Vedānta (2, 405)
manana reflection, thought (33)
manas mind, mental organ (243, 328)
manovṛtti mental modification, "mental organ's vṛtti" (331)

mantṛ thinker, act of thinking or reflecting (310)
mantra incantation, sacred formula (306)
mandarabhūbhṛta Mount Mandara, center of the universe (6)
marīcikā mirage (161)
maryādā goal (350)
mastaka head, skull (282)
mahatva greatness (181)
mahādeva great god, "great One" (408)
maharṣi great sage (192, 145, etc.)
mahākāya Great-bodied (said of Viṣṇu) (303)
mahāpuruṣa Supreme Spirit, God (Viṣṇu) (216, 220)
mahāprabhu "Supreme-God" (249)
mahābhrama Great Illusion (of the universe) (35)
mahābhrānti Great Illusion (of the universe) (45)
mahāmukti final emancipation (345)
mahāmokṣa final emancipation, summit of emancipation (373)
mahitva greatness (8)
mahiman majesty (3, 4, 11)
mātṛ mother (46, 309)
mātra full measure, totality (170)
mātrāpara beyond measure (8)
māna standard, measure, appraisal (35, 36, 420)
māyā Illusion, power of Illusion (160, 364, 365, 375)
māyākalpita characterized by or made of māyā (372)
māyāmaya consisting of māyā, characterized by māyā (368, 375)
māyāvādin Illusionist (Non-dualist) (59)
māyin Illusionist (Non-dualist) (67, 340)
māyika illusory (with "na," real—336), marked by māyā (376)
māyitvaśruti scriptural passages dealing with māyā (370)
mārga road, path (317, 382)
mālā row, series, sequence (115, etc.)
māhātmyavārdhi "ocean of majesty" (said of Scripture) (351)
mithyā illusory, false (168, 190, etc.)
mithyājñāna false way of thinking, illusion (66)
mithyātva illusoriness (140, 358)
mithyātvaśruti passages in Scripture which refer to "illusion" (358)
mithyāvādita error-speaking (31)
mukta liberated, freed, released (one) (330, 345, 376, 418)
mukti release, liberation (298, 333, 335, 345, 405, 416)
mukha mouth (33, 155); face (118, 272, 273, 275, 277, 279, 281, 285, 288, 290, 291, 292, 293, 294, 369)
mukhacandra "moon-faced" (288)
mukhacchāyā face-image (in a mirror) (287)
mukhyatva—pre-eminence, literalness (as opposed to figurativeness); also "faceness" (punningly) (292)
mukhyārtha the primary, most immediate, or literal sense or meaning (of a word or text) (212, 355, 401)
muni sage, seer (177, 187, etc.)

munimārga path or way of the seer or sage (191)
mṛti death (321)
mṛṣātva illusoriness, illusion (138, 141, etc.)
maitreya the sage Maitreya (188)
mokṣa liberation, release (34, 262 373)

yajñakartṛ performer of a sacrifice (321)
yatana effort, endeavor, attention (389)
yatna effort, exertion (174)
yāga sacrifice (39, 320)
yācñā prayer (196)
yātanā agony, acute irritation, punishment (244, 248, etc.)
yātrākaraṇa pilgrimage (305)
yukta proper, correct, appropriate (142, etc.)
yukti proof, argument (77, etc.); fitness, sense (267, etc.)
yuktimat fit, correct, logical, right (370, etc.)
yujir yoge the verbal root of the derivation "sāyujya" (373)
yoga connection, relation, union, alliance (146, 147, 205, etc.)
yogaja arising from or generated by contact (162)
yogāvinābhūtabheda a difference characterized by an inseparable unity (374)
yogin yogi (37)
yogīndra Yogi-Prince (34, 64)
yogyatā fitness, suitableness, aptitude (163)

rakṣaka protecting, protector (350)
rakṣā care, protection, safeguard (174, 263, etc.)
rajata silver (43, 92, 307, 360)
rajju rope (307)
rajjusarpa rope-snake (147)
ratna jewel (175, 415, 416)
ratnatāṭaṅka bejewelled earring (355)
ratnamālā jewel necklace (217)
ramāpati Lakṣmī's Lord (Viṣṇu) (261)
rājan King (56, 176, 255, 348, 418)
rājādhirāja King of kings (Viṣṇu) (257)
rāddhānta guaranteed truth, creed (190, 369)
rāma Rāma (50)
rāmadeva Rāma (53)
rāṣṭra country, empire, dominion (348)
rudra Śiva (47, 187)
rūpa form, formed like, shaped like, having the nature of, constituted by, consisting of (85, 91, 106, 211, etc.)
rūpatā (grammatical) character (21); essence (29)
rūpya silver (79, 147, 163, 164, 360)
rūpyatva having the quality of silver, silveriness (163)

lakṣaṇā indirect expression (396)
lakṣmīśa Lord of wealth (Viṣṇu) (299)

laya dissolution, disappearance (234, 235, etc.)
liṅga essential character (54); mark (of sin) (415)
līlā amusement, sport (46)
lupti annihilation, suppression (160)
lepa stain, taint (264)
loka world (252, 256, etc.)
laukika ordinary man, mankind (172, 287, etc.)

vaktra face (121)
vacas speech, words (62, 352, etc.)
vaṁcaka fraudulent, fraud (195)
vaṁcakatā fraudulence (36, 38)
vaṁcana illusion, deception (61, 226, etc.)
valmīka ant-hill (300)
vaśin controller (3)
vasiṣṭha Vaṣiṣṭha, a great sage (192)
vastu thing, substance (69, 80, 81, 290, etc.)
vahni fire (284)
vākya statement, declaration (13, 17, etc.)
vāc word, words, expression, text, interpretation (15, 16, 18, 26, etc.)
vāṇī language (210); eloquent words (190)
vāda doctrine, thesis, belief (103, etc.)
vādin speaker, proponent (179, etc.)
vādirāja Vādirāja, the author (421)
vāsudeva Vāsudeva (Viṣṇu) (55, 56, 60)
vikāra altered condition (359)
vikriyā agitation, modification (243)
vikṣepa projection, illusory projection (of Ignorance over the Pure Consciousness of Brahman) (72, 86, 126)
vicakṣana clear-sighted, intelligent man (235, 308)
vicāra interrogation (208)
vicāraṇa investigation, analysis (15, 27, 413)
vijñāna knowledge, discernment (172)
vitarka debate, dispute (176)
vid man of knowledge (360)
vidyā (true) knowledge (86)
vidhavā widow (81)
vidhā methodology (137)
vināśa destruction (113)
vinirṇaya ascertainment, determination (319)
vipakṣa opposing thesis (271)
viparīta reversed, opposite (275)
vipra inspired sage (219)
vibhinnatā difference (53)
vibhrama illusion, delusion, error (74)
vibhrānti (vibhrāṁti) illusory appearance (69)
viruddha obstructed, contradicted, contradicting (127, 137, etc.)
virodha opposition, contradiction, annulment (140, 189, 205, etc.)

virodhitva ability to annul or contradict (85)
vilakṣaṇasvabhāva intrinsically different (266)
vivarta illusory world appearance (127)
vivāda dispute (391)
viveka discrimination (129)
vivekin one who discriminates, wise person (191, etc.)
viśiṣṭa distinguished, qualified by (394, etc.)
viśeṣa distinction, something distinctive, peculiar characteristic, attribute, difference (42, 44, 60, 167, 203, 204)
viśeṣya bare substance of something, actual substance present (162)
viṣaya object, object of the senses, thing seen (129, 268)
viṣavṛkṣa "poison tree" (337)
viṣṇu Viṣṇu (8, 49, 54, 177, 186, 394, 417)
visadṛśatva dissimilarity (276)
vṛtti a particular mode of mind, an instant of consciousness, a momentary condition of mind, mental modification (74, 91, 102, 106, 109, 112, 113, 114, 116, 133, 154, 160, 170, 171, 172, 331); sense (of a word) (214, 215); also see "parokṣavṛtti" and "aparokṣavṛtti"
vṛddhi well-being, prosperity (394)
veṅkaṭapati Master of Veṅkaṭa, a sacred hill on top of which is a famous temple dedicated to Viṣṇu; said of Viṣṇu (305)
vettṛ knower, one who is aware (195)
vettṛtā act of knowing (311)
veda the Vedas, Scripture (36, 39, 45, 194, 225, etc.)
vedadraṣṭṛ Vedic visionary (194)
vedanā (act of) perception (33, etc.)
vedavyāsa Vedavyāsa, Vyāsa (194); also see "vyāsa"
vedokti words of Scripture (216)
vaikalya defectiveness, state of being flawed (88, 128)
vaijātya diverseness, heterogeneity (339)
vaidika conforming to the Vedas (257)
vairataḥ (due to) spite, hostility (253)
vaiśiṣṭyavat distinguished by (335)
vaisādṛśya dissimilarity (296)
vyatyāsa subversion, opposition (358)
vyathā torment, anguish (247)
vyartha (something) meaningless, false (208)
vyavasthā see "pratikarmavyavasthā"
vyavahartṛtā the condition of one who is involved in some activity, activity (104)
vyavahāra everyday life (41); activity (104)
vyāpta pervading (414)
vyāvahārika merely conventional or conventionally true, only empirically valid (35, 40, 200, 201, 202, 216, 359, 372, 374)
vyāvahārikatā the Non-dualist position which holds that all reality short of Brahman is merely conventionally real (67, 96, 97, 103, 190, 209, 222, 377)
vyāvahārikī only conventionally true or valid (221)
vyāsa Vyāsa (the omniscient compiler of the Scriptures and composer of the *Brahmasūtra* (100, 101, 385)

vyāsaṅga "complete standoff" (205)

śakti force, power, purport (27, 72, 86, 158, etc.)
śaṅkara Śiva (185)
śaṅkā fear (145, etc.); doubt, uncertainty (229)
śaṅkāpaṅka "mire of fear" (393)
śapatha oath, imprecation (210)
śabda Revelation (15, 21, 27, etc.); word (168, etc.)
śayana sleeping (300)
śara arrow ("can" for rhyme effect—233) (312)
śaśaśṛṅga hare's horn (something unknown, never seen) (307, 362)
śākunika soothsayer (383)
śāstra sacred book(s), canonical work(s) (36, 420)
śikṣā teaching, instruction (82); punishment (255)
śiromaṇi crest-jewel (350)
śilā stone, rock, boulder (280, 304)
śiva Śiva (54, 394)
śiśu baby (174, 175)
śiṣṭa one who is learned (195)
śiṣṭācāra practice or conduct of wise or learned men (208)
śuka Śuka (narrator of the *Bhāgavata Purāṇa*) (63, 65, 196, 364, 403)
śukti shell, mother-of-pearl (70, 149, 163, 307)
śuktirūpya shell which is mistaken for silver, "shell-silver" (70, 94, 149)
śuddhānantacit purified eternal consciousness (in liberation) (416)
śuddhi purity, freedom (from defilement) (415)
śūnya void, empty (173)
śaila one of the seven mountain ranges dividing the earth into regions (304)
śodhana examination, investigation, test (133, 183)
śrayaṇa recourse to, "counting on" (396)
śrī Lakṣmī, Viṣṇu's consort (1)
śrīpati Lord (11)
śruti scriptural test, Scripture (especially the Upaniṣads) (4, 9, 11, 25, etc.)
śrutistrī "Scripture-wife" (313)
śraiṣṭhya superiority, sovereignty (40, etc.)
śrotavyamantavyadhyeyatva capacity to be heard of, reflected, on, meditated on (315)
śrotṛ hearer, hearing (310)
śloka verse, stanza (220)

ṣa(ṣ)ṭhyartha the genitive case or meaning (24)

saṁyoga union, contact (93)
saṁvāda consent, agreement (391)
saṁśaya doubt (18, etc.)
saṁsat council, assembly (32, etc.)
saṁsāra round of rebirths, transmigratory existence (236)
saṁkoca curtailment, limitation (71)
saṅga attached (said of karma with respect to Brahman) (203)
saṅgama contact (76, 244, etc.)

saṁcaya multitude (394)
saṁcaraṇa activity (408, 409, etc.)
saṁcāra activity (409, 411)
sat being, truth (32, etc.); real, true (139, etc.); something real, reality; existent (141, etc.)
sattā reality, truth (76, 96, etc.)
sat(t)ra great Soma sacrifice (176)
sat(t)va truth (198)
satya true, truth (4, 41, 210, etc.)
satyatā truth (208, 209, etc.)
satyārthaśruti Scripture passage which teaches that things are real (358)
santoṣa happiness (224)
sapta the seventh, or locative case (400)
saptamī locative case (20)
sambandha relation, union (24, 115, 116, etc.)
sambhava existence (90)
samatā equality, equivalence (178, 366)
samatva equality (180)
sarasvatī Sarasvatī River, one of India's most sacred waterways (176)
sarpa snake (307); the serpent Ananta (Unending) (300)
sarvajña omniscient, all-knowing (134, 299, 385, 392)
sarvanāśa destruction of the whole (352)
sarveśvara Lord of all (3)
savikalpa determinate (knowledge) based on distinction-making (419)
sahāyin united with (208)
sākṣātkāra direct perception (246)
sākṣin witnessing self, inner witness (77)
sācivya alliance, derivation from (311)
sādṛśya likeness, resemblance, similarity (164, 288)
sādhya established (420)
sāmarthya purport (15); capability (183, 185, 191, etc.)
sāmānādhikaraṇya same (grammatical) case (16); consubstantiality (of subjective and objective capacities) (315)
sāmya similarity, likeness (289, etc.)
sāyujya perfect union (of the soul with God) (373)
sārasvata relating to the Sarasvatī River (219)
sārvajñya omniscience (186)
siṁha lion (289)
siddha established, confirmed (178, etc.)
siddhatva establishment, correctness (131)
siddhānta orthodox, accepted teaching (246)
siddhi establishment, fulfilment, corroboration, settlement (383, 384, 420)
sindhu ocean(s) (304)
sudhī wise or intelligent man (272, etc.)
supti sleep, especially deep (dreamless) sleep (234, 235)
sura god (7)
sūtrakāra author of the Scriptures (Vyāsa) (287)
sūtrakṛt author of the Scriptures (Vyāsa) (256, 284, 392)

sūri sage, wise man, oracle (89, 164, etc.)
sūrya sun (75, 111, 282)
sṛṣṭi creation (131)
sevā worship (220)
skandha shoulder(s) (294)
sthāpana causing to stand, placing (412)
sthita abiding, situated (123, etc.)
sthitatva situating, "situatedness" (293)
snātṛ swimmer (275)
snāna bathing (305)
spaṣṭatva clarity, obviousness (144)
smaraṇa recollection, remembering (247, 258)
smṛti sacred Epics and Purāṇas, Purāṇa texts (10, 11, 178, 199, 200 etc.)
sraṣṭṛ begetter (297)
svajñāna Self-Knowledge (149)
svatantra self-dependent, non-contingent, independent (298)
svadṛṣṭa experienced by oneself (388)
svanāśajagannāśa "the destruction of the self and the destruction of the world" (353)
svaprakāśa self-luminous, the self-luminous (One) (324)
svaprakāśatva self-luminosity (of Brahman) (311)
svapratikarma self-refuting (87)
svabhāva nature, intrinsic nature (11, 49, 152, etc.)
svabhāvatas by nature, due to one's nature (126)
svarūpa intrinsically real (164, 167); essential nature, own substance (338)
svarga heaven (241)
svardeha heaven-body (or spiritual body) (320, 321)
svaśaktitas by its own power (114)
svasṛ sister (309)
svasvākāra separate, distinct nature (415)
svājñāna ignorant oneself, one's own ignorance (371)
svādṛṣṭa not experienced (by oneself) (384)
svāmin master, lord (368)
svārtha true meaning, real truth (200, 205, 209, etc.)

hari Viṣṇu (3, 230, 248, 252, 254, 256, 296, 376, 403)
harītakī myrobalan tree (155)
hartṛ slayer (6)
hasta hand (52, 118); (elephant's) trunk (379)
hastīndrahasta "king elephant's trunk" (379)
hāni loss, extinction, cessation (239, 321)
hīnatā depravity, baseness (45)
huṅkāra the sound *hum* (expressive of contempt), hiss (145)
hṛd heart (sometimes meaning the soul) (112, 232, etc.)
hetu basis, cause (of), reason (for) (272, 330); resulting in (320)

CORRECTIONS

[Excepting a few lapses in punctuation and diacritics]

page	*line*	*for*	*read*
1	4	doctrined	doctrine
3	17	indifferentiated	undifferentiated
16	13	which	while
21	14	pun	pun on
65	21	—o what	—or as what
65	25	under-or ever-exclusiveness	under-or over-inclusiveness
67	7	knowledge	knowledge is
71	13	is	are
72	21	true	as true
87	29	(identity-and-difference-)	(identity- and difference-)
89	7	and te	and the
110	8	Madhava	Madhva
116	6 (from bottom)	carth	earth
118	9 (from bottom)	objectives	objectness
123	17	there	then
125	14 (from bottom)	thus	also
131	15	The	It is the
131	15	*delete* 'at a lower level'	
133	2	as	As
139	18	?	.
140	25	We	COMMENT : We
142	7	dear	clear
146	11	Madhava	Madhva
148	9	*delete* '(pareṇa)	
148	4 (from bottom)	united.	united,
161	11	counsel	council
161	2 (from bottom)	costituting	constituting